PENGUIN BOOKS

THE PENGUIN GANDHI READER

Mohandas Karamchand Gandhi was born on 2 October 1869 in Porbander. He was called to the Bar. He was not very successful as a Barrister-at-law in India and he moved to South Africa in 1893. In South Africa, he was unable to accept the official policy of racial discrimination and launched a series of non-violent protests.

On the basis of his South African experience, Gandhi elaborated a critique of Western civilization and a theory of passive resistance. In India he began his political career by organizing protests against the oppressive Rowlatt Act and by the peaceful mobilization of peasants in Champaran in Bihar and in Kheda in Gujarat. He was the key figure in the three great mass movements—the Non-Co-operation Movement (1920–22), the Civil Disobedience Movement (1931–32) and the Quit India Movement (1942)—which were the most important milestones in India's struggle for freedom. He was a champion of handspun cloth, Hindu–Muslim unity and the removal of untouchability. Non-violence remained right through his life the first article of his creed.

Gandhi chose to absent himself from the celebrations in New Delhi which marked India's independence on 15 August 1947. He could not accept the two nation theory and its logical sequel, the partition of the subcontinent into India and Pakistan.

He was assassinated by a Hindu fanatic on 30 January 1948 while he was addressing a prayer meeting.

*

Rudrangshu Mukherjee was born in 1952 and educated at Presidency College, Calcutta, Jawaharlal Nehru University, Delhi and St Edmund Hall, Oxford. He was awarded a D.Phil. in Modern History in 1981 by the University of Oxford. He is the author of *Awadh in Revolt 1857–58: A Study of Popular Resistance*; and an editor of *Trade and the Indian Ocean World: Essays in Honour of Ashin Das Gupta*.

Rudrangshu Mukherjee is Editor, Editorial Pages, *The Telegraph* and lives in Calcutta.

The Penguin Gandhi Reader

Edited By

Rudrangshu Mukherjee

PENGUIN BOOKS

Penguin Books India (P) Ltd., 210 Chiranjiv Tower, 43 Nehru Place, New Delhi 110 019 India
Penguin Books Ltd., 27 Wrights Lane, London W8 5TZ, UK
Penguin Books USA Inc., 375 Hudson Street, New York, New York 10014, USA
Penguin Books Australia Ltd., Ringwood, Victoria, Australia
Penguin Books Canada Ltd., 10 Alcorn Avenue, Suite 300, Toronto, Ontario, MAV 3B2, Canada
Penguin Books (NZ) Ltd., 182-190 Wairau Road, Auckland, 10, New Zealand

First published by Penguin Books India (P) Ltd. 1993

10 9 8 7 6 5 4

Typeset in Times Roman by Fortune Publishers, New Delhi

For GC, PC, NA and D who help me to scrabble through life.

Contents

Contents

My language is aphoristic, it lacks precision.
It is therefore open to several interpretations.

—Gandhi to Dharmadev

●

My life is my message.

—Gandhi to Shanti Sena Dal

Preface

General and scholarly interest in Mahatma Gandhi continues to thrive. The principal reason for this is the universal appeal of his message of non-violence in a world torn by strife. There is something compelling about the simplicity of his life and the persuasive powers of his writings. Even the most ardent admirer of Gandhi will find it difficult to read through his *Collected Works* which is already ninety volumes long. This *Reader* selects certain themes from Gandhi's staggering output so that the general reader interested in Gandhi can get to know his style and his views without having to plough through 90 volumes.

In India, Gandhi has been made into an icon. As a result deification or its obverse, debunking, have replaced critical evaluation. The introduction tries to outline some of the tensions and contradictions in Gandhi's life and thought.

The iconization of Gandhi is not without irony. As a country, India has turned its back on Gandhi and his ideas. The very process through which India gained independence, by accepting the two nation theory, was a betrayal of one of Gandhi's fundamental beliefs. Much before 1947, Jawaharlal Nehru in his autobiography had written off the ideas contained in Gandhi's *Hind Swaraj* as 'utterly wrong . . . and impossible of achievement'. The quest for modernity and the building of a powerful nation-state had no time or space for an anti-modern and anti-industrial manifesto. Yet Gandhi continues to be venerated as the Father of the Nation; he is the object of ritual, if hypocritical, genuflection. If independent India has turned its back on Gandhi, he too made his attitude clear by staying away from the celebrations in New Delhi on 15 August 1947. The irony fully manifested itself when somebody on 15 August 1947 put a fez on Gandhi's statue in Karachi.

The power of Gandhi's message has taken its appeal beyond the borders of India. His importance in the history of the 20th century will be based not only on his achievements as the architect of India's freedom but also on the fact that he devised and deployed a remarkable method of fighting oppression. This book will serve its purpose if it takes readers nearer to understanding Gandhi.

In commemoration of the fiftieth death anniversary of Mahatma Gandhi.

January 1998   RUDRANGSHU MUKHERJEE
Calcutta

Introduction

Mohandas Karamchand Gandhi was born on 2 October 1869 at Porbander in the western coast of India. His father was an official of a small native state. He had an orthodox upbringing but went to London to train as a lawyer. He enrolled at the Inner Temple and was called to the Bar in the summer of 1891. Back in India, he could not make a successful career as a lawyer and moved to South Africa in 1893. Confronted with the rampant racism in vogue there, he began the first of, what he was to call later, his 'experiments with truth'. The main thrust of this experiment was to resist racial discrimination non-violently. It involved the peaceful violation of certain laws, the courting of arrests collectively, hartals and spectacular marches.

The South African experiment was to serve as a model of Gandhi's involvement in mass movements in India. In the first two decades of the twentieth century, the Indian National Congress and the Indian national movement was in disarray. In the aftermath of the swadeshi movement in Bengal, the Indian National Congress was split between Moderates and Extremists. There was, however, a growing awareness in the country of the various dimensions of imperialist exploitation and oppression. It was in this atmosphere that Gandhi made his first mark in Indian politics by organizing mass, non-violent protests in Champaran, Kheda and against the Rowlatt Act.

But before his emergence in the Indian political scene, Gandhi had already worked out some of his fundamental ideas. He articulated these in a booklet called *Hind Swaraj*. All commentators on Gandhi recognize this to be the most coherent exposition of Gandhi's world-view.[1] Gandhi himself saw the text as representing 'the views...held by many Indians not touched by what is known as civilization.' His motive, he said, was 'to serve my country, to find out the Truth and to follow it.'[2]

Hind Swaraj is a trenchant critique of modern civilization but it also contains a statement of Gandhi's alternative to modern civilization and a programme for Indians to actualize such an alternative. Gandhi was emphatic about the superiority of Indian

xi

civilization and its inherent ability to withstand the onslaughts of modernity. Throughout his life, in all his major writings, Gandhi returned again and again to these themes.

The critique attacked all the major aspects of the 'modern philosophy of life,'—Gandhi emphasized that it was called 'Western' because its principal site was the West.[3] On the surface, Gandhi's position has similarities with the romantic criticism of the moral and social depredations of advancing capitalism. Indeed, the two major influences on Gandhi, in the formulation of these ideas, were Edward Carpenter's *Civilization: Its Cause and Cure* and John Ruskin's *Unto This Last.* The former influenced Gandhi's ideas on science especially modern medicine. And Gandhi liked especially Carpenter's argument that the ever-increasing powers of production engendered by modern science and technology alienated man '(1) from Nature (2) from his true self (3) from his Fellows' and it worked 'in every way to disintegrate and corrupt man...to *break up* the unity of his nature.'[4] From Ruskin came the criticism of 'political economy based on self-interest.' Ruskin's suggestion that 'that country is richest which nourishes the greatest number of noble and happy human beings; that man is richest who, having perfected the functions of his own life to the utmost, has also the widest helpful influence, both personal, and by means of his possessions, over the lives of others'[5] had Gandhi's approval. From Lev Tolstoy's political writings Gandhi took his ideas about the essentially repressive character of the State and about the moral imperative of non-violence. There is always the danger while discussing the lineages of Gandhi's ideas of overemphasizing the influences. Gandhi was thoroughly eclectic and his borrowings were not impaired by any considerations of scientific and theoretical rigour. Thus, while Gandhi borrowed from Ruskin and Carpenter, he rejected completely some other aspects of their thought. This distinguished Gandhi from the romantic critique of capitalism. Carpenter, for example, argued, drawing, in his own turn, from Lewis Morgan and Engels, that civilization transformed the nature of 'property' and thereby destroyed man's unity with nature. Such theories did not attract Gandhi.

Ruskin, again, was a historicist influenced by German idealism especially by Hegel. He was also a believer in the virtues of 'modernity' caring intensely, as R.G. Collingwood noted, 'for science and progress, for political reform, for the advancement of knowledge and for new movements in art and letters.'[6] His attack on political economy did not call for a jettisoning of Reason and a falling back on 'conscience' and 'faith.'[7]

This was, of course, completely unacceptable to Gandhi. He did not share this confidence in Reason and Science. He asserted that the scientific mode of knowledge was applicable only to very limited areas of human living. The assumption that rationality and science could provide solutions to all problems led to insanity and impotence.'...mere intellect,' Gandhi wrote, 'makes one insane or unmanly....The reasoning faculty will raise a thousand issues. Only one thing will save us from these and that is faith.'[8] There were very few things, Gandhi felt, that reason could help explain: where reason failed, faith worked. Similarly, he was not willing to accept arguments based on history. 'To believe that what has not occurred in history will not occur at all is to argue disbelief in the dignity of man,' he declared. What history records are aberrations; history is 'a record of an interruption of the course of nature.'[9] Neither science nor history has any privileged access to Truth. Truth was in morality, in one's own conscience and in the performance of one's duty.[10]

Gandhi thus not only made a critique of modern civilization, civil society and its various institutions; the intellectual developments associated with modern civilization—Reason, Science, History, the dominant themes of post-enlightenment thought—met with his utter and complete disapproval and rejection. This rejection gave his arguments a uniquely self-contained character. The epistemic vantage point for Gandhi was outside civil society and post-enlightenment thought. Unlike the romantics his critique was not an elaboration of the historical contradictions of civil society as comprehended from within it.[11]

Thus the alternative to modern civilization that Gandhi posed had to be located outside the domain of civil society and the influences of modern civilization. And India was uniquely placed to provide this alternative, indeed, only India could provide the alternative since millions of Indians who lived in the villages had not been lured by the trappings of modern civilization.

'Real civilization' was to be found in the villages of India. The 'traditional' village world, autonomous of modern civilization, was the complete opposite of the individualistic world of civil society. Life was governed by a communal morality where each member performed his duty. It was to the 'common people' living 'independently' that Gandhi turned: India, 'to me,' he wrote, 'means its teeming millions on whom depends the existence of its princes and our own.'[12] The hope of India lay in the peasantry.

Gandhi's challenge to the presence of modern civilization in India, i.e., British rule, would come from the peasantry since it was untouched by modern civilization. This meant the challenge would have to be non-violent since, according to Gandhi, the Indian peasantry had never been violent.[13] Moreover, an armed resistance to British rule would Europeanize India whereas Gandhi's aim was exactly the opposite. He called this mode of resistance satyagraha. Complete non-co-operation would lead to the collapse of any government. The deployment of satyagraha would force the British to leave India. That, however, would not, according to Gandhi, bring swaraj. Swaraj would only be possible with the disappearance of tyranny and exploitation.

Since passive resistance, the only road to swaraj, was possible through personal suffering it followed that swaraj could only be 'experienced by each one for himself.'[14] Every individual who chose the path of satyagraha would learn to regulate his own life by observing perfect chastity, adopting poverty, following truth and cultivating fearlessness.[15] A moral life on the part of every individual was the necessary pre-condition for swaraj. A community of self-regulated individuals, each performing his moral duty would give to national life a completely different character:

> The power to control national life through national representatives is called political power. Representatives will become unnecessary if the national life becomes so perfect as to be self-controlled. It will then be a state of enlightened anarchy in which each person will become his own ruler. He will conduct himself in such a way that his behaviour will not hamper the well-being of his neighbours. In an ideal State there will be no political institution and therefore no political power.16

This is Gandhi's political ideal where there was continual and complete reciprocity among and participation by every member of the polity. He called this utopia Ramarajya, a society where there was no gulf between the ruler and the ruled, where the former always expressed the collective morality:

> In my opinion swaraj and Ramarajya are one and the same thing....We call a State Ramarajya when both the ruler and his subjects are straightforward, when both are pure in heart, when both are inclined towards self-sacrifice, when both exercise restraint and self-control while enjoying worldly pleasures, and, when the relationship between the two is as good as that between a father and a son. It is because we have forgotten this that we talk of democracy or the government of the people. Although this is the age of democracy, I do not know what the word connotes; however, I would say that democracy exists where the people's voice is heard, where love of the people holds a place of prime importance. In my Ramarajya, however, public opinion cannot be measured by counting of heads or raising of hands. I would not regard this as a measure of public opinion;...The rishis and the munis [wisemen/philoso-phers of ancient India] after doing penance came to the conclusion that public opinion is the opinion of people who practice penance and who have the good of the people at heart.[17]

In Ramarajya the production would be organized according to the four-fold *varna* (the four castes, the Brahmins, the Kshatriyas [the warriors], the Vaishyas [the professionals] and the Shudras [the menial caste]) scheme of specialization i.e., according to the caste system. A perfect system of reciprocity in the exchange of commodities and services would guarantee that there was no competition and no differences in status. The whole of society would be held together by equal, self-regulating individuals, each performing his duty:

The law of *varna* means that everyone shall follow as a matter of *dharma*—duty—the hereditary calling of his forefathers, in so far as it is not inconsistent with fundamental ethics. He will earn his livelihood by following that calling. He may not hoard riches, but devote the balance for the good of the people.

The four *varnas* have been compared in the Vedas to the four members of the body, and no simile could be happier. If they are members of one body, how can one be superior or inferior to another? If the members of the body had the power of expression and each of them were to say that it was higher and better than the rest, the body would go to pieces. Even so, our body politic, the body of humanity, would go to pieces, if it were to perpetuate the canker of superiority or inferiority. It is this canker that is at the root of the various ills of our time, especially class wars and civil strife....All callings would be equally reputable—whether that of the minister or of the lawyer, of the doctor or of the leather-worker, of the carpenter or the scavenger, of the soldier or the trader, of the farmer or the spiritual teacher. In this ideal state of things, there would be no room for the monstrous anomaly of the three *varnas* lording it over the Shudra, or of the Kshatriya and the Vaishya enjoying themselves in their palaces and the Brahmin contenting himself with a cottage and the Shudra toiling for the rest and living in a hovel....Under such dispensation, all property will be held by its respective holders in trust for the community. No one will claim it as his own. The king will hold his palace in trust for his people and will collect the taxes only to be used for the benefit of the people.[18]

Indian civilization had as its foundation this kind of a system: that is why it was more longlasting than and superior to modern/ Western civilization. 'Indian civilization,' Gandhi reiterated, 'is the best and the European is a nine days' wonder.'[19]

Beginning as a critique of modern civilization and civil society, Gandhi's is at the end also an invocation of an extreme nationalist position i.e., the intrinsic superiority of India to the West. This superiority is, however, evident, as we have seen, in that part of Indian society which is the least affected by modern civilization. The challenge to modern civilization, British rule, would be located there. The Indian peasantry, therefore, would be the main agency of Indian nationalism. And that nationalism would articulate itself through non-violence since that is the peasantry's main instrument of resistance. Further, perfect morality is an essential pre-requisite of all passive resisters if swaraj is to be achieved. It might be argued that Gandhi's vision of swaraj was that of an alternative society and therefore his arguments transcend the nationalist goal of getting political independence from British rule. Without gainsaying Gandhi's vision of an alternative society, which indeed *Hind Swaraj* sketches, it needs to be emphasized that that alternative was also essentially Indian: it was embedded in what Gandhi thought to be the foundation and also the superiority of Indian civilization. Such a view of Indian civilization has a strong nationalist hue to it. It also needs to be underscored that from within Gandhi's own framework it is impossible to dismantle his propositions. He pre-empted any counter-argument premised on History or Reason. Thus, an argument that proceeded to show through historical examples that the *varna* system never actually worked the way Gandhi described or that the peasants of India had not always been non-violent would actually be of no relevance to Gandhi. What *has been* is for Gandhi no argument against what *should be* or *should have been.*

Gandhi's ideas by their very nature could be used in very many different directions. Gandhi, himself, would go on to show the power of political movements whose mass base was the peasantry, whose principal modality was non-violence and whose direction from its inception was sought to be regulated. It would lead to other nationalist leaders discovering the peasantry and also becoming aware of their 'responsibility' towards them: witness Jawaharlal Nehru:

> I was filled with shame and sorrow, shame at my own
> easy-going and comfortable life and our petty politics of

the city which ignored this vast multitude of semi-naked sons and daughters of India, sorrow at the degradation and overwhelming poverty of India. A new picture of India seemed to rise before me, naked, starving, crushed and utterly miserable. And their faith in us...embarrassed me and filled me with a new responsibility that frightened me.[20]

Yet, nationalist leaders aspiring for political power could never reconcile themselves with Gandhi's ideas of swaraj and 'enlightened anarchy.' Nehru, the archetypal spokesman of the nation state, could admit, despite his loyalty to Gandhi, that the ideas of *Hind Swaraj* represented an 'utterly wrong and harmful doctrine, and impossible of achievement.'[21] Similarly, the emphasis on Ramarajya and the *varna* system—both essentially Hindu ideas—had the possibility of alienating non-Hindus. And when Gandhi wrote, 'Those in whose name we speak we do not know...' he was, of course, unaware of any irony: the Indian peasants would, indeed, respond to the message of the Mahatma in ways that Gandhi had not quite anticipated. During the three great mass upsurges associated with the name of Gandhi—the Non-co-operation movement (1920–1922), the Civil Disobedience movement (1930–1933) and the Quit India movement (1942)—the common people responded to Gandhi's call but did so often on their own terms and initiative. It is a cliché of modern Indian historiography that Gandhi brought politics to the masses. Recent research is emphasizing that the masses had their own politics, their own ways of resisting British rule and it was within these that they tried to adapt the 'message of the Mahatma.'

In a remarkable essay Shahid Amin has shown the interface between the 'official' Congress projection of Gandhi and the popular perceptions of him in Gorakhpur in Uttar Pradesh.[22] Gandhi was invited to Gorakhpur in October 1920 and he came to address a public meeting in February 1921. The nationalist leadership of the district made it clear that the reception of Gandhi would be the work of the local élite. The common people would follow a set pattern: they would come for darshan and return to their inert and oppressed existence. The local élite did not reckon with the fact that the peasants often undertook the journey for such darshan defying landlord opposition. Such defiance was not only a political act but it often entailed on the part of the common villager an independent decoding of Gandhi's message. Indeed, when Gandhi arrived in Gorakhpur thousands gathered in every station to see him, to greet him and to offer donations to him. But this reception seemed to acquire a certain militancy. Mahadev Desai, Gandhi's secretary, recorded how during the return journey people came armed with lathis and torches and shouting and demanding to see Gandhi almost as if it was their right to have darshan. Desai commented disapprovingly on the people's *hathagraha* (mule-like obstinacy) and on their 'love-mad insolence.'

Gandhi spoke in Gorakhpur on familiar themes: Hindu-Muslim unity; forbade the use of violence; the abandonment of gambling, drinking and whoring; the importance of non-co-operation with the government; the importance of spinning and khadi and; the imminence of swaraj. Gandhi's message, however, came to be endowed with a very different and profound significance amongst the people of Gorakhpur. Gandhi's ideas were interpreted by them in terms of Hindu popular beliefs and the material culture of the peasantry. Gorakhpur was flooded with 'stories' of Gandhi's *pratap* (power). All these 'stories' or rumours centred around boons and punishments that people had received because they had either obeyed or disobeyed the orders of the Mahatma. Gandhi was thus given magical and miraculous powers: he came to be endowed with a saintliness. In Gorakhpur, Gandhi's name lent itself as a label to all kinds of meetings, pamphlets and to swaraj. 'Gandhi papers' and 'Gandhi notes' came to be circulated, and the non-acceptance of these came to be interpreted by the villagers as opposition to Gandhi. Gandhi, thus, emerged as an alternative source of authority and this took place independently of the district leadership of the Congress. And the people of Gorakhpur used this authority to legitimize actions which were not sanctioned by the Congress or by the Gandhian code of non-violence. As Amin writes:

> There was no single authorized version of the Mahatma
> to which the peasants of eastern UP and north Bihar
> may be said to have subscribed in 1921. Indeed their
> ideas about Gandhi's 'orders' and 'powers' were often at

variance with those of the local Congress-Khilafat leadership and clashed with the basic tenets of Gandhism itself. The violence at Chauri-Chaura was rooted in this paradox.[23]

The violence which led to the death of twenty-two policemen resulted in Gandhi's decision to withdraw the Non-co-operation movement.

Gandhi's principled insistence on non-violence occasioned the withdrawal of a mass movement; the same principle, however, also, ensured that a political struggle against the British would not snowball into a radical social revolution seeking to turn the world upside down. This basic guarantee made Gandhian mobilization attractive not only to rich and dominant peasants but also to Indian business groups. And, it was mounting pressure from the latter that made Gandhi call off the Civil Disobedience movement.[24]

The impact of Gandhi on the course of mass resistance was ambiguous. Gandhi succeeded in drawing in the masses but he did so by keeping mass activity confined within certain forms predetermined by the leader. 'The peasants,' as one commentator has noted, 'were meant to become willing participants in a struggle wholly conceived and directed *by others.*'[25]

The ambiguity which, despite Gandhi's anti-capitalism, allowed so much manoeuvrability to the Indian capitalist class had other profound consequences. In the Forties, especially after the end of the Second World War, when the British intentions to leave India became evident, the Indian capitalists and sections of the Congress leadership engaged themselves in trying to ensure a negotiated transfer of power. There were many radical mass movements in the Forties, all outside Congress control.[26] In the circumstances, another mass confrontation seemed risky to the Congress leadership while a negotiated transfer of power would guarantee control over the independent Indian State. Gandhi, at this stage, found himself completely isolated, shunned by the men he, himself, had made. He could see that a negotiated transfer of power would mean the division of the country and the aggravation of Hindu-Muslim tension. With this he would brook no compromise. Thus, while India celebrated independence, the 'Father of the Nation' kept his own tryst with destiny in the slums of east Calcutta. His isolation evoked, perhaps, the image of Eliot's *Gerontion:*

> *I have no ghosts,*
> *An old man in a draughty house*
> *Under a windy knob.*

This book tries, within a short compass, to present the richness and the ambiguity of Gandhi's ideas. It will have served its purpose if it helps the readers to seek their own Gandhi.

Critique Of Modern Civilization

Hind Swaraj[1]

Preface

I have written some chapters on the subject of Indian Home Rule which I venture to place before the readers of *Indian Opinion*. I have written because I could not restrain myself. I have read much, I have pondered much, during the stay, for four months in London, of the Transvaal Indian deputation. I discussed things with as many of my countrymen as I could. I met, too, as many Englishmen as it was possible for me to meet. I consider it my duty now to place before the readers of *Indian Opinion* the conclusions, which appear to me to be final. The Gujarati subscribers of *Indian Opinion* number about 800. I am aware that, for every subscriber, there are at least ten persons who read the paper with zest. Those who cannot read Gujarati have the paper read out to them. Such persons have often questioned me about the condition of India. Similar questions were addressed to me in London. I felt, therefore, that it might not be improper for me to ventilate publicly the views expressed by me in private.

These views are mine, and yet not mine. They are mine because I hope to act according to them. They are almost a part of my being. But, yet, they are not mine, because I lay no claim to originality. They have been formed after reading several books. That which I dimly felt received support from these books.

The views I venture to place before the reader are, needless to say, held by many Indians not touched by what is known as civilization, but I ask the reader to believe me when I tell him that they are also held by thousands of Europeans. Those who wish to dive deep, and have time, may read certain books themselves. If time permits me, I hope to translate portions of such books for the benefit of the readers of *Indian Opinion*.

If the readers of *Indian Opinion* and others who may see the following chapters will pass their criticism on to me, I shall feel obliged to them.

The only motive is to serve my country, to find out the Truth, and to follow it. If, therefore, my views are proved to be wrong, I shall have no hesitation in rejecting them. If they are proved to be right, I would naturally wish, for the sake of the motherland, that others should adopt them.

To make it easy reading, the chapters are written in the form of a dialogue between the reader and the editor.

Kildonan Castle   *Mohandas Karamchand Gandhi*
22-11-1909

Chapter I : The Congress and its Officials

READER: Just at present there is a Home Rule wave passing over India. All our countrymen appear to be pining for National Independence. A similar spirit pervades them even in South Africa. Indians seem to be eager to acquire rights. Will you explain your views in this matter?

EDITOR: You have put the question well, but the answer is not easy. One of the objects of a newspaper is to understand popular feeling and to give expression to it; another is to arouse among the people certain desirable sentiments; and the third is fearlessly to expose popular defects. The exercise of all these three functions is involved in answering your question. To a certain extent the people's will has to be expressed; certain sentiments will need to be fostered, and defects will have to be brought to light. But, as you have asked the question, it is my duty to answer it.

READER: Do you then consider that a desire for Home Rule has been created among us?

EDITOR: That desire gave rise to the National Congress. The choice of the word "National" implies it.

READER: That, surely, is not the case. Young India seems to ignore the Congress. It is considered to be an instrument for perpetuating British Rule.

EDITOR: That opinion is not justified. Had not the Grand Old Man of India prepared the soil, our young men could not have even spoken about Home Rule. How can we forget what Mr Hume has written, how he has lashed us into action, and with that effort he has awakened us, in order to achieve the objects of the Congress? Sir William Wedderburn has given his body, mind and money to the same cause. His writings are worthy of perusal to this day. Professor Gokhale, in order to prepare the nation, embraced poverty and gave twenty years of his life. Even now, he is living in poverty. The late Justice Budruddin Tyebji was also one of those who, through the Congress, sowed the seed of Home Rule. Similarly, in Bengal, Madras, the Punjab and other places, there have been lovers of India and members of the Congress, both Indian and English.

READER: Stay, stay; you are going too far, you are straying away from my question. I have asked you about Home - or Self-Rule; you

5

are discussing foreign rule. I do not desire to hear English names, and you are giving me such names. In these circumstances, I do not think we can ever meet. I shall be pleased if you will confine yourself to Home Rule. All other talk will not satisfy me.

EDITOR: You are impatient. I cannot afford to be likewise. If you will bear with me for a while, I think you will find that you will obtain what you want. Remember the old proverb that the tree does not grow in one day. The fact that you have checked me and that you do not want to hear about the well-wishers of India shows that, for you at any rate, Home Rule is yet far away. If we had many like you, we would never make any advance. This thought is worthy of your attention.

READER: It seems to me that you simply want to put me off by talking round and round. Those whom you consider to be well-wishers of India are not such in my estimation. Why, then, should I listen to your discourse on such people? What has he whom you consider to be the Father of the Nation done for it? He says that the English Governors will do justice and that we should co-operate with them.

EDITOR: I must tell you, with all gentleness, that it must be a matter of shame for us that you should speak about that great man in terms of disrespect. Just look at his work. He has dedicated his life to the service of India. We have learned what we know from him. It was the respected Dadabhai who taught us that the English had sucked our life-blood. What does it matter that, today, his trust is still in the English nation? Is Dadabhai less to be honoured because, in the exuberance of youth, we are prepared to go a step further? Are we, on that account, wiser than he? It is a mark of wisdom not to kick away the very step from which we have risen higher. The removal of a step from a staircase brings down the whole of it. When, out of infancy, we grow into youth, we do not despise infancy, but, on the contrary, we recall with affection the days of our childhood. If, after many years of study, a teacher were to teach me something, and if I were to build a little more on the foundation laid by that teacher, I would not, on that account, be considered wiser than the teacher. He would always command my respect. Such is the case with the Grand Old Man of India. We must admit that he is the author of nationalism.

READER: You have spoken well. I can now understand that we must look upon Mr Dadabhai with respect. Without him and men like him, we should probably not have the spirit that fires us. How can the same be said of Professor Gokhale? He has constituted himself a great friend of the English; he says that we have to learn a great deal from them, that we have to learn their political wisdom, before we can talk of Home Rule. I am tired of reading his speeches.

EDITOR: If you are tired, it only betrays your impatience. We believe that those, who are discontented with the slowness of their parents and are angry because the parents would not run with their children, are considered disrespectful to their parents. Professor Gokhale occupies the place of a parent. What does it matter if he cannot run with us? A nation that is desirous of securing Home Rule cannot afford to despise its ancestors. We shall become useless, if we lack respect for our elders. Only men with mature thoughts are capable of ruling themselves and not the hasty-tempered. Moreover, how many Indians were there like Professor Gokhale, when he gave himself to Indian education? I verily believe that whatever Professor Gokhale does, he does with pure motives and with a view to serving India. His devotion to the Motherland is so great that he would give his life for it, if necessary. Whatever he says is said not to flatter anyone but because he believes it to be true. We are bound, therefore, to entertain the highest regard for him.

READER: Are we, then, to follow him in every respect?

EDITOR: I never said any such thing. If we conscientiously differed from him, the learned Professor himself would advise us to follow the dictates of our conscience rather than him. Our chief purpose is not to decry his work, but to believe that he is infinitely greater than we are, and to feel assured that compared with his work for India, ours is infinitesimal. Several newspapers write disrespectfully of him. It is our duty to protest against such writings. We should consider men like Professor Gokhale to be the pillars of Home Rule. It is a bad habit to say that another man's thoughts are bad and ours only are good and that those holding different views from ours are the enemies of the country.

READER: I now begin to understand somewhat your meaning. I shall have to think the matter over. But what you say about Mr Hume and Sir William Wedderburn is beyond my comprehension.

EDITOR: The same rule holds good for the English as for the Indians. I can never subscribe to the statement that all Englishmen are bad. Many Englishmen desire Home Rule for India. That the English people are somewhat more selfish than others is true, but that does not prove that every Englishman is bad. We who seek justice will have to do justice to others. Sir William does not wish ill to India—that should be enough for us. As we proceed, you will see that, if we act justly, India will be sooner free. You will see, too, that if we shun every Englishman as an enemy, Home Rule will be delayed. But if we are just to them, we shall receive their support in our progress towards the goal.

READER: All this seems to me at present to be simply nonsensical. English support and the obtaining of Home Rule are two contradictory things. How can the English people tolerate Home Rule for us? But I do not want you to decide this question for me just yet. To spend time over it is useless. When you have shown how we can have Home Rule, perhaps I shall understand your views. You have prejudiced me against you by discoursing on English help. I would, therefore, beseech you not to continue this subject.

EDITOR: I have no desire to do so. That you are prejudiced against me is not a matter for much anxiety. It is well that I should say unpleasant things at the commencement. It is my duty patiently to try to remove your prejudice.

READER: I like that last statement. It emboldens me to say what I like. One thing still puzzles me. I do not understand how the Congress laid the foundation of Home Rule.

EDITOR: Let us see. The Congress brought together Indians from different parts of India, and enthused us with the idea of nationality. The Government used to look upon it with disfavour. The Congress has always insisted that the Nation should control revenue and expenditure. It has always desired self-government after the Canadian model. Whether we can get it or not, whether we desire it or not, and whether there is not something more desirable, are different questions. All I have to show is that the Congress gave us a foretaste of Home Rule. To deprive it of the honour is not proper, and for us to do so would not only be ungrateful, but retard the fulfilment of our object. To treat the Congress as an institution inimical to our growth as a nation would disable us from using that body.

Chapter II : The Partition of Bengal

READER: Considering the matter as you put it, it seems proper to say that the foundation of Home Rule was laid by the Congress. But you will admit that this cannot be considered a real awakening. When and how did the real awakening take place?

EDITOR: The seed is never seen. It works underneath the ground, is itself destroyed, and the tree which rises above the ground is alone seen. Such is the case with the Congress. Yet, what you call the real awakening took place after the Partition of Bengal. For this we have to be thankful to Lord Curzon. At the time of the Partition, the people of Bengal reasoned with Lord Curzon, but in the pride of power he disregarded all their prayers. He took it for granted that Indians could only prattle, that they could never take any effective steps. He used insulting language, and in the teeth of all opposition partitioned Bengal. That day may be considered to be the day of the partition of the British Empire. The shock the British power received through the Partition has never been equalled by any other act. This does not mean that the other injustices done to India are less glaring than that done by the Partition. The salt-tax is not a small injustice. We shall see many such things later on. But the people were ready to resist the Partition. At that time feeling ran high. Many leading Bengalis were ready to lose their all. They knew their power; hence the conflagration. It is now well-nigh unquenchable; it is not necessary to quench it either. The Partition will go, Bengal will be reunited, but the rift in the English barque will remain; it must daily widen. India awakened is not likely to fall asleep. The demand for the abrogation of the Partition is tantamount to a demand for Home Rule. Leaders in Bengal know this. British officials realize it. That is why the Partition still remains. As time passes, the Nation is being forged. Nations are not formed in a day; the formation requires years.

READER: What, in your opinion, are the results of the Partition?

EDITOR: Hitherto we have considered that for redress of grievances we must approach the throne, and if we get no redress we must sit still, except that we may still petition. After the Partition, people saw that petitions must be backed up by force, and that they must be capable of suffering. This new spirit must be

9

considered to be the chief result of the Partition. That spirit was seen in the outspoken writings in the Press. That which the people said tremblingly and in secret began to be said and to be written publicly. The Swadeshi movement was inaugurated. People; young and old, used to run away at the sight of an English face; it now no longer awes them. They do not fear even a row, or being imprisoned. Some of the best sons of India are at present in banishment. This is something different from mere petitioning. Thus are the people moved. The spirit generated in Bengal has spread in the north to the Punjab, and in the south to Cape Comorin.

READER: Do you suggest any other striking result?

EDITOR: The Partition has not only made a rift in the English ship but has made it in ours also. Great events always produce great results. Our leaders are divided into two parties: the Moderates and the Extremists. These may be considered as the slow party and the impatient party. Some call the Moderates the timid party, and the Extremists the bold party. All interpret the two words according to their preconceptions. This much is certain—that there has arisen an enmity between the two. The one distrusts the other and imputes motives. At the time of the Surat Congress there was almost a fight. I think that this division is not a good thing for the country, but I think also that such divisions will not last long. It all depends upon the leaders how long they will last.

Chapter III : Discontent and Unrest

READER: Then you consider the Partition to be a cause of the awakening? Do you welcome the unrest which has resulted from it?

EDITOR: When a man rises from sleep, he twists his limbs and is restless. It takes some time before he is entirely awakened. Similarly, although the Partition has caused an awakening, the comatose condition has not yet disappeared. We are still twisting our limbs and are still restless, and just as the state between sleep and awakening must be considered to be necessary, so may the present unrest in India be considered a necessary and, therefore, a proper state. The knowledge that there is unrest will, it is highly probable, enable us to outgrow it. Rising from sleep, we do not continue in a comatose state, but according to our ability, sooner or later, we are completely restored to our senses. So shall we be free from the present unrest which no one likes.

READER: What is the other form of unrest?

EDITOR: Unrest is, in reality, discontent. The latter is only now described as unrest. During the Congress period, it was labelled discontent. Mr Hume always said that the spread of discontent in India was necessary. This discontent is a very useful thing. As long as a man is contented with his present lot, so long is it difficult to persuade him to come out of it. Therefore it is that every reform must be preceded by discontent. We throw away things we have, only when we cease to like them. Such discontent has been produced among us after reading the great works of Indians and Englishmen. Discontent has led to unrest, and the latter has brought about many deaths, many imprisonments, many banishments. Such a state of things will still continue. It must be so. All these may be considered good signs but they may also lead to bad results.

Chapter IV : What is Swaraj?

READER: I have now learnt what the Congress has done to make India one nation, how the Partition has caused an awakening, and how discontent and unrest have spread through the land. I would now like to know your views on swaraj. I fear that our interpretation is not the same as yours.

EDITOR: It is quite possible that we do not attach the same meaning to the term. You and I and all Indians are impatient to obtain swaraj, but we are certainly not decided as to what it is. To drive the English out of India is a thought heard from many mouths, but it does not seem that many have properly considered why it should be so. I must ask you a question. Do you think that it is necessary to drive away the English, if we get all we want?

READER: I should ask of them only one thing, that is: "Please leave our country." If, after they have complied with this request, their withdrawal from India means that they are still in India, I should have no objection. Then we would understand that, in their language, the word "gone" is equivalent to "remained".

EDITOR: Well then, let us suppose that the English have retired. What will you do then?

READER: That question cannot be answered at this stage. The state after withdrawal will depend largely upon the manner of it. If, as you assume, they retire, it seems to me we shall still keep their constitution and shall carry on the Government. If they simply retire for the asking, we should have an army, etc., ready at hand. We should, therefore, have no difficulty in carrying on the Government.

EDITOR: You may think so; I do not. But I will not discuss the matter just now. I have to answer your question, and that I can do well by asking you several questions. Why do you want to drive away the English?

READER: Because India has become impoverished by their Government. They take away our money from year to year. The most important posts are reserved for themselves. We are kept in a state of slavery. They behave insolently towards us and disregard our feelings.

EDITOR: If they do not take our money away, become gentle, and give us responsible posts, would you still consider their presence to be harmful?

READER: That question is useless. It is similar to the question whether there is any harm in associating with a tiger if he changes his nature. Such a question is sheer waste of time. When a tiger changes his nature, Englishmen will change theirs. This is not possible, and to believe it to be possible is contrary to human experience.

EDITOR: Supposing we get Self-Government similar to what the Canadians and the South Africans have, will it be good enough?

READER: That question also is useless. We may get it when we have the same powers; we shall then hoist our own flag. As is Japan, so must India be. We must own our navy, our army, and we must have our own splendour, and then will India's voice ring through the world.

EDITOR: You have drawn the picture well. In effect it means this: that we want English rule without the Englishman. You want the tiger's nature, but not the tiger; that is to say, you would make India English. And when it becomes English, it will be called not Hindustan but *Englistan*. This is not the swaraj that I want.

READER: I have placed before you my idea of swaraj as I think it should be. If the education we have received be of any use, if the works of Spencer, Mill and others be of any importance, and if the

English Parliament be the Mother of Parliaments, I certainly think that we should copy the English people, and this to such an extent that, just as they do not allow others to obtain a footing in their country, so we should not allow them or others to obtain it in ours. What they have done in their own country has not been done in any other country. If is, therefore, proper for us to import their institutions. But now I want to know your views.

EDITOR: There is need for patience. My views will develop of themselves in the course of this discourse. It is as difficult for me to understand the true nature of swaraj as it seems to you to be easy. I shall therefore, for the time being, content myself with endeavouring to show that what you call swaraj is not truly swaraj.

Chapter V : The Condition of England

READER: Then from your statement I deduce that the Government of England is not desirable and not worth copying by us.

EDITOR: Your deduction is justified. The condition of England at present is pitiable. I pray to God that India may never be in that plight. That which you consider to be the Mother of Parliaments is like a sterile woman and a prostitute. Both these are harsh terms, but exactly fit the case. That Parliament has not yet, of its own accord, done a single good thing. Hence I have compared it to a sterile woman. The natural condition of the Parliament is such that, without outside pressure, it can do nothing. It is like a prostitute because it is under the control of ministers who change from time to time. Today it is under Mr Asquith, tomorrow it may be under Mr Balfour.

READER: You have said this sarcastically. The term "sterile woman" is not applicable. The Parliament, being elected by the people, must work under public pressure. This is its quality.

EDITOR: You are mistaken. Let us examine it a little more closely. The best men are supposed to be elected by the people. The members serve without pay and therefore, it must be assumed, only for the public weal. The electors are considered to be educated and therefore we should assume that they would not generally make mistakes in their choice. Such a Parliament should not need the spur of petitions or any other pressure. Its work should be so smooth that its effects would be more apparent day by day. But, as a matter of fact, it is generally acknowledged that the members are hypocritical and selfish. Each thinks of his own little interest. It is fear that is the guiding motive. What is done today may be undone tomorrow. *It is not possible to recall a single instance in which finality can be predicted for its work.* When the greatest questions are debated, its members have been seen to stretch themselves and to doze. Sometimes the members talk away until the listeners are disgusted. Carlyle has called it the "talking shop of the world". Members vote for their party without a thought. Their so-called discipline binds them to it. If any member, by way of exception, gives an independent vote, he is considered a renegade. If the money and the time wasted by Parliament were entrusted to a few good men, the English nation would be occupying today a much higher platform. Parliament is simply a costly toy of the nation. These views are by no means peculiar to me. Some great English thinkers have expressed them. One of the members of that Parliament recently said that a true Christian could not become a member of it. Another said that it was a baby. And if it has remained a baby after an existence of seven hundred years, when will it outgrow its babyhood?

READER: You have set me thinking; you do not expect me to accept at once all you say. You give me entirely novel views. I shall have to digest them. Will you now explain the epithet "prostitute"?

EDITOR: That you cannot accept my views at once is only right. If you will read the literature on this subject, you will have some idea of it. Parliament is without a real master. Under the Prime Minister, its movement is not steady but it is buffeted about like a prostitute. The Prime Minister is more concerned about his power than about the welfare of Parliament. His energy is concentrated upon securing the success of his party. His care is not always that Parliament shall do right. Prime Ministers are known to have made Parliament do things merely for party advantage. All this is worth thinking over.

READER: Then you are really attacking the very men whom we have hitherto considered to be patriotic and honest?

EDITOR: Yes, that is true; I can have nothing against Prime Ministers, but what I have seen leads me to think that they cannot be considered really patriotic. If they are to be considered honest because they do not take what are generally known as bribes, let them be so considered, but they are open to subtler influence. In order to gain their ends, they certainly bribe people with honours. I do not hesitate to say that they have neither real honesty nor a living conscience.

READER: As you express these views about Parliament, I would like to hear you on the English people, so that I may have your view of their Government.

EDITOR: To the English voters their newspaper is their Bible. They take their cue from their newspapers which are often dishonest. The same fact is differently interpreted by different newspapers, according to the party in whose interests they are edited. One newspaper would consider a great Englishman to be a paragon of honesty, another would consider him dishonest. What must be the condition of the people whose newspapers are of this type?

READER: You shall describe it.

EDITOR: These people change their views frequently. It is said that they change them every seven years. These views swing like the pendulum of a clock and are never steadfast. The people would follow a powerful orator or a man who gives them parties, receptions, etc. As are the people, so is their Parliament. They have certainly one quality very strongly developed. They will never allow their country to be lost. If any person were to cast an evil eye on it, they would pluck out his eyes. But that does not mean that the nation possesses every other virtue or that it should be imitated. If India copies England, it is my firm conviction that she will be ruined.

READER: To what do you ascribe this state of England?

EDITOR: It is not due to any peculiar fault of the English people, but the condition is due to modern civilization. It is a civilization only in name. Under it the nations of Europe are becoming degraded and ruined day by day.

Chapter VI : Civilization

READER: Now you will have to explain what you mean by civilization.

EDITOR: It is not a question of what I mean. Several English writers refuse to call that civilization which passes under that name. Many books have been written upon that subject. Societies have been formed to cure the nation of the evils of civilization. A great English writer has written a work called *Civilization: Its Cause and Cure*. Therein he had called it a disease.

READER: Why do we not know this generally?

EDITOR: The answer is very simple. We rarely find people arguing against themselves. Those who are intoxicated by modern civilization are not likely to write against it. Their care will be to find out facts and arguments in support of it, and this they do unconsciously, believing it to be true. A man, whilst he is dreaming, believes in his dream; he is undeceived only when he is awakened from his sleep. A man labouring under the bane of civilization is like a dreaming man. What we usually read are the works of defenders of modern civilization, which undoubtedly claims among its votaries very brilliant and even some very good men. Their writings hypnotize us. And so, one by one, we are drawn into the vortex.

READER: This seems to be very plausible. Now will you tell me something of what you have read and thought of this civilization?

EDITOR: Let us first consider what state of things is described by the word "civilization". Its true test lies in the fact that people living in it make bodily welfare the object of life. We will take some examples. The people of Europe today live in better-built houses than they did a hundred years ago. This is considered an emblem of civilization, and this is also a matter to promote bodily happiness. Formerly, they wore skins, and used spears as their weapons. Now, they wear long trousers, and, for embellishing their bodies, they wear a variety of clothing, and, instead of spears, they carry with them revolvers containing five or more chambers. If people of a certain country, who have hitherto not been in the habit of wearing much clothing, boots, etc., adopt European clothing, they are supposed to have become civilized out of savagery. Formerly, in

Europe, people ploughed their lands mainly by manual labour. Now, one man can plough a vast tract by means of steam engines and can thus amass great wealth. This is called a sign of civilization. Formerly, only a few men wrote valuable books. Now, anybody writes and prints anything he likes and poisons people's minds. Formerly, men travelled in waggons. Now, they fly through the air in trains at the rate of four hundred and more miles per day. This is considered the height of civilization. It has been stated that, as men progress, they shall be able to travel in airships and reach any part of the world in a few hours. Men will not need the use of their hands and feet. They will press a button, and they will have their clothing by their side. They will press another button, and they will have their newspaper. A third, and a motor-car will be in waiting for them. They will have a variety of delicately dished up food. Everything will be done by machinery. Formerly, when people wanted to fight with one another, they measured between them their bodily strength; now it is possible to take away thousands of lives by one man working behind a gun from a hill. This is civilization. Formerly, men worked in the open air only as much as they liked. Now thousands of workmen meet together and for the sake of maintenance work in factories or mines. Their condition is worse than that of beasts. They are obliged to work, at the risk of their lives, at most dangerous occupations, for the sake of millionaires. Formerly, men were made slaves under physical compulsion. Now they are enslaved by temptation of money and of the luxuries that money can buy. There are now diseases of which people never dreamt before, and an army of doctors is engaged in finding out their cures, and so hospitals have increased. This is a test of civilization. Formerly, special messengers were required and much expense was incurred in order to send letters; today, anyone can abuse his fellow by means of a letter for one penny. True, at the same cost, one can send one's thanks also. Formerly, people had two or three meals consisting of home-made bread and vegetables; now, they require something to eat every two hours so that they have hardly leisure for anything else. What more need I say? All this you can ascertain from several authoritative books. These are all true tests of civilization. And if anyone speaks to the contrary, know that he is ignorant. This civilization takes note neither of morality nor of religion. Its votaries calmly state that their business is not to teach religion. Some even consider it to be a superstitious growth. Others put on the cloak of religion, and prate about morality. But after twenty years' experience, I have come to the conclusion that immorality is often taught in the name of morality. Even a child can understand that in all I have described above there can be no inducement to morality. Civilization seeks to increase bodily comforts, and it fails miserably even in doing so.

This civilization is irreligion, and it has taken such a hold on the people in Europe that those who are in it appear to be half mad. They lack real physical strength or courage. They keep up their energy by intoxication. They can hardly be happy in solitude. Women, who should be the queens of households, wander in the streets or they slave away in factories. For the sake of a pittance, half a million women in England alone are labouring under trying circumstances in factories or similar institutions. This awful fact is one of the causes of the daily growing Suffragette Movement.

This civilization is such that one has only to be patient and it will be self-destroyed. According to the teaching of Mahomed this would be considered a Satanic Civilization. Hinduism calls it the Black Age. I cannot give you an adequate conception of it. It is eating into the vitals of the English nation. It must be shunned. Parliaments are really emblems of slavery. If you will sufficiently think over this, you will entertain the same opinion and cease to blame the English. They rather deserve our sympathy. They are a shrewd nation and I therefore believe that they will cast off the evil. They are enterprising and industrious, and their mode of thought is not inherently immoral. Neither are they bad at heart. I therefore respect them. Civilization is not an incurable disease, but it should never be forgotten that the English people are at present afflicted by it.

Chapter VII : Why was India Lost?

READER: You have said much about civilization—enough to make me ponder over it. I do not now know what I should adopt and what I should avoid from the nations of Europe but one question comes to my lips immediately. If civilization is a disease and if it has attacked England, why has she been able to take India, and why is she able to retain it?

EDITOR: Your question is not very difficult to answer, and we shall presently be able to examine the true nature of swaraj; for I am aware that I have still to answer that question. I will, however, take up your previous question. The English have not taken India; we have given it to them. They are not in India because of their strength, but because we keep them. Let us now see whether these propositions can be sustained. They came to our country originally for purposes of trade. Recall the Company Bahadur. Who made it Bahadur? They had not the slightest intention at the time of establishing a kingdom. Who assisted the Company's officers? Who was tempted at the sight of their silver? Who bought their goods? History testifies that we did all this. In order to become rich all at once we welcomed the Company's officers with open arms. We assisted them. If I am in the habit of drinking *bhang* and a seller thereof sells it to me, am I to blame him or myself? By blaming the seller, shall I be able to avoid the habit? And, if a particular retailer is driven away, will not another take his place? A true servant of India will have to go to the root of the matter. If an excess of food has caused me indigestion, I shall certainly not avoid it by blaming water. He is a true physician who probes the cause of a disease, and if you pose as a physician for the disease of India, you will have to find out its true cause.

READER: You are right. Now I think you will not have to argue much with me to drive your conclusions home. I am impatient to know your further views. We are now on a most interesting topic. I shall, therefore, endeavour to follow your thought, and stop you when I am in doubt.

EDITOR: I am afraid that, in spite of your enthusiasm, as we proceed further, we shall have differences of opinion. Nevertheless, I shall argue only when you stop me. We have already seen that the English merchants were able to get a footing in India because we encouraged them. When our princes fought among themselves, they sought the assistance of Company Bahadur. That corporation was versed alike in commerce and war. It was unhampered by questions of morality. Its object was to increase its commerce and to make money. It accepted our assistance, and increased the number of its warehouses. To protect the latter it employed an army which was utilized by us also. Is it not then useless to blame the English for what we did at that time? The Hindus and the Mahomedans were at daggers drawn. This, too, gave the Company its opportunity and thus we created the circumstances that gave the Company its control over India. Hence it is truer to say that we gave India to the English than that India was lost.

READER: Will you now tell me how they are able to retain India?

EDITOR: The causes that gave them India enable them to retain it. Some Englishmen state that they took and they hold India by the sword. Both these statements are wrong. The sword is entirely useless for holding India. We alone keep them. Napoleon is said to have described the English as a nation of shop-keepers. It is a fitting description. They hold whatever dominions they have for the sake of their commerce. Their army and their navy are intended to protect it. When the Transvaal offered no such attractions, the late Mr Gladstone discovered that it was not right for the English to hold it. When it became a paying proposition, resistance led to war. Mr Chamberlain soon discovered that England enjoyed a suzerainty over the Transvaal. It is related that someone asked the late President Kruger whether there was gold in the moon. He replied that it was highly unlikely because, if there were, the English would have annexed it. Many problems can be solved by remembering that money is their God. Then it follows that we keep the English in India for our base self-interest. We like their commerce; they please us by their subtle methods and get what they want from us. To blame them for this is to perpetuate their power. We further strengthen their hold by quarrelling amongst ourselves. If you accept the above statements, it is proved that the English entered India for the purposes of trade. They remain in it for the same purpose and we help them to do so. Their arms and ammunition are perfectly useless. In this connection I remind you that it is the British flag which is waving in Japan and not the Japanese. The English have a treaty with Japan for the sake of their commerce, and you will see that if they can manage it, their commerce will greatly expand in that country. They wish to convert the whole world into a vast market for their goods. That they cannot do so is true, but the blame will not be theirs. They will leave no stone unturned to reach the goal.

Chapter VIII : The Condition of India

READER: I now understand why the English hold India. I should like to know your views about the condition of our country.

EDITOR: It is a sad condition. In thinking of it my eyes water and my throat gets parched. I have grave doubts whether I shall be able sufficiently to explain what is in my heart. It is my deliberate opinion that India is being ground down, not under the English heel, but under that of modern civilization. It is groaning under the monster's terrible weight. There is yet time to escape it, but every day makes it more and more difficult. Religion is dear to me and my first complaint is that India is becoming irreligious. Here I am not thinking of the Hindu or the Mahomedan or the Zoroastrian religion but of that religion which underlies all religions. We are turning away from God.

READER: How so?

EDITOR: There is a charge laid against us that we are a lazy people and that Europeans are industrious and enterprising. We have accepted the charge and we therefore wish to change our condition. Hinduism, Islam, Zoroastrianism, Christianity and all other religions teach that we should remain passive about worldly pursuits and active about godly pursuits, that we should set a limit to our worldly ambition and that our religious ambition should be illimitable. Our activity should be directed into the latter channel.

READER: You seem to be encouraging religious charlatanism. Many a cheat has, by talking in a similar strain, led the people astray.

EDITOR: You are bringing an unlawful charge against religion. Humbug there undoubtedly is about all religions. Where there is light, there is also shadow. I am prepared to maintain that humbugs in worldly matters are far worse than the humbugs in religion. The humbug of civilization that I am endeavouring to show to you is not to be found in religion.

READER: How can you say that? In the name of religion Hindus and Mahomedans fought against one another. For the same cause Christians fought Christians. Thousands of innocent men have been murdered, thousands have been burned and tortured in its name. Surely, this is much worse than any civilization.

EDITOR: I certainly submit that the above hardships are far more bearable than those of civilization. Everybody understands that the cruelties you have named are not part of religion although they have been practised in its name; therefore there is no aftermath to these cruelties. They will always happen so long as there are to be found ignorant and credulous people. But there is no end to the victims destroyed in the fire of civilization. Its deadly effect is that people come under its scorching flames believing it to be all good. They become utterly irreligious and, in reality, derive little advantage from the world. Civilization is like a mouse gnawing while it is soothing us. When its full effect is realized, we shall see that religious superstition is harmless compared to that of modern civilization. I am not pleading for a continuance of religious superstitions. We shall certainly fight them tooth and nail, but we can never do so by disregarding religion. We can only do so by appreciating and conserving the latter.

READER: Then you will content that the Pax Britannica is a useless encumbrance?

EDITOR: You may see peace if you like; I see none.

READER: You make light of the terror that the Thugs, the Pindaris and the Bhils were to the country.

EDITOR: If you give the matter some thought, you will see that the terror was by no means such a mighty thing. If it had been a very substantial thing, the other people would have died away before the English advent. Moreover, the present peace is only nominal, for by it we have become emasculated and cowardly. We are not to assume that the English have changed the nature of the Pindaris and the Bhils. It is, therefore, better to suffer the Pindari peril than that someone else should protect us from it and thus render us effeminate. I should prefer to be killed by the arrow of a Bhil than to seek unmanly protection. India without such protection was an India full of valour. Macaulay betrayed gross ignorance when he libelled Indians as being practically cowards. They never merited the charge. Cowards living in a country inhabited by hardy mountaineers and infested by wolves and tigers must surely find an early grave. Have you ever visited our fields? I assure you that our agriculturists sleep fearlessly on their farms even today; but the English and you and I would hesitate to sleep where they sleep. Strength lies in absence of fear, not in the quantity of flesh and muscle we may have on our bodies. Moreover, I must remind you who desire Home Rule that, after all, the Bhils, the Pindaris, and the Thugs are our own countrymen. To conquer them is your and my work. So long as we fear our own brethren, we are unfit to reach the goal.

Chapter IX : The Condition of India (continued) : Railways

READER: You have deprived me of the consolation I used to have regarding peace in India.

EDITOR: I have merely given you my opinion on the religious aspect, but when I give you my views as to the poverty of India, you will perhaps begin to dislike me because what you and I have hitherto considered beneficial for India no longer appears to me to be so.

READER: What may that be?

EDITOR: Railways, lawyers and doctors have impoverished the country so much so that, if we do not wake up in time, we shall be ruined.

READER: I do now, indeed, fear that we are not likely to agree at all. You are attacking the very institutions which we have hitherto considered to be good.

EDITOR: It is necessary to exercise patience. The true inwardness of the evils of civilization you will understand with difficulty. Doctors assure us that a consumptive clings to life even when he is about to die. Consumption does not produce apparent hurt—it even produces a seductive colour about a patient's face so as to induce the belief that all is well. Civilization is such a disease and we have to be very wary.

READER: Very well, then. I shall hear you on the railways.

EDITOR: It must be manifest to you that, but for the railways, the English could not have such a hold on India as they have. The railways, too, have spread the bubonic plague. Without them, the masses could not move from place to place. They are the carriers of plague germs. Formerly, we had natural segregation. Railways have also increased the frequency of famines because, owing to facility of means of locomotion, people sell out their grain and it is sent to the dearest markets. People become careless and so the pressure of famine increases. Railways accentuate the evil nature of man. Bad men fulfil their evil designs with greater rapidity. The holy places of India have become unholy. Formerly, people went to these places with very great difficulty. Generally, therefore, only the real devotees visited such places. Nowadays rogues visit them in order to practise their roguery.

READER: You have given a one-sided account, good men can visit these places as well as bad men. Why do they not take the fullest advantage of the railways?

EDITOR: Good travels at a snail's pace—it can, therefore, have little to do with the railways. Those who want to do good are not selfish, they are not in a hurry, they know that to impregnate people with good requires a long time. But evil has wings. To build a house takes time. Its destruction takes none. So the railways can become a distributing agency for the evil one only. It may be a debatable matter whether railways spread famines, but it is beyond dispute that they propagate evil.

READER: Be that as it may, all the disadvantages of the railways are more than counterbalanced by the fact that it is due to them that we see in India the new spirit of nationalism.

EDITOR: I hold this to be a mistake. The English have taught us that we were not one nation before and that it will require centuries before we become one nation. This is without foundation. We were one nation before they came to India. One thought inspired us. Our mode of life was the same. It was because we were one nation that they were able to establish one kingdom. Subsequently they divided us.

READER: This requires an explanation.

EDITOR: I do not wish to suggest that because we were one nation we had no differences, but it is submitted that our leading men travelled throughout India either on foot or in bullock-carts. They learned one another's languages and there was no aloofness between them. What do you think could have been the intention of those farseeing ancestors of ours who established Setubandha (Rameshwar) in the South, Jagannath in the East and Hardwar in the North as places of pilgrimage? You will admit they were no fools. They knew that worship of God could have been performed just as well at home. They taught us that those whose hearts were aglow with righteousness had the Ganges in their own homes. But they saw that India was one undivided land so made by nature. They, therefore, argued that it must be one nation. Arguing thus, they established holy places in various parts of India, and fired the people with an idea of nationality in a manner unknown in other parts of the world. And we Indians are one as no two Englishmen are. Only you and I and others who consider ourselves civilized and superior persons imagine that we are many nations. It was after the advent of railways that we began to believe in distinctions, and you are at liberty now to say that it is through the railways that we are beginning to abolish those distinctions. An opium-eater may argue the advantage of opium-eating from the fact that he began to understand the evil of the opium habit after having eaten it. I would ask you to consider well what I had said on the railways.

READER: I will gladly do so, but one question occurs to me even now. You have described to me the India of the pre-Mahomedan period, but now we have Mahomedan, Parsis and Christians. How can they be one nation? Hindus and Mahomedans are old enemies. Our very proverbs prove it. Mahomedans turn to the West for worship, whilst Hindus turn to the East. The former look down on the Hindus as idolaters. The Hindus worship the cow, the Mahomedans kill her. The Hindus believe in the doctrine of non-killing, the Mahomedans do not. We thus meet with differences at every step. How can India be one nation?

Chapter X : The Condition of India (continued) : The Hindus & the Mahomedans

EDITOR: Your last question is a serious one and yet, on careful consideration, it will be found to be easy of solution. The question arises because of the presence of the railways, of the lawyers and of the doctors. We shall presently examine the last two. We have already considered the railways. I should, however, like to add that man is so made by nature as to require him to restrict his movements as far as his hands and feet will take him. If we did not rush about from place to place by means of railways and such other maddening conveniences, much of the confusion that arises would be obviated. Our difficulties are of our own creation. God set a limit to man's locomotive ambition in the construction of his body. Man immediately proceeded to discover means of overriding the limit. God gifted man with intellect that he might know his Maker. Man abused it so that he might forget his Maker. I am so constructed that I can only serve my immediate neighbours, but in my conceit I pretend to have discovered that I must with my body serve every individual in the Universe. In thus attempting the impossible, man comes in contact with different natures, different religions, and is utterly confounded. According to this reasoning, it must be apparent to you that railways are a most dangerous institution. Owing to them, man has gone further away from his Maker.

READER: But I am impatient to hear your answer to my question. Has the introduction of Mahomedanism not unmade the nation?

EDITOR: India cannot cease to be one nation because people belonging to different religions live in it. The introduction of foreigners does not necessarily destroy the nation; they merge in it. A country is one nation only when such a condition obtains in it. That country must have a faculty for assimilation. India has ever been such a country. In reality, there are as many religions as there are individuals; but those who are conscious of the spirit of nationality do not interfere with one another's religion. If they do, they are not fit to be considered a nation. If the Hindus believe that India should be peopled only by Hindus, they are living in dreamland. The Hindus, the Mahomedans, the Parsis and the Christians who have made India their country are fellow countrymen, and they will have to live in unity, if only for their own interest. In no part of the world are one nationality and one religion synonymous terms; nor has it ever been so in India.

READER: But what about the inborn enmity between Hindus and Mahomedans?

EDITOR: That phrase has been invented by our mutual enemy. When the Hindus and Mahomedans fought against one another, they certainly spoke in that strain. They have long since ceased to fight. How, then, can there be any inborn enmity? Pray remember this too, that we did not cease to fight only after British occupation. The Hindus flourished under Moslem sovereigns and Moslems under the Hindu. Each party recognized that mutual fighting was suicidal, and that neither party would abandon its religion by force of arms. Both parties, therefore, decided to live in peace. With the English advent quarrels recommenced.

The proverbs you have quoted were coined when both were fighting; to quote them now is obviously harmful. Should we not remember that many Hindus and Mahomedans own the same ancestors and the same blood runs through their veins? Do people become enemies because they change their religion? Is the God of the Mahomedan different from the God of the Hindu? Religions are different roads converging to the same point. What does it matter that we take different roads so long as we reach the same goal? Wherein is the cause for quarrelling?

Moreover, there are deadly proverbs as between the followers of Shiva and those of Vishnu, yet nobody suggests that these two do not belong to the same nation. It is said that the Vedic religion is different from Jainism, but the followers of the respective faiths are not different nations. The fact is that we have become enslaved and, therefore, quarrel and like to have our quarrels decided by a third party. There are Hindu iconoclasts as there are Mahomedan. The more we advance in true knowledge, the better we shall understand that we need not be at war with those whose religion we may not follow.

READER: Now I would like to know your views about cow-protection.

EDITOR: I myself respect the cow, that is, I look upon her with affectionate reverence. The cow is the protector of India because, being an agricultural country, she is dependent on the cow. The cow is a most useful animal in hundreds of ways. Our Mahomedan brethren will admit this.

But, just as I respect the cow, so do I respect my fellow-men. A man is as just as useful as a cow no mattter whether he be a Mahomedan or a Hindu. Am I, then, to fight with or kill a Mahomedan in order to save a cow? In doing so, I would become an enemy of the Mahomedan as well as of the cow. Therefore, the only method I know of protecting the cow is that I should approach my Mahomedan brother and urge him for the sake of the country to join me in protecting her. If he would not listen to me I should let the cow go for the simple reason that the matter is beyond my ability. If I were overfull of pity for the cow, I should sacrifice my life to save her but not take my brother's. This, I hold, is the law of our religion.

When men become obstinate, it is a difficult thing. If I pull one way, my Moslem brother will pull another. If I put on superior airs, he will return the compliment. If I bow to him gently, he will do it much more so; and if he does not, I shall not be considered to have done wrong in having bowed. When the Hindus became insistent, the killing of cows increased. In my opinion, cow-protection societies may be considered cow-killing societies. It is a disgrace to us that we should need such societies. When we forgot how to protect cows, I suppose we needed such societies.

What am I to do when a blood-brother is on the point of killing a cow? Am I to kill him, or to fall down at his feet and implore him? If you admit that I should adopt the latter course, I must do the same to my Moslem brother.

Who protects the cow from destructions by Hindus when they cruelly ill-treat her? Whoever reasons with the Hindus when they mercilessly belabour the progeny of the cow with their sticks? But this has not prevented us from remaining one nation.

Lastly, if it be true that the Hindus believe in the doctrine of non-killing and the Mahomedans do not, what, pray, is the duty of the former? It is not written that a follower of the religion of ahimsa (non-killing) may kill a fellow-man. For him the way is straight. In order to save one being, he may not kill another. He can only plead—therein lies his sole duty.

But does every Hindu believe in ahimsa? Going to the root of the matter, not one man really practises such a religion because we do destroy life. We are said to follow that religion because we want to obtain freedom from liability to kill any kind of life. Generally speaking, we may observe that many Hindus partake of meat and are not, therefore, followers of ahimsa. It is, therefore, preposterous to suggest that the two cannot live together amicably because the Hindus believe in ahimsa and the Mahomedans do not.

These thoughts are put into our minds by selfish and false religious teachers. The English put the finishing touch. They have a habit of writing history; they pretend to study the manners and customs of all peoples. God has given us a limited mental capacity, but they usurp the function of the Godhead and indulge in novel experiments. They write about their own researches in most laudatory terms and hypnotize us into believing them. We in our ignorance then fall at their feet.

Those who do not wish to misunderstand things may read up the Koran, and they will find therein hundreds of passages acceptable to the Hindus: and the Bhagavad Gita contains passages to which not a Mahomedan can take exception. Am I to dislike a Mahomedan because there are passages in the Koran I do not understand or like? It takes two to make a quarrel. If I do not want to quarrel with a Mahomedan, the latter will be powerless to foist a quarrel on me; and, similarly, I should be powerless if a Mahomedan refuses his assistance to quarrel with me. An arm striking the air will become disjointed. If everyone will try to understand the core of his own religion and adhere to it, and will not allow false teachers to dictate to him, there will be no room left for quarrelling.

READER: But will the English ever allow the two bodies to join hands?

EDITOR: This question arises out of your timidity. It betrays our shallowness. If two brothers want to live in peace, is it possible for a third party to separate them? If they were to listen to evil counsels we would consider them to be foolish. Similarly, we Hindus and Mahomedans would have to blame our folly rather than the English, if we allowed them to put us asunder. A clay pot would break through impact, if not with one stone, then with another. The way to save the pot is not to keep it away from the danger point but to bake it so that no stone would break it. We have then to make our hearts of perfectly baked clay. Then we shall be steeled against all danger. This can be easily done by the Hindus. They are superior in numbers; they pretend that they are more educated; they are, therefore, better able to shield themselves from attack on their amicable relations with the Mahomedans.

There is mutual distrust between the two communities. The Mahomedans, therefore, ask for certain concessions from Lord Morley. Why should the Hindus oppose this? If the Hindus desisted, the English would notice it, the Mahomedans would gradually begin to trust the Hindus, and brotherliness would be the outcome. We should be ashamed to take our quarrels to the English. Everyone can find out for himself that the Hindus can lose nothing by desisting.

That man who has inspired confidence in another has never lost anything in this world.

I do not suggest that the Hindus and the Mahomedans will never fight. Two brothers living together often do so. We shall sometimes have our heads broken. Such a thing ought not to be necessary, but all men are not equitable. When people are in a rage, they do many foolish things. These we have to put up with. But when we do quarrel, we certainly do not want to engage counsel and resort to English or any law courts. Two men fight; both have their heads broken, or one only. How shall a third party distribute justice amongst them? Those who fight may expect to be injured.

Chapter XI : The Condition of India (continued) : Lawyers

READER: You tell me that when two men quarrel they should not go to a law court. This is astonishing.

EDITOR: Whether you call it astonishing or not, it is the truth. And your question introduces us to the lawyers and the doctors. My firm opinion is that the lawyers have enslaved India, have accentuated Hindu-Mahomedan dissensions and have confirmed English authority.

READER: It is easy enough to bring these charges, but it will be difficult for you to prove them. But for the lawyers, who would have shown us the road to independence? Who would have protected the poor? Who would have secured justice? For instance, the late Manomohan Ghose defended many a poor man free of charge. The Congress, which you have praised so much, is dependent for its existence and activity upon the work of the lawyers. To denounce such an estimable class of men is to spell injustice, and you are abusing the liberty of the Press by decrying lawyers.

EDITOR: At one time I used to think exactly like you. I have no desire to convince you that they have never done a single good thing. I honour Mr Ghose's memory. It is quite true that he helped the poor. That the Congress owes the lawyers something is believable. Lawyers are also men, and there is something good in every man. Whenever instances of lawyers having done good can be brought forward, it will be found that the good is due to them as men rather than as lawyers. All I am concerned with is to show you that the profession teaches immorality; it is exposed to temptation from which few are saved.

The Hindus and the Mahomedans have quarrelled. An ordinary man will ask them to forget all about it; he will tell them that both must be more or less at fault, and will advise them no longer to quarrel. But they go to lawyers. The latter's duty is to side with their clients and to find out ways and arguments in favour of the clients, to which they (the clients) are often strangers. If they do not do so, they will be considered to have degraded their profession. The lawyers, therefore, will, as a rule, advance quarrels instead of repressing them. Moreover, men take up that profession, not in order to help others out of their miseries, but to enrich themselves. It is one of the avenues of becoming wealthy and their interest exists in multiplying disputes. It is within my knowledge that they are glad when men have disputes. Petty pleaders actually manufacture them. Their touts, like so many leeches, suck the blood of the poor people. Lawyers are men who have little to do. Lazy people, in order to indulge in luxuries, take up such professions. This is a true statement. Any other argument is a mere pretension. It is the lawyers who have discovered that theirs is an honourable profession. They frame laws as they frame their own praises. They decide what fees they will charge and they put on so much side that poor people almost consider them to be heaven-born.

Why do they want more fees than common labourers? Why are their requirements greater? In what way are they more profitable to the country than the labourers? Are those who do good entitled to greater payment? And, if they have done anything for the country for the sake of money, how shall it be counted as good?

Those who know anything of the Hindu-Mahomedan quarrels know that they have been often due to the intervention of lawyers. Some families have been ruined through them; they have made brothers enemies. Principalities, having come under the lawyers' power, have become loaded with debt. Many have been robbed of their all. Such instances can be multiplied.

But the greatest injury they have done to the country is that they have tightened the English grip. Do you think that it would be possible for the English to carry on their Government without law courts? It is wrong to consider that courts are established for the benefit of the people. Those who want to perpetuate their power do so through the courts. If people were to settle their own quarrels, a third party would not be able to exercise any authority over them. Truly, men were less unmanly when they settled their disputes either by fighting or by asking their relative to decide for them. They became more unmanly and cowardly when they resorted to the courts of law. It was certainly a sign of savagery when they settled their disputes by fighting. Is it any the less so, if I ask a third party to decide between you and me? Surely, the decision of a third party is not always right. The parties alone know who is right. We, in our simplicity and ignorance, imagine that a stranger, by taking our money, gives us justice.

The chief thing, however, to be remembered is that without lawyers courts could not have been established or conducted and without the latter the English could not rule. Supposing that there were only English judges, English pleaders and English police, they could only rule over the English. The English could not do without Indian judges and Indian pleaders. How the pleaders were made in the first instance and how they were favoured you should understand well. Then you will have the same abhorrence for the profession that I have. If pleaders were to abandon their profession, and consider it just as degrading as prostitution, English rule would break up in a day. They have been instrumental in having the charge laid against us that we love quarrels and courts as fish love water. What I have said with reference to the pleaders necessarily applies to the judge; they are first cousins; and the one gives strength to the other.

Chapter XII : The Condition of India (continued) : Doctors

READER: I now understand the lawyers; the good they may have done is accidental. I feel that profession is certainly hateful. You, however, drag in the doctors also, how is that?

EDITOR: The views I submit to you are those I have adopted. They are not original. Western writers have used stronger terms regarding both lawyers and doctors. One writer has likened the whole modern system to the upas tree. Its branches are represented by parasitical professions, including those of law and medicine, and over the trunk has been raised the axe of true religion. Immorality is the root of the tree. So you will see that the views do not come right out of my mind but represent the combined experiences of many. I was at one time a great lover of the medical profession. It was my intention to become a doctor for the sake of the country. I no longer hold that opinion. I now understand why the medicine men (the vaids) among us have not occupied a very honourable status.

The English have certainly effectively used the medical profession for holding us. English physicians are known to have used their profession with several Asiatic potentates for political gain.

Doctors have almost unhinged us. Sometimes I think that quacks are better than highly qualified doctors. Let us consider: the business of a doctor is to take care of the body, or, properly speaking, not even that. Their business is really to rid the body of diseases that may afflict it. How do these diseases arise? Surely by our negligence or indulgence. I overeat, I have indigestion, I go to a doctor, he gives me medicine, I am cured. I overeat again, I take his pills again. Had I not taken the pills in the first instance, I would have suffered the punishment deserved by me and I would not have overeaten again. The doctor intervened and helped me to indulge myself. My body thereby certainly felt more at ease; but my mind became weakened. A continuance of a course of medicine must, therefore, result in loss of control over the mind.

I have indulged in vice, I contract a disease, a doctor cures me, the odds are that I shall repeat the vice. Had the doctor not intervened, nature would have done its work, and I would have acquired mastery over myself, would have been freed from vice and would have become happy.

Hospitals are institutions for propagating sin. Men take less care of their bodies and immorality increases. European doctors are the worst of all. For the sake of a mistaken care of the human body, they kill annually thousands of animals. They practise vivisection. No religion sanctions this. All say that it is not necessary to take so many lives for the sake of our bodies.

These doctors violate our religious instinct. Most of their

33

medical preparations contain either animal fat or spirituous liquors; both of these are tabooed by Hindus and Mahomedans. We may pretend to be civilized, call religious prohibitions a superstition and want only to indulge in what we like. The fact remains that the doctors induce us to indulge, and the result is that we have become deprived of self-control and have become effeminate. In these circumstances, we are unfit to serve the country. To study European medicine is to deepen our slavery.

It is worth considering why we take up the profession of medicine. It is certainly not taken up for the purpose of serving humanity. We become doctors so that we may obtain honours and riches. I have endeavoured to show that there is no real service of humanity in the profession, and that it is injurious to mankind. Doctors make a show of their knowledge, and charge exorbitant fees. Their preparations, which are intrinsically worth a few pence, cost shillings. The populace, in its credulity and in the hope of ridding itself of some disease, allows itself to be cheated. Are not quacks then, whom we know, better than the doctors who put on an air of humaneness?

Chapter XIII : What is True Civilization?

READER: You have denounced railways, lawyers and doctors. I can see that you will discard all machinery. What, then, is civilization?

EDITOR: The answer to that question is not difficult. I believe that the civilization India has evolved is not to be beaten in the world. Nothing can equal the seeds sown by our ancestors. Rome went, Greece shared the same fate; the might of the Pharaohs was broken; Japan has become westernized; of China nothing can be said; but India is still, somehow or other, sound at the foundation. The people of Europe learn their lessons from the writings of the men of Greece or Rome, which exist no longer in their former glory. In trying to learn from them, the Europeans imagine that they will avoid the mistakes of Greece and Rome. Such is their pitiable condition. In the midst of all this India remains immovable and that is her glory. It is a charge against India that her people are so uncivilized, ignorant and stolid, that it is not possible to induce them to adopt any changes. It is a charge really against our merit. What we have tested and found true on the anvil of experience, we dare not change. Many thrust their advice upon India, and she remains steady. This is her beauty: it is the sheet-anchor of our hope.

Civilization is that mode of conduct which points out to man the path of duty. Performance of duty and observance of morality are convertible terms. To observe morality is to attain mastery over our mind and our passions. So doing, we know ourselves. The Gujarati equivalent for civilization means "good conduct".

If this definition be correct, then India, as so many writers have shown, has nothing to learn from anybody else, and this is as it should be. We notice that the mind is a restless bird; the more it gets the more it wants, and still remains unsatisfied. The more we indulge our passions, the more unbridled they become. Our ancestors, therefore, set a limit to our indulgences. They saw that happiness was largely a mental condition. A man is not necessarily happy because he is rich, or unhappy because he is poor. The rich are often seen to be unhappy, the poor to be happy. Millions will always remain poor. Observing all this, our ancestors dissuaded us from luxuries and pleasures. We have managed with the same kind of plough as existed thousands of years ago. We have retained the same kind of cottages that we had in former times and our indigenous education remains the same as before. We have had no system of life-corroding competition. Each followed his own occupation or trade and charged a regulation wage. It was not that we did not know how to invent machinery, but our forefathers knew that, if we set our hearts after such things, we would become slaves and lose our moral fibre. They, therefore, after due deliberation decided that we should only do what we could with our hands and feet. They saw that our real happiness and health consisted in a proper use of our hands and feet. They further reasoned that large cities were a snare and a useless encumbrance and that people would not be happy in them, that there would be gangs of thieves and robbers, prostitution and vice flourishing in them and that poor men would be robbed by rich men. They were, therefore, satisfied with small villages. They saw that kings and their swords were inferior to the sword of ethics, and they, therefore, held the sovereigns of the earth to be inferior to the Rishis and the Fakirs. A nation with a constitution like this is fitter to teach others than to learn from others. This nation had courts, lawyers and doctors, but

35

they were all within bounds. Everybody knew that these professions were not particularly superior; moreover, these vakils and vaids did not rob people; they were considered people's dependants, not their masters. Justice was tolerably fair. The ordinary rule was to avoid courts. There were no touts to lure people into them. This evil, too, was noticeable only in and around capitals. There common people lived independently and followed their agricultural occupation. They enjoyed true Home Rule.

And where this cursed modern civilization has not reached, India remains as it was before. The inhabitants of that part of India will very properly laugh at your new-fangled notions. The English do not rule over them, nor will you ever rule over them. Those in whose name we speak we do not know, nor do they know us. I would certainly advise you and those like you who love the motherland to go into the interior that has yet been not polluted by the railways and to live there for six months; you might then be patriotic and speak of Home Rule.

Now you see what I consider to be real civilization. Those who want to change conditions such as I have described are enemies of the country and are sinners.

READER: It would be all right if India were exactly as you have described it, but it is also India where there are hundreds of child widows, where two-year-old babies are married, where twelve-year-old girls are mothers and housewives, where women practise polyandry, where the practice of Niyoga obtains, where, in the name of religion, girls dedicate themselves to prostitution, and in the name of religion sheep and goat are killed. Do you consider these also symbols of the civilization that you have described?

EDITOR: You make a mistake. The defects that you have shown are defects. Nobody mistakes them for ancient civilization. They remain in spite of it. Attempts have always been made and will be made to remove them. We may utilize the new spirit that is born in us for purging ourselves of these evils. But what I have described to you as emblems of modern civilization are accepted as such by its votaries. The Indian civilization, as described by me, has been so described by its votaries. In no part of the world, and under no civilization, have all men attained perfection. The tendency of the Indian civilization is to elevate the moral being, that of the Western civilization is to propagate immorality. The latter is godless, the former is based on a belief in God. So understanding and so believing, it behoves every lover of India to cling to the old Indian civilization even as a child clings to the mother's breast.

Chapter XIV : How Can India Become Free?

READER: I appreciate your views about civilization. I will have to think over them. I cannot take them in all at once. What, then, holding the views you do, would you suggest for freeing India?

EDITOR: I do not expect my views to be accepted all of a sudden. My duty is to place them before readers like yourself. Time can be trusted to do the rest. We have already examined the conditions for freeing India, but we have done so indirectly; we will now do so directly. It is a world-known maxim that the removal of the cause of a disease results in the removal of the disease itself. Similarly if the cause of India's slavery be removed, India can become free.

READER: If Indian civilization is, as you say, the best of all, how do you account for India's slavery?

EDITOR: This civilization is unquestionably the best, but it is to be observed that all civilizations have been on their trial. That civilization which is permanent outlives it. Because the sons of India were found wanting, its civilization has been placed in jeopardy. But its strength is to be seen in its ability to survive the shock. Moreover, the whole of India is not touched. Those alone who have been affected by Western civilization have become enslaved. We measure the universe by our own miserable foot-rule. When we are slaves, we think that the whole universe is enslaved. Because we are in an abject condition, we think that the whole of India is in that condition. As a matter of fact, it is not so, yet it is as well to impute our slavery to the whole of India. But if we bear in mind the above fact, we can see that if we become free, India is free. And in this thought you have a definition of swaraj. It is swaraj when we learn to rule ourselves. It is, therefore, in the palm of our hands. Do not consider this swaraj to be like a dream. There is no idea of sitting still. The swaraj that I wish to picture is such that, after we have once realized it, we shall endeavour to the end of our life-time to persuade others to do likewise. But such swaraj has to be experienced, by each one for himself. One drowning man will never save another. Slaves ourselves, it would be a mere pretension to think of freeing others. Now you will have seen that it is not necessary for us to have as our goal the expulsion of the English. If the English become Indianized, we can accommodate them. If they wish to remain in India along with their civilization, there is no room for them. It lies with us to bring about such a state of things.

READER: It is impossible that Englishmen should ever become Indianized.

EDITOR: To say that is equivalent to saying that the English have no humanity in them. And it is really beside the point whether they become so or not. If we keep our own house in order, only those who are fit to live in it will remain. Others will leave of their own accord. Such things occur within the experience of all of us.

READER: But it has not occurred in history.

EDITOR: To believe that what has not occurred in history will not occur at all is to argue disbelief in the dignity of man. At any rate, if behoves us to try what appeals to our reason. All countries are not similarly conditioned. The condition of India is unique. Its strength is immeasurable. We need not, therefore, refer to the history of other countries. I have drawn attention to the fact that, when other civilizations have succumbed, the Indian has survived many a shock.

READER: I cannot follow this. There seems little doubt that we shall have to expel the English by force of arms. So long as they are in the country we cannot rest. One of our poets says that slaves cannot even dream of happiness. We are day by day becoming weakened owing to the presence of the English. Our greatness is gone; our people look like terrified men. The English are in the country like a blight which we must remove by every means.

EDITOR: In your excitement, you have forgotten all we have been considering. We brought the English, and we keep them. Why do you forget that our adoption of their civilization makes their presence in India at all possible? Your hatred against them ought to be transferred to their civilization. But let us assume that we have to drive away the English by fighting, how is that to be done?

READER: In the same way as Italy did it. What was possible for Mazzini and Garibaldi is possible for us. You cannot deny that they were very great men.

Chapter XV : Italy and India

EDITOR: It is well that you have instanced Italy. Mazzini was a great and good man; Garibaldi was a great warrior. Both are adorable; from their lives we can learn much. But the condition of Italy was different from that of India. In the first instance, the difference between Mazzini and Garibaldi is worth noting. Mazzini's ambition was not and has not yet been realized regarding Italy. Mazzini has shown in his writings on the duty of man that every man must learn how to rule himself. This has not happened in Italy. Garibaldi did not hold this view of Mazzini's. Garibaldi gave and very Italian took arms. Italy and Austria had the same civilization; they were cousins in this respect. It was a matter of tit for tat. Garibaldi simply wanted Italy to be free from the Austrian yoke. The machinations of Minister Cavour disgrace that portion of the history of Italy. And what has been the result? If you believe that because Italians rule Italy the Italian nation is happy, you are groping in darkness. Mazzini has shown conclusively that Italy did not become free. Victor Emmanuel (II) gave one meaning to the expression; Mazzini gave another. According to Emmanuel, Cavour and even Garibaldi, Italy meant the King of Italy and his henchmen. According to Mazzini, it meant the whole of the Italian people, that is, its agriculturists. Emmanuel was only its servant. The Italy of Mazzini still remains in a state of slavery. At the time of the so-called national war, it was a game of chess between two rival kings with the people of Italy as pawns. The working classes in that land are still unhappy. They, therefore, indulge in assassination, rise in revolt, and rebellion on their part is always expected. What substantial gain did Italy obtain after the withdrawal of the Austrian troops? The gain was only nominal. The reforms for the sake of which the war was supposed to have been undertaken have not yet been granted. The condition of the people in general still remains the same. I am sure you do not wish to reproduce such a condition in India. I believe that you want the millions of India to be happy, not that you want the reins of government in your hands. If that be so, we have to consider only one thing: how can the millions obtain self-rule? You will admit that people under several Indian princes are being ground down. The latter mercilessly crush them. Their

39

tyranny is greater than that of the English, and if you want such tyranny in India, then we shall never agree. My patriotism does not teach me that I am to allow people to be crushed under the heel of Indian princes if only the English retire. If I have the power, I should resist the tyranny of Indian princes just as much as that of the English. By patriotism I mean the welfare of the whole people, and if I could secure it at the hands of the English, I should bow down my head to them. If any Englishman dedicated his life to securing the freedom of India, resisting tyranny and serving the land, I should welcome that Englishman as an Indian.

Again, India can fight like Italy only when she has arms. You have not considered this problem at all. The English are splendidly armed; that does not frighten me, but it is clear that, to pit ourselves against them in arms, thousands of Indians must be armed. If such a thing be possible, how many years will it take? Moreover, to arm India on a large scale is to Europeanize it. Then her condition will be just as pitiable as that of Europe. This means, in short, that India must accept European civilization, and if that is what we want, the best thing is that we have among us those who are so well trained in that civilization. We will then fight for a few rights, will get what we can and so pass our days. But the fact is that the Indian nation will not adopt arms, and it is well that it does not.

READER: You are over-stating the facts. All need not be armed. At first, we shall assassinate a few Englishmen and strike terror; then, a few men who will have been armed will fight openly. We may have to lose a quarter of a million men, more or less, but we shall regain our land. We shall undertake guerrilla warfare, and defeat the English.

EDITOR: That is to say, you want to make the holy land of India unholy. Do you not tremble to think of freeing India by assassination? What we need to do is to sacrifice ourselves. It is a cowardly thought, that of killing others. Whom do you suppose to free by assassination? The millions of India do not desire it. Those who are intoxicated by the wretched modern civilization think these things. Those who will rise to power by murder will certainly not make the nation happy. Those who believe that India has gained by Dhingra's act and other similar acts in India make a serious mistake. Dhingra was a patriot, but his love was blind. He gave his body in a wrong way; its ultimate result can only be mischievous.

READER: But you will admit that the English have been frightened by these murders, and that Lord Morley's reforms are due to fear.

EDITOR: The English are both a timid and a brave nation. England is, I believe, easily influenced by the use of gunpowder. It is possible that Lord Morley has granted the reforms through fear, but what is granted under fear can be retained only so long as the fear lasts.

Chapter XVI : Brute Force

READER: This is a new doctrine, that what is gained through fear is retained only while the fear lasts. Surely, what is given will not be withdrawn?

EDITOR: Not so. The Proclamation of 1857 was given at the end of a revolt, and for the purpose of preserving peace. When peace was secured and people became simple-minded, its full effect was toned down. If I cease stealing for fear of punishment, I would recommence the operation as soon as the fear is withdrawn from me. This is almost a universal experience. We have assumed that we can get men to do things by force and, therefore, we use force.

READER: Will you not admit that you are arguing against yourself? You know that what the English obtained in their own country they obtained by using brute-force. I know you have argued that what they have obtained is useless, but that does not affect my argument. They wanted useless things and they got them. My point is that their desire was fulfilled. What does it matter what means they adopted? Why should we not obtain our goal, which is good, by any means whatsoever, even by using violence? Shall I think of the means when I have to deal with a thief in the house? My duty is to drive him out anyhow. You seem to admit that we have received nothing, and that we shall receive nothing, by petitioning. Why, then, may we not do so by using brute-force? And, to retain what we may receive, we shall keep up the fear by using the same force to the extent that it may be necessary. You will not find fault with a continuance of force to prevent a child from thrusting its foot into fire? Somehow or other we have to gain our end.

EDITOR: Your reasoning is plausible. It has deluded many. I have used similar arguments before now. But I think I know better now, and I shall endeavour to undeceive you. Let us first take the argument that we are justified in gaining our end by using brute-force because the English gained theirs by using similar means. It is perfectly true that they used brute-force and that it is possible for us to do likewise, but by using similar means we can get only the same thing that they got. You will admit that we do not want that. Your belief that there is no concession between the means and the end is a great mistake. Through that mistake even men who have been considered religious have committed grievous crimes. Your reasoning is the same as saying that we can get a rose through planting a noxious weed. If I want to cross the ocean, I can do so only by means of a vessel; if I were to use a cart for that purpose, both the cart and I would soon find the bottom. "As is the God, so is the votary", is a maxim worth considering. Its meaning has been distorted and men have gone astray. The means may be likened to a seed, the end to a tree; and there is just the same inviolable connection between the means and the end as there is between the seed and the tree. I am not likely to obtain the result flowing from the worship of God by laying myself prostrate before Satan. If, therefore, anyone were to say: "I want to worship god; it does not matter that I do so by means of Satan", it would be set down as ignorant folly. We reap exactly as we sow. The English in 1833 obtained greater voting power by violence. Did they by using brute-force better appreciate their duty? They wanted the right of voting, which they obtained by using physical force. But real rights are a result of performance of duty; these rights they have not obtained. We, therefore, have before us in England the farce of everybody wanting and insisting on his rights, nobody thinking of his duty. And, where everybody wants rights, who shall give them to whom? I do not wish to imply that they do no duties. They don't perform the duties corresponding to those rights; and as they do not perform that particular duty, namely, acquire fitness, their rights have proved a burden to them. In other words, what they have obtained is an exact result of the means they adopted. They used the means corresponding to the end. If I want to deprive you of your watch, I shall certainly have to fight for it; if I want to buy your watch, I shall have to pay you for it; and if I want a gift I shall have to plead for it; and, according to the means I employ, the watch is stolen property, my own property, or a donation. Thus we see three different results from three different means. Will you still say that means do not matter?

Now we shall take the example given by you of the thief to be driven out. I do not agree with you that the thief may be driven out by any means. If it is my father who has come to steal I shall use one kind of means. If it is an acquaintance I shall use another; and in the case of a perfect stranger I shall use a third. If it is a white man, you will perhaps say you will use means different from those you will adopt with an Indian thief. If it is a weakling, the means will be different from those to be adopted for dealing with an equal in physical strength; and if the thief is armed from top to toe, I shall simply remain quiet. Thus we have a variety of means between the father and the armed man. Again, I fancy that I should pretend to be sleeping whether the thief was my father or that strong armed man. The reason for this is that my father would also be armed and I should succumb to the strength possessed by either and allow my things to be stolen. The strength of my father would make me weep with pity; the strength of the armed man would rouse in me anger and we should become enemies. Such is the curious situation. From these examples we may not be able to agree as to the means to be adopted in each case. I myself seem clearly to see what should be done in all these cases, but the remedy may frighten you. I therefore hesitate to place it before you. For the time being I will leave you to guess it, and if you cannot, it is clear you will have to adopt different means in each case. You will also have seen that any means will not avail to drive away the thief. You will have to adopt means to fit each case. Hence it follows that your duty is *not* to drive away the thief by any means you like.

Let us proceed a little further. That well-armed man has stolen your property; you have harboured the thought of his act; you are filled with anger; you argue that you want to punish that rogue, not for your own sake, but for the good of your neighbours; you have collected a number of armed men, you want to take his house by assault; he is duly informed of it, he runs away; he too is incensed. He collects his brother-robbers, and sends you a defiant message that he will commit robbery in broad daylight. You are strong, you do not fear him, you are prepared to receive him. Meanwhile, the robber pesters your neighbours. They complain before you. You reply that you are doing all for their sake, you do not mind that your own goods have been stolen. Your neighbours reply that the robber never pestered them before, and that he commenced his depredations only after you declared hostilities against him. You are between Scylla and Charybdis. You are full of pity for the poor men. What they say is true. What are you to do? You will be disgraced if you now leave the robber alone. You, therefore, tell the poor men: "Never mind. Come, my wealth is yours, I will give you arms, I will teach you how to use them; you should belabour the rogue; don't you leave him alone." And so the battle grows; the robbers increase in numbers; your neighbours have deliberately put themselves to incovenience. Thus the result of wanting to take revenge upon the robber is that you have disturbed your own peace; you are in perpetual fear of being robbed and assaulted; your courage has given place to cowardice. If you will patiently examine the argument, you will see that I have not overdrawn the picture. This is one of the means. Now let us examine the other. You set this armed robber down as an ignorant brother; you intend to reason with him at a suitable opportunity: you argue that he is, after all, a fellow man; you do not know what prompted him to steal. You, therefore, decide that, when you can, you will destroy the man's motive for stealing. Whilst you are thus reasoning with yourself, the man comes again to steal. Instead of being angry with him, you take pity on him. You think that this stealing habit must be a disease with him. Henceforth, you, therefore, keep your doors and windows open, you change your sleeping-place, and you keep your things in a manner most accessible to him. The robber comes again and is confused as all this is new to him; nevertheless, he takes away your things. But his mind is agitated. He enquires about you in the village, he comes to learn about your broad and loving heart, he repents, he begs your pardon, returns you your things, and leaves off the stealing habit. He becomes your servant, and you find for him honourable employment. This is the second method. Thus, you see, different means have brought about totally different results. I do not wish to deduce from this that robbers will act in the above manner or that all will have the same pity and love like you, but I only wish to show that fair means alone can produce fair results, and that, at least in the majority of cases, if not indeed in all, the force of love and pity is infinitely greater than the force of arms.

There is harm in the exercise of brute-force, never in that of pity.

Now we will take the question of petitioning. It is a fact beyond dispute that a petition, without the backing of force, is useless. However, the late Justice Ranade used to say that petitions served a useful purpose because they were a means of educating people. They give the latter an idea of their condition and warn the rulers. From this point of view, they are not altogether useless. A petition of an equal is a sign of courtesy; a petition from a slave is a symbol of his slavery. A petition backed by force is a petition from an equal and, when he transmits his demand in the form of a petition, it testifies to his nobility. Two kinds of force can back petitions. "We shall hurt you if you do not give this", is one kind of force; it is the force of arms, whose evil results we have already examined. The second kind of force can thus be stated: "If you do not concede our demand, we shall be no longer your petitioners. You can govern us only so long as we remain the governed; we shall no longer have any dealings with you." The force implied in this may be described as love-force, soul-force, or, more popularly but less accurately, passive resistance. This force is indestructible. He who uses it perfectly understands his position. We have an ancient proverb which literally means: "One negative cures thirty-six diseases." The force of arms is powerless when matched against the force of love or the soul.

Now we shall take your last illustration, that of the child thrusting its foot into fire. It will not avail you. What do you really do to the child? Supposing that it can exert so much physical force that it renders you powerless and rushes into fire, then you cannot prevent it. There are only two remedies open to you—either you must kill it in order to prevent it from perishing in the flames, or you must give your own life because you do not wish to see it perish before your very eyes. You will not kill it. If your heart is not quite full of pity, it is possible that you will not surrender yourself by preceding the child and going into the fire yourself. You, therefore, helplessly allow it to go into the flames. Thus, at any rate, you are not using physical force. I hope you will not consider that it is still physical force, though of a low order, when you would forcibly prevent the child from rushing towards the fire if you could. That force is of a different order and we have to understand what it is.

Remember that, in thus preventing the child, you are minding entirely its own interest, you are exercising authority for its sole benefit. Your example does not apply to the English. In using brute-force against the English you consult entirely your own, that is the national, interest. There is no question here either of pity or of love. If you say that the actions of the English, being evil, represent fire, and that they proceed to their actions through ignorance, and that therefore they occupy the position of a child and that you want to protect such a child, then you will have to overtake every evil action of that kind by whomsoever committed and, as in the case of the evil child, you will have to sacrifice yourself. If you are capable of such immeasurable pity, I wish you well in its exercise.

Chapter XVII : Passive Resistance

READER: Is there any historical evidence as to the success of what you have called soul-force or truth-force? No instance seems to have happened of any nation having risen through soul-force. I still think that the evil-doers will not cease doing evil without physical punishment.

EDITOR: The poet Tulsidas has said: "Of religion, pity, or love, is the root, as egotism of the body. Therefore, we should not abandon pity so long as we are alive." This appears to me to be a scientific truth. I believe in it as much as I believe in two and two being four. The force of love is the same as the force of the soul or truth. We have evidence of its working at every step. The universe would disappear without the existence of that force. But you ask for historical evidence. It is, therefore, necessary to know what history means. The Gujarati equivalent means: "It so happened." If that is the meaning of history, it is possible to give copious evidence. But, if it means the doings of kings and emperors, there can be no evidence of soul-force or passive resistance is such history. You cannot expect silver ore in a tin mine. History, as we know it, is a record of the wars of the world, and so there is a proverb among Englishmen that a nation which has no history, that is, no wars, is a happy nation. How kings played, how they became enemies of one another, how they murdered one another, is found accurately recorded in history, and if this were all that had happened in the world, it would have been ended long ago. If the story of the universe had commenced with wars, not a man would have been found alive today. Those people who have been warred against have disappeared as, for instance, the natives of Australia of whom hardly a man was left alive by the intruders. Mark, please, that these natives did not use soul-force in self-defence, and it does not require much foresight to know that the Australians will share the same fate as their victims. "Those that take the sword shall perish by the sword." With us the proverb is that professional swimmers will find a watery grave.

The fact that there are so many men still alive in the world shows that it is based not on the force of arms but on the force of truth or love. Therefore, the greatest and most unimpeachable evidence of the success of this force is to be found in the fact that, in spite of the wars of the world, it still lives on.

Thousands, indeed tens of thousands, depend for their existence on a very active working of this force. Little quarrels of millions of families in their daily lives disappear before the exercise of this force. Hundreds of nations live in peace. History does not and cannot take note of this fact. History is really a record of every interruption of the even working of the force of love or of the soul. Two brothers quarrel; one of them repents and re-awakens the love that was lying dormant in him; the two again begin to live in peace; nobody takes note of this. But if the two brothers, through the intervention of solicitors or some other reason take up arms or go to law—which is another form of the exhibition of brute force—their doings would be immediately noticed in the Press, they would be the talk of their neighbours and would probably go down to history. And what is true of families and communities is true of nations. There is no reason to believe that there is one law for families and another for nations. History, then, is a record of an interruption of the course of nature. Soul-force, being natural, is not noted in history.

READER: According to what you say, it is plain that instances of this kind of passive resistance are not to be found in history. It is necessary to understand this passive resistance more fully. It will be better, therefore, if you enlarge upon it.

EDITOR: Passive resistance is a method of securing rights by personal suffering; it is the reverse of resistance by arms. When I refuse to do a thing that is repugnant to my conscience, I use soul-force. For instance, the Government of the day has passed a law which is applicable to me. I do not like it. If by using violence I force the Government to repeal the law, I am employing what may be termed body-force. If I do not obey the law and accept the penalty for its breach, I use soul-force. It involves sacrifice of self.

Everybody admits that sacrifice of self is infinitely superior to sacrifice of others. Moreover, if this kind of force is used in a cause that is unjust, only the person using it suffers. He does not make others suffer for his mistakes. Men have before now done many things which were subsequently found to have been wrong. No man can claim that he is absolutely in the right or that a particular thing is wrong because he thinks so, but it is wrong for him so long as that is his deliberate judgment. It is therefore meet that he should not do that which he knows to be wrong, and suffer the consequence whatever it may be. This is the key to the use of soul-force.

READER: You would then disregard laws—this is rank disloyalty. We have always been considered a law-abiding nation. You seem to be going even beyond the Extremists. They say that we must obey the laws that have been passed, but that if the laws be bad, we must drive out the law-givers even by force.

EDITOR: Whether I go beyond them or whether I do not is a matter of no consequence to either of us. We simply want to find out what is right and to act accordingly. The real meaning of the statement that we are a law-abiding nation is that we are passive resisters. When we do not like certain laws, we do not break the heads of law-givers but we suffer and do not submit to the laws. That we should obey laws whether good or bad is a new-fangled notion. There was no such thing in former days. The people disregarded those laws they did not like and suffered the penalties for their breach. It is contrary to our manhood if we obey laws repugnant to our conscience. Such teaching is opposed to religion and means slavery. If the Government were to ask us to go about without any clothing, should we do so? If I were a passive resister, I would say to them that I would have nothing to do with their law.

But we have so forgotten ourselves and become so compliant that we do not mind any degrading law.

A man who has realized his manhood, who fears only God, will fear no one else. Man-made laws are not necessarily binding on him. Even the Government does not expect any such thing from us. They do not say: "You must do such and such a thing", but they say: "If you do not do it, we will punish you." We are sunk so low that we fancy that it is our duty and our religion to do what the law lays down. If man will only realize that it is unmanly to obey laws that are unjust, no man's tyranny will enslave him. This is the key to Self Rule or Home Rule.

It is a superstition and ungodly thing to believe that an act of a majority binds a minority. Many examples can be given in which acts of majorities will be found to have been wrong and those of minorities to have been right. All reforms owe their origin to the initiation of minorities in opposition to majorities. If among a band of robbers a knowledge of robbing is obligatory, is a pious man to accept the obligation? So long as the superstition that men should obey unjust laws exists, so long will their slavery exist. And a passive resister alone can remove such a superstition.

To use brute-force, to use gunpowder, is contrary to passive resistance, for it means that we want our opponent to do by force that which we desire but he does not. And if such a use of force is justifiable, surely he is entitled to do likewise by us. And so we should never come to an agreement. We may simply fancy, like the blind horse moving in a circle round a mill, that we are making progress. Those who believe that they are not bound to obey laws which are repugnant to their conscience have only the remedy of passive resistance open to them. Any other must lead to disaster.

READER: From what you say I deduce that passive resistance is a splendid weapon of the weak, but that when they are strong they may take up arms.

EDITOR: This is gross ignorance. Passive resistance, that is soul-force, is matchless. It is superior to the force of arms. How, then, can it be considered only a weapon of the weak? Physical-force men are strangers to the courage that is requisite in a passive resister. Do you believe that a coward can ever disobey a law that he dislikes? Extremists are considered to be advocates of brute-force. Why do they, then, talk about obeying laws? I do not blame them. They can say nothing else. When they succeed in driving out the English and they themselves become governors, they will want you and me to obey their laws. And that is a fitting thing for their constitution. But a passive resister will say he will not obey a law that is against his conscience, even though he may be blown to pieces at the mouth of a cannon.

What do you think? Wherein is courage required—in blowing others to pieces from behind a cannon, or with a smiling face to approach a cannon and be blown to pieces? Who is the true warrior—he who keeps death always as a bosom-friend, or he who controls the death of others? Believe me that a man devoid of courage and manhood can never be a passive resister.

This, however, I will admit: that even a man weak in body is capable of offering this resistance. One man can offer it just as well as millions. Both men and women can indulge in it. It does not require the training of an army; it needs no jiu-jitsu. Control over the mind is alone necessary, and when that is attained, man is free like the king of the forest and his very glance withers the enemy.

Passive resistance is an all-sided sword, it can be used anyhow; it blesses him who uses it and him against whom it is used. Without drawing a drop of blood it produces far-reaching results. It never rusts and cannot be stolen. Competition between passive resisters does not exhaust. The sword of passive resistance does not require a scabbard. It is strange indeed that you should consider such a weapon merely of the weak.

READER: You have said that passive resistance is a speciality of India. Have cannons never been used in India?

EDITOR: Evidently, in your opinion, India means its few princes. To me it means its teeming millions on whom depends the existence of its princes and our own.

Kings will always use their kingly weapons. To use force is bred in them. They want to command, but those who have to obey commands do not want guns: and these are in a majority throughout the world. They have to learn either body-force or soul-force. Where they learn the former, both the rulers and the ruled become like so many madmen; but where they learn soul-force, the commands of the rulers do not go beyond the point of their swords, for true men disregard unjust commands. Peasants have never been subdued by the sword, and never will be. They do not know the use of the sword, and they are not frightened by the use of it by others. That nation is great which rests its head upon death as its pillow. Those who defy death are free from all fear. For those who are labouring under the delusive charms of brute-force, this picture is not overdrawn. The fact is that, in India, the nation at large has generally used passive resistance in all departments of life. We cease to co-operate with our rulers when they displease us. This is passive resistance.

I remember an instance when, in a small principality, the villagers were offended by some command issued by a prince. The former immediately began vacating the village. The prince became nervous, apologized to his subjects and withdrew his command. Many such instances can be found in India. Real Home Rule is possible only where passive resistance is the guiding force of the people. Any other rule is foreign rule.

READER: Then you will say that it is not at all necessary for us to train the body?

EDITOR: I will certainly not say any such thing. It is difficult to become a passive resister unless the body is trained. As a rule, the mind, residing in a body that has become weakened by pampering, is also weak, and where there is no strength of mind there can be no strength of soul. We shall have to improve our physique by getting rid of infant marriages and luxurious living. If I were to ask a man with a shattered body to face a cannon's mouth, I should make a laughing stock of myself.

READER: From what you say, then, it would appear that it is not a small thing to become a passive resister, and, if that is so, I should like you to explain how a man may become one.

EDITOR: To become a passive resister is easy enough but it is also equally difficult. I have known a lad of fourteen years become a passive resister; I have known also sick people do likewise; and I have also known physically strong and otherwise happy people unable to take up passive resistance. After a great deal of experience it seems to me that those who want to become passive resisters for the service of the country have to observe perfect chastity, adopt poverty, follow truth, and cultivate fearlessness.

Chastity is one of the greatest disciplines without which the mind cannot attain requisite firmness. A man who is unchaste loses stamina, becomes emasculated and cowardly. He whose mind is given over to animal passions is not capable of any great effort. This can be proved by innumerable instances. What, then, is a married person to do is the question that arises naturally; and yet it need not. When a husband and wife gratify the passions, it is of less an animal indulgence on that account. Such an indulgence, except for perpetuating the race, is strictly prohibited. But a passive resister has to avoid even that very limited indulgence because he can have no desire for progeny. A married man, therefore, can observe perfect chastity. This subject is not capable of being treated at greater length. Several questions arise: How is one to carry one's wife with one, what are her rights, and other similar questions. Yet those who wish to take part in a great work are bound to solve these puzzles.

Just as there is necessity for chastity, so is there for poverty. Pecuniary ambition and passive resistance cannot well go together. Those who have money are not expected to throw it away, but they *are* expected to be indifferent about it. They must be prepared to lose every penny rather than give up passive resistance.

Passive resistance has been described in the course of our discussion as truth-force. Truth, therefore, has necessarily to be followed and that at any cost. In this connection, academic questions such as whether a man may not lie in order to save a life, etc., arise, but these questions occur only to those who wish to justify lying. Those who want to follow truth every time are not placed in such a quandary; and if they are, they are still saved from a false position.

Passive resistance cannot proceed a step without fearlessness. Those alone can follow the path of passive resistance who are free from fear, whether as to their possessions, false honour, their relatives, the government, bodily injuries or death.

These observances are not to be abandoned in the belief that they are difficult. Nature has implanted in the human breast ability to cope with any difficulty or suffering that may come to man unprovoked. These qualities are worth having, even for those who do not wish to serve the country. Let there be no mistake, as those who want to train themselves in the use of arms are also obliged to have these qualities more or less. Everybody does not become a warrior for the wish. A would-be warrior will have to observe chastity and to be satisfied with poverty as his lot. A warrior without fearlessness cannot be conceived of. It may be thought that he would not need to be exactly truthful, but that quality follows real fearlessness. When a man abandons truth, he does so owing to fear in some shape or form. The above four attributes, then, need not frighten anyone. It may be as well here to note that a physical-force man has to have many other useless qualities which a passive resister never needs. And you will find that whatever extra effort a swordsman needs is due to lack of fearlessness. If he is an embodiment of the latter, the sword will drop from his hand that very moment. He does not need its support. One who is free from hatred requires no sword. A man with a stick suddenly came face to face with a lion and instinctively raised his weapon in self-defence. The man saw that he had only prated about fearlessness when there was none in him. That moment he dropped the stick and found himself free from all fear.

Chapter XVIII : Education

READER: In the whole of our discussion, you have not demonstrated the necessity for education; we always complain of its absence among us. We notice a movement for compulsory education in our country. The Maharaja of Gaekwar has introduced it in his territories. Every eye is directed towards them. We bless the Maharaja for it. Is all this effort then of no use?

EDITOR: If we consider our civilization to be the highest, I have regretfully to say that much of the effort you have described is of no use. The motive of the Maharaja and other great leaders who have been working in this direction is perfectly pure. They, therefore, undoubtedly deserve great praise. But we cannot conceal from ourselves the result that is likely to flow from their effort.

What is the meaning of education? It simply means a knowledge of letters. It is merely an instrument, and an instrument may be well used or abused. The same instrument that may be used to cure a patient may be used to take his life, and so may a knowledge of letters. We daily observe that many men abuse it and very few make good use of it; and if this is a correct statement, we have proved that more harm has been done by it than good.

The ordinary meaning of education is a knowledge of letters. To teach boys reading, writing and arithmetic is called primary education. A peasant earns his bread honestly. He has ordinary knowledge of the world. He knows fairly well how he should behave towards his parents, his wife, his children and his fellow-villagers. He understands and observes the rules of morality. But he cannot write his own name. What do you propose to do by giving him a knowledge of letters? Will you add an inch to his happiness? Do you wish to make him discontented with his cottage or his lot? And even if you want to do that, he will not need such an education. Carried away by the flood of Western thought we came to the conclusion, without weighing pros and cons, that we should give this kind of education to the people.

Now let us take higher education. I have learned Geography, Astronomy, Algebra, Geometry, etc. What of that? In what way have I benefited myself or those around me? Why have I learned these things? Professor Huxley has thus defined education:

> That man I think has had a liberal education who has been so trained in youth that his body is the ready servant of his will and does with ease and pleasure all the work that as a mechanism it is capable of; whose intellect is a clear, cold, logic [al] engine with all its parts of equal strength and in smooth working order...whose mind is stored with a knowledge of the fundamental truths of nature...whose passions are trained to come to heel by a vigorous will, the servant of a tender conscience...who has learnt to hate all vileness and to respect others as himself. Such a one and no other, I conceive, has had a liberal education, for he is in harmony with nature. He will make the best of her and she of him.

If this is true education, I must emphatically say that the sciences I have enumerated above I have never been able to use for controlling my senses. Therefore, whether you take elementary education or higher education, it is not required for the main thing. It does not make men of us. It does not enable us to do our duty.

READER: If that is so, I shall have to ask you another question. What enables you to tell all these things to me? If you had not received higher education, how would you have been able to explain to me the things that you have?

EDITOR: You have spoken well. But my answer is simple: I do not for one moment believe that my life would have been wasted, had I not received higher or lower education. Nor do I consider that I necessarily serve because I speak. But I do desire to serve and in endeavouring to fulfil that desire, I make use of the education I have received. And, if I am making good use of it, even then it is not for the millions, but I can use it only for such as you, and this supports my contention. Both you and I have come under the bane of what is mainly false education. I claim to have become free from its ill effect, and I am trying to give you the benefit of my experience and in doing so, I am demonstrating the rottenness of this education.

Moreover, I have not run down a knowledge of letters in all circumstances. All I have now shown is that we must not make of it a fetish. It is not our *kamadhuk*. In its place it can be of use and it has its place when we have brought our senses under subjection and put our ethics on a firm foundation. And then, if we feel inclined to receive that education, we may make good use of it. As an ornament it is likely to sit well on us. It now follows that it is not necessary to make this education compulsory. Our ancient school system is enough. Character-building has the first place in it and that is primary education. A building erected on that foundation will last.

READER: Do I then understand that you do not consider English education necessary for obtaining Home Rule?

EDITOR: My answer is yes and no. To give millions a knowledge of English is to enslave them. The foundation that Macaulay laid of education has enslaved us. I do not suggest that he had any such intention, but that has been the result. It it not a sad commentary that we should have to speak of Home Rule in a foreign tongue?

And it is worthy of note that the systems which the Europeans have discarded are the systems in vogue among us. Their learned men continually make changes. We ignorantly adhere to their cast-off systems. They are trying each division to improve its own status. Wales is a small portion of England. Great efforts are being made to revive a knowledge of Welsh among Welshmen. The English Chancellor, Mr Lloyd George, is taking a leading part in the movement to make Welsh children speak Welsh. And what is our condition? We write to each other in faulty English, and from this even our M.A.s are not free; our best thoughts are expressed in English; the proceedings of our Congress are conducted in English; our best newspapers are printed in English. If this state of things continues for a long time, posterity will—it is my firm opinion—condemn and curse us.

It is worth noting that, by receiving English education, we have enslaved the nation. Hypocrisy, tyranny, etc., have increased; English-knowing Indians have not hesitated to cheat and strike terror into the people. Now, if we are doing anything for the people at all, we are paying only a portion of the debt due to them.

Is it not a painful thing that, if I want to go to a court of justice, I must employ the English language as a medium, that when I become a barrister, I may not speak my mother-tongue and that someone else should have to translate to me from my own language? Is not this absolutely absurd? Is it not a sign of slavery? Am I to blame the English for it or myself? It is we, the English-knowing Indians, that have enslaved India. The curse of the nation will rest not upon the English but upon us.

I have told you that my answer to your last question is both yes and no. I have explained to you why it is yes. I shall now explain why it is no.

We are so much beset by the disease of civilization, that we cannot altogether do without English education. Those who have already received it may make good use of it wherever necessary. In our dealings with the English people, in our dealings with our own people, when we can only correspond with them through that language, and for the purpose of knowing how disgusted they (the English) have themselves become with their civilization, we may use or learn English, as the case may be. Those who have studied English will have to teach morality to their progeny through their mother-tongue and to teach them another Indian language; but when they have grown up, they may learn English, the ultimate aim being that we should not need it. The object of making money thereby should be eschewed. Even in learning English to such a limited extent we shall have to consider what we should learn through it and what we should not. It will be necessary to know what sciences we should learn. A little thought should show you that immediately we cease to care for English degrees, the rulers will prick up their ears.

READER: Then what education shall we give?

EDITOR: This has been somewhat considered above, but we will consider it a little more. I think that we have to improve all our languages. What subjects we should learn through them need not be elaborated here. Those English books which are valuable, we should translate into the various Indian languages. We should abandon the pretension of learning many sciences. Religious, that is ethical, education will occupy the first place. Every cultured Indian will know in addition to his own provincial language, if a Hindu, Sanskrit; if a Mahomedan, Arabic; if a Parsee, Persian; and all, Hindi. Some Hindus should know Arabic and Persian; some Mahomedans and Parsees, Sanskrit. Several Northerners and Westerners should learn Tamil. A universal language for India should be Hindi, with the option of writing it in Persian or Nagari characters. In order that the Hindus and the Mahomedans may have closer relations, it is necessary to know both the characters. And, if we can do this, we can drive the English language out of the field in a short time. All this is necessary for us, slaves. Through our slavery the nation has been enslaved, and it will be free with our freedom.

READER: The question of religious education is very difficult.

EDITOR: Yet we cannot do without it. India will never be godless. Rank atheism cannot flourish in this land. The task is indeed difficult. My head begins to turn as I think of religious education. Our religious teachers are hypocritical and selfish; they will have to be approached. The Mullas, the Dasturs and the Brahmins hold the key in their hands, but if they will not have the good sense, the energy that we have derived from English education will have to be devoted to religious education. This is not very difficult. Only the fringe of the ocean has been polluted and it is those who are within the fringe who alone need cleansing. We who come under this category can even cleanse ourselves because my remarks do not apply to the millions. In order to restore India to its pristine condition, we have to return to it. In our own civilization there will naturally be progress, retrogression, reforms, and reactions; but one effort is required, and that is to drive out Western civilization. All else will follow.

Chapter XIX : Machinery

READER: When you speak of driving out Western civilization, I suppose you will also say that we want no machinery?

EDITOR: By raising this question, you have opened the wound I have received. When I read Mr Dutt's *Economic History of India*, I wept; and as I think of it again my heart sickens. It is machinery that has impoverished India. It is difficult to measure the harm that Manchester has done to us. It is due to Manchester that Indian handicraft has all but disappeared.

But I make a mistake. How can Manchester be blamed? We wore Manchester cloth and this is why Manchester wove it. I was delighted when I read about the bravery of Bengal. There were no cloth-mills in that Presidency. They were, therefore, able to restore the original hand-weaving occupation. It is true Bengal encourages the mill-industry of Bombay. If Bengal had proclaimed a boycott of *all* machine-made goods, it would have been much better.

Machinery has begun to desolate Europe. Ruination is now knocking at the English gates. Machinery is the chief symbol of modern civilization; it represents a great sin.

The workers in the mills of Bombay have become slaves. The condition of the women working in the mills is shocking. When there were no mills, these women were not starving. If the machinery craze grows in our country, it will become an unhappy land. It may be considered a heresy, but I am bound to say that it were better for us to send money to Manchester and to use flimsy Manchester cloth than to multiply mills in India. By using Manchester cloth we only waste our money; but by reproducing Manchester in India, we shall keep our money at the price of our blood, because our very moral being will be sapped, and I call in support of my statement the very mill-hands as witnesses. And those who have amassed wealth out of factories are not likely to be better than other rich men. It would be folly to assume that an Indian Rockefeller would be better than the American Rockefeller. Impoverished India can become free, but it will be hard for any India made rich through immorality to regain its freedom. I fear we shall have to admit that moneyed men support British rule; their interest is bound up with its stability. Money renders a man helpless. The other thing which is equally harmful is sexual vice. Both are poison. A snakebite is a lesser poison than these two, because the former merely destroys the body but the latter destroy body, mind and soul. We need not, therefore, be pleased with the prospect of the growth of the mill-industry.

READER: Are the mills, then, to be closed down?

EDITOR: That is difficult. It is no easy task to do away with a thing that is established. We, therefore, say that the non-beginning of a thing is supreme wisdom. We cannot condemn millowners; we can but pity them. It would be too much to expect them to give up their mills, but we may implore them not to increase them. If they would be good they would gradually contract their business. They can establish in thousands of households the ancient and sacred handlooms and they can buy out the cloth that may be thus woven. Whether the millowners do this or not, people can cease to use machine-made goods.

READER: You have so far spoken about machine-made cloth, but there are innumerable machine-made things. We have either to import them or to introduce machinery into our country.

EDITOR: Indeed, our gods even are made in Germany. What need, then, to speak of matches, pins and glassware? My answer can be only one. What did India do before these articles were introduced? Precisely the same should be done today. As long as we cannot make pins without machinery, so long will we do without them. The tinsel splendour of glassware we will have nothing to do with, and we will make wicks, as of old, with home-grown cotton and use hand-made earthen saucers or lamps. So doing, we shall save our eyes and money and support swadeshi and so shall we attain Home Rule.

It is not to be conceived that all men will do all these things at one time or that some men will give up all machine-made things at once. But if the thought is sound, we shall always find out what we can give up and gradually cease to use it. What a few may do, others will copy; and the movement will grow like the coconut of the mathematical problem. What the leaders do, the populace will gladly do in turn. The matter is neither complicated nor difficult. You and I need not wait until we can carry others with us. Those will be the losers who will not do it, and those who will not do it, although they appreciate the truth, will deserve to be called cowards.

READER: What, then, of the tram-cars and electricity?

EDITOR: This question is now too late. It signifies nothing. If we are to do without the railways we shall have to do without the tram-cars. Machinery is like a snake-hole which may contain from one to a hundred snakes. Where there is machinery there are large cities; and where there are large cities, there are tram-cars and railways; and there only does one see electric light. English villages do not boast of any of these things. Honest physicians will tell you that where means of artificial locomotion have increased, the health of the people has suffered. I remember that when in a European town there was a scarcity of money, the receipts of the tramway company, of the lawyers and of the doctors went down and people were less unhealthy. I cannot recall a single good point in connection with machinery. Books can be written to demonstrate its evils.

READER: Is it a good point or a bad one that all you are saying will be printed through machinery?

EDITOR: This is one of those instances which demonstrate that sometimes poison is used to kill poison. This, then, will not be a good point regarding machinery. As it expires, the machinery, as it were, says to us: "Beware and avoid me. You will derive no benefits from me and the benefit that may accrue from printing will avail only those who are infected with the machinery-craze."

Do not, therefore, forget the main thing. It is necessary to realize that machinery is bad. We shall then be able gradually to do away with it. Nature has not provided any way whereby we may reach a desired goal all of a sudden. If, instead of welcoming machinery as a boon, we should look upon it as an evil, it would ultimately go.

Chapter XX : Conclusion

READER: From your views I gather that you would form a third party. You are neither an Extremist nor a Moderate.

EDITOR: That is a mistake. I do not think of a third party at all. We do not all think alike. We cannot say that all the Moderates hold identical views. And how can those who want only to serve have a party? I would serve both the Moderates and the Extremists.

Where I differ from them, I would respectfully place my position before them and continue my service.

READER: What, then, would you say to both the parties?

EDITOR: I would say to the Extremists: "I know that you want Home Rule for India; it is not to be had for your asking. Everyone will have to take it for himself. What others get for me is not Home Rule but foreign rule; therefore, it would not be proper for you to say that you have obtained Home Rule if you have merely expelled the English. I have already described the true nature of Home Rule. This you would never obtain by force of arms. Brute-force is not natural to Indian soil. You will have therefore, to rely wholly on soul-force. You must not consider that violence is necessary at any stage for reaching our goal."

I would say to the Moderates: "Mere petitioning is derogatory; we thereby confess inferiority. To say that British rule is indispensable is almost a denial of the godhead. We cannot say that anybody or anything is indispensable except God. Moreover, commonsense should tell us that to state that, for the time being, the presence of the English in India is a necessity, is to make them conceited.

"If the English vacated India, bag and baggage, it must not be supposed that she would be widowed. It is possible that those who are forced to observe peace under their pressure would fight after their withdrawal. There can be no advantage in suppressing an eruption; it must have its vent. If, therefore, before we can remain at peace, we must fight amongst ourselves, it is better that we do so. There is no occasion for a third party to protect the weak. It is this so-called protection which has unnerved us. Such protection can only make the weak weaker. Unless we realize this, we cannot have Home Rule. I would paraphrase the thought of an English divine and say that anarchy under Home Rule were better than orderly foreign rule. Only, the meaning that the learned divine attached to Home Rule is different from Indian Home Rule according to my conception. We have to learn, and to teach others, that we do not want the tyranny of either English rule or Indian rule."

If this idea were carried out, both the Extremists and the Moderates could join hands. There is no occasion to fear or distrust one another.

READER: What, then, would you say to the English?

EDITOR: To them I would respectfully say: "I admit you are my rulers. It is not necessary to debate the question whether you hold India by the sword or by my consent. I have no objection to your remaining in my country, but although you are the rulers, you will have to remain as servants of the people. It is not we who have to do as you wish, but it is you who have to do as we wish. You may keep the riches that you have drained away from this land, but you may not drain riches henceforth. Your function will be, if you so wish, to police India; you must abandon the idea of deriving any commercial benefit from us. We hold the civilization that you support to be the reverse of civilization. We consider our civilization to be far superior to yours. If you realize this truth, it will be to your advantage and, if you do not, according to your own proverb, you should only live in our country in the same manner as we do. You must not do anything that is contrary to our religions. It is your duty as rulers that for the sake of the Hindus you should eschew beef, and for the sake of Mahomedans you should avoid bacon and ham. We have hitherto said nothing because we have been cowed down, but you need not consider that you have not hurt our feelings by your conduct. We are not expressing our sentiments either through base selfishness or fear, but because it is our duty now to speak out boldly. We consider your schools and law courts to be useless. We want our own ancient schools and courts to be restored. The common language of India is not English but Hindi. You should, therefore, learn it. We can hold communication with you only in our national language.

"We cannot tolerate the idea of you spending money on railways and the military. We see no occasion for either. You may fear Russia; we do not. When she comes we shall look after her. If you are with us, we may then receive her jointly. We do not need any European cloth. We shall manage with articles produced and manufactured at home. You may not keep one eye on Manchester and the other on India. We can work together only if our interests are identical.

"This has not been said to you in arrogance. You have great military resources. Your naval power is matchless. If we wanted to fight with you on your own ground, we should be unable to do so, but if the above submissions be not acceptable to you, we cease to play the part of the ruled. You may, if you like, cut us to pieces.

You may shatter us at the cannon's mouth. If you act contrary to our will, we shall not help you; and without our help, we know that you cannot move one step forward.

"It is likely that you will laugh at all this in the intoxication of your power. We may not be able to disillusion you at once; but if there be any manliness in us, you will see shortly that your intoxication is suicidal and that your laugh at our expense is an aberration of intellect. We believe that at heart you belong to a religious nation. We are living in a land which is the source of religions. How we came together need not be considered, but we can make mutual good use of our relations.

"You, English, who have come to India are not good specimens of the English nation, nor can we almost half-Anglicized Indians, be considered good specimens of the real Indian nation. If the English nation were to know all you have done, it would oppose many of your actions. The mass of the Indians have had few dealings with you. If you will abandon your so-called civilization and search into your own scriptures, you will find that our demands are just. Only on condition of our demands being fully satisfied may you remain in India; and if you remain under those conditions, we shall learn several things from you and you will learn many from us. So doing we shall benefit each other and the world. But that will happen only when the root of our relationship is sunk in a religious soil."

READER: What will you say to the nation?

EDITOR: Who is the nation?

READER: For our purposes it is the nation that you and I have been thinking of, that those of us who are affected by European civilization, and who are eager to have Home Rule.

EDITOR: To these I would say: "It is only those Indians who are imbued with real love who will be able to speak to the English in the above strain without being frightened, and only those can be said to be so imbued who conscientiously believe that Indian civilization is the best and that the European is a nine days' wonder. Such ephemeral civilizations have often come and gone and will continue to do so. Those only can be considered to be so imbued who, having experienced the force of the soul within themselves, will not cower before brute-force, and will not, on any account, desire to use brute-force. Those only can be considered to have been so imbued who are intensely dissatisfied with the present pitiable condition, having already drunk the cup of poison.

"If there be only one such Indian, he will speak as above to the English and the English will have to listen to him.

"These are not demands, but they show our mental state. We shall get nothing by asking; we shall have to take what we want, and we need the requisite strength for the effort and that strength will be available to him only who will act thus:

- He will only on rare occasions make use of the English language.
- If a lawyer, he will give up his profession, and take up a handloom.
- If a lawyer, he will devote his knowledge to enlightening both his people and the English.
- If a lawyer, he will not meddle with the quarrels between parties but will give up the courts, and from his experience induce the people to do likewise.
- If a lawyer, he will refuse to be a judge, he will give up his profession.
- If a doctor, he will give up medicine, and understand that rather than mending bodies, he should mend souls.
- If a doctor, he will understand that no matter to what religion he belongs, it is better that bodies remain diseased rather than that they are cured through the instrumentality of the diabolical vivisection that is practised in European schools of medicine.
- Although a doctor, he will take up a handloom, and if any patients come to him, will tell them the cause of their diseases, and will advise them to remove the cause rather than pamper them by giving useless drugs; he will understand that if by not taking drugs, perchance the patient dies, the world will not come to grief and that he will have been really merciful to him.
- Although a wealthy man, yet regardless of his wealth, he will speak out his mind and fear no one.

64

- If a wealthy man, he will devote his money to establishing handlooms, and encourage others to use hand-made goods by wearing them himself.
- Like every other Indian, he will know that this is a time for repentance, expiation and mourning.
- Like every other Indian, he will know that to blame the English is useless, that they came because of us, and remain also for the same reason, and that they will either go or change their nature only when we reform ourselves.
- Like others, he will understand that at a time of mourning, there can be no indulgence, and that, whilst we are in a fallen state, to be in gaol or in banishment is much the best.
- Like others, he will know that it is superstition to imagine it necessary that we should guard against being imprisoned in order that we may deal with the people.
- Like others, he will know that action is much better than speech; that it is our duty to say exactly what we think and face the consequences and that it will be only then that we shall be able to impress anybody with our speech.
- Like others, he will understand that we shall become free only through suffering.
- Like others, he will understand that deportation for life to the Andamans is not enough expiation for the sin of encouraging European civilization.
- Like others, he will know that no nation has risen without suffering; that, even in physical warfare, the true test is suffering and not the killing of others, much more so in the warfare of passive resistance.
- Like others, he will know that it is an idle excuse to say that we shall do a thing when the others also do it; that we should do what we know to be right, and that others will do it when they see the way; that when I fancy a particular delicacy, I do not wait till others taste it; that to make a national effort and so

suffer are in the nature of delicacies; and that to
suffer under pressure is no suffering."

READER: This is a large order. When will all carry it out?
EDITOR: You make a mistake. You and I have nothing to do with the
others. Let each do his duty. If I do my duty, that is, serve myself,
I shall be able to serve others. Before I leave you, I will take the
liberty of repeating:

- Real Home Rule is Self Rule or self-control.
- The way to it is passive resistance: that is soul-force
  or love-force.
- In order to exert this force, swadeshi in every sense is
  necessary.
- What we want to do should be done, not because we
  object to the English or because we want to retaliate
  but because it is our duty to do so. Thus, supposing
  that the English remove the salt-tax, restore our
  money, give the highest posts to Indians, withdraw
  the English troops, we shall certainly not use their
  machine-made goods, nor use the English language,
  nor many of their industries. It is worth noting that
  these things are, in their nature, harmful; hence we do
  not want them. I bear no enmity towards the English
  but I do towards their civilization.

In my opinion, we have used the term "swaraj" without
understanding its real significance. I have endeavoured to explain it
as I understand it, and my conscience testifies that my life
henceforth is dedicated to its attainment.

Swaraj And Swadeshi

Pure Swadeshi [11 July 1920]

[...] It is very necessary to understand thoroughly some fundamental principles of swadeshi. Will it advance the cause of swadeshi if Muslims take the swadeshi vow in their hundreds of thousands? I think it will, provided that either there is an increase in the production of swadeshi goods to meet their needs or they and others reduce their requirements of cloth.

The cloth which our cotton mills produce is not enough for India's needs and the mills are not in a position to increase the production of cloth in the immediate future. Their weaving capacity is greater than their spinning capacity. If, therefore, we use mill-yarn for handloom cloth, it will mean that the mills will produce less correspondingly and not that there will be an increase in the total production of cloth. The result will be large imports, not of cloth, but of yarn. That will leave us just where we are. We need not believe that we shall be saving on weaving, for yarn will cost more. This is not swadeshi.

The swadeshi of our conception safeguards both *dharma* and *artha*. Not to be able to serve our own neighbours, our own kith and kin—to wrest a morsel from their mouths and put it into those of strangers, surely this would not be serving the higher end of life, this would not be compassion. That would only mean our deserting our own field of duty. We are, therefore, morally bound to encourage our sisters who spin and our weavers. In the process, we shall be sending sixty crores of rupees to the homes of our starving millions and this will safeguard *artha*. The swadeshi *dharma* is thus the royal road for safeguarding both our *dharma* and *artha*.

We can follow this only if we take to hand-spinning and hand-weaving. The true and genuine swadeshi movement, therefore, consists in increasing the production of yarn, getting the yarn woven and then marketing the cloth thus produced. It is, therefore, my suggestion to all lovers of swadeshi and to all owners of swadeshi stores that they should get women to spin and should popularize the cloth woven out of the yarn they produce. I know that this work is difficult and heart-breaking. But no progress is ever possible without our venturing on a path beset with difficulties. The way to the Dhaulagiri peak is strewn with the bones of countless travellers. The weak of heart lose their enthusiasm right at the foot; there is no way, though, except through hills and valleys. If, therefore, those who take up the swadeshi cause do so after fully understanding the basic principle of swadeshi, they will save themselves from disappointment. It does not matter if every worker does no more than spin and infects a few with his zeal; but there will be great harm, if the swadeshi movement does not make headway, in being satisfied with what goes under the name of swadeshi. No piece of brass, however shining, can serve for gold; nor a bit of glass for a diamond. Just as mistakenly accepting glass as diamond will only delay our getting the latter, in the same way we shall only retard the progress of swadeshi if we accept spurious swadeshi as genuine swadeshi.

Some people may wonder why, if the idea is to produce yarn, some ten or twenty new mills should not be set up instead of trying to persuade millions of women to spin. I have already answered this question in *Navajivan*. New mills are not easily set up. Nor does anyone need especially to make the effort. The rich make the attempt on their own and keep adding to the number. But the setting up of new mills will mean being permanently dependent on foreigners for machinery. It is, besides, no remedy for the hunger of the millions, nor does it enable us to put sixty crores of rupees in circulation among them every year. India's population numbering millions and spread over a length of 1,900 miles will never be saved from starvation till we introduce a subsidiary occupation into the homes of the millions living on agriculture. Such an occupation can only be hand-spinning and, to some extent, hand-weaving. This industry flourished in India a hundred-and-fifty years ago and at that time we were not as miserably poor as we are today.

A True Congressman
[19 November 1925]

[...] A Congressman to be true must be above suspicion. Let him remember that he is out to gain swaraj by 'legitimate and peaceful means'. We have been a long time getting it. The obvious inference is that we have not at all adopted even in our mutual intercourse means that can bear scrutiny. Indeed, a correspondent once suggested that, whilst we must be truthful and peaceful towards opponents, we need not be that in our mutual dealings. But experience shows that we cannot be truthful and peaceful on some occasions and for some people only, if we are not so on all occasions. And if we will not be considerate towards one another, we shall not be considerate to the world outside. All the prestige acquired by the Congress will be gone if we are not scrupulously clean in our dealings within or without in every detail. Pounds will take care of themselves if we could but take care of the pennies.

A true Congressman is a true servant. He ever gives, never wants service. He is easily satisfied so long as his own comfort is concerned. He is always content to take a back seat. He is never communal or provincial. His country is his paramount consideration. He is brave to a fault because he has shed all earthly ambition, fear of Death himself. And he is generous because he is brave, forgiving because he is humble and conscious of his own failings and limitations.

If such Congressmen are rare, swaraj is far off and we must revise our creed. The fact that we have not got swaraj as yet is proof presumptive that we have not as many true Congressmen as we want. Be that however as it may, if I have placed on record the ugly incidents which can be multiplied, I must bear grateful testimony to the fact that there are nameless Congressmen, no doubt few today, but daily growing in number, who fulfil all the tests I have mentioned. They are unknown to fame. It is well that they are. Work would be impossible if they wanted to shine in the limelight and expected honourable mention in Congress dispatches. Those who obtain even Victoria Crosses are by no means and necessarily always the bravest humanitarians.

To the end of time the real heroes of the world will be never known. Their deeds remain imperishable. They are their own reward. Such men are the real scavengers without whom the earth will be a plague spot not worth living in. It has been my lot to meet such men and women in the Congress ranks. But for them the Congress will not be an institution to which it would be a pride to belong. There is no doubt at the present moment a hunt for offices and an unhealthy competition to capture the Congress. It is a disease which has come to the surface and it is bound to give place in the course of time to health. That will not happen if the Congress becomes anything but an institution for hard, honest and selfless toil.

Let the Congress be ever so democratic, but democracy must not be brag and bluster, a passport to receiving service from people. If *Vox populi* is to be *Vox dei,* it must be the voice of honesty, bravery, gentleness, humility and complete self-sacrifice. A woman is to guide the Congress next year. Woman is nothing if she is no self-sacrifice and purity personified. Let us men and women of the Congress humble ourselves, purify our hearts and be worthy representatives of the dumb millions.

Independence vs Swaraj
[12 January 1928]

[...] Let us, therefore, understand what we mean by independence. England, Russia, Spain, Italy, Turkey, Chile, Bhutan have all their independence. Which independence do we want? I must not be accused of begging the question. For, if I were told that it is Indian independence that is desired, it is possible to show that no two persons will give the same definition. The fact of the matter is that we do not know our distant goal. It will be determined not by our definitions but by our acts, voluntary and involuntary. If we are wise, we will take care of the present and the future will take care of itself. God has given us only a limited sphere of action and a limited vision. Sufficient unto the day is the good thereof.

I submit that swaraj is an all-satisfying goal for all time. We the English-educated Indians often unconsciously make the terrible mistake of thinking that the microscopic minority of English-speaking Indians is the whole of India. I defy anyone to give for independence a common Indian word intelligible to the masses. Our goal at any rate may be known by an indigenous word understood of the three hundred millions. And we have such a word in 'swaraj' first used in the name of the nation by Dadabhai Naoroji. It is infinitely greater than and includes independence. It is a vital word. It has been sanctified by the noble sacrifices of thousands of Indians. It is a word which, if it has not penetrated the remotest corner of India, has at least got the largest currency of any similar word. It is a sacrilege to displace that word by a foreign importation of doubtful value. This Independence Resolution is perhaps the final reason for conducting Congress proceedings in Hindustani and that alone. No tragedy like that of the Independence Resolution would then have been possible. The most valiant speakers would then have ornamented the native meaning of the word 'swaraj' and attempted all kinds of definitions, glorious and inglorious. Would that the independents would profit by their experience and resolve henceforth to work among the masses for whom they desire freedom and taboo English speech in its entirety in so far as meetings such as the Congress are concerned.

Personally, I crave not for 'independence', which I do not

understand, but I long for freedom from the English yoke. I would pay any price for it. I would accept chaos in exchange for it. For the English peace is the peace of the grave. Anything would be better than this living death of a whole people. This Satanic rule has well-nigh ruined this fair land materially, morally and spiritually. I daily see its law courts denying justice and murdering truth. I have just come from terrorized Orissa. This rule is using my own countrymen for its sinful sustenance. I have a number of affidavits swearing that, in the district of Khurda, acknowledgments of enhancement of revenue are being forced from the people practically at the point of the bayonet. The unparalleled extravagance of this rule has demented the Rajas and the Maharajas who, unmindful of consequences, ape it and grind their subjects to dust. In order to protect its immoral commerce, this rule regards no means too mean, and in order to keep three hundred millions under the heels of a hundred thousand, it carries a military expenditure which is keeping millions in a state of semi-starvation and polluting thousands of mouths with intoxicating liquor.

But my creed is non-violence under all circumstances. My method is conversion, not coercion; it is self-suffering, not the suffering of the tyrant. I know that method to be infallible. I know that a whole people can adopt it without accepting it as its creed and without understanding its philosophy. People generally do not understand the philosophy of all their acts. My ambition is much higher than independence. Through the deliverance of India, I seek to deliver the so-called weaker races of the earth from the crushing heels of Western exploitation in which England is the greatest partner. If India converts, as it can convert, Englishmen, it can become the predominant partner in a world commonwealth of which England can have the privilege of becoming a partner if she chooses. India has the right, if she only knew, of becoming the predominant partner by reason of her numbers, geographical position and culture inherited for ages. This is big talk, I know. For a fallen India to aspire to move the world and protect weaker races is seemingly an impertinence. But in explaining my strong opposition to this cry for independence, I can no longer hide the light under a bushel. Mine is an ambition worth living for and worth dying for. In no case do I want to reconcile myself to a state lower than the best for fear of consequences. It is, therefore, not out of expedience that

I oppose independence as my goal. I want India to come to her own and that state cannot be better defined by any single word than 'swaraj'. Its content will vary with the action that the nation is able to put forth at a given moment. India's coming to her own will mean every nation doing likewise.

The Law of Swadeshi [18 June 1931]

Swadeshi is the law of laws enjoined by the present age. Spiritual laws, like Nature's laws, need no enacting; they are self-acting. But through ignorance or other causes man often neglects or disobeys them. It is then vows are needed to steady one's course. A man who is by temperament a vegetarian needs no vow to strengthen his vegetarianism. For, the sight of animal food, instead of tempting him, would only excite his disgust. The law of swadeshi is ingrained in the basic nature of man but it has today sunk into oblivion. Hence the necessity for the vow of swadeshi. In its ultimate and spiritual sense swadeshi stands for the final emancipation of the human soul from its earthly bondage. For, this earthly tabernacle is not its natural or permanent abode, it is a hindrance in its onward journey, it stands in the way of its realizing its oneness with other lives. A votary of swadeshi therefore, in his striving to identify himself with the entire creation, seeks to be emancipated from the bondage of the physical body.

If this interpretation of swadeshi be correct, then it follows that its votary will as a first duty dedicate himself to the service of his immediate neighbours. This involves exclusion or even sacrifice of the interests of the rest but the exclusion or the sacrifice would be apparent only. Pure service of one's neighbours can never, from its very nature, result in disservice to those who are remotely situated, rather the contrary. 'As with the individual so with the universe' is an unfailing principle which we would do well to lay to heart. On the other hand, a man who allows himself to be lured by 'the distant scene' and runs to the ends of the earth for service is not only foiled in his ambition but fails in his duty towards his neighbours also. Take a concrete instance. In the particular place where I live I have certain persons as my neighbours, some relations and dependents. Naturally, they all feel, as they have a right to, that they have a claim on me and look to me for help and support. Suppose now I leave them all at once and set out to serve people in a distant place. My decision would throw my little world of neighbours and dependents out of gear while my gratuitous knight-errantry would more likely than not disturb the atmosphere in the new place. Thus a culpable neglect of my immediate neighbours and an unintended disservice to the people whom I wish to serve would be the first fruits of my violation of the principles of swadeshi.

It is not difficult to multiply such instances. That is why the Gita says: 'It is better to die performing one's duty or *swadharma,* but *paradharma,* or another's duty, is fraught with danger.' Interpreted in terms of one's physical environment this gives us the law of swadeshi. What the Gita says with regard to *swadharma* equally applies to swadeshi also, for swadeshi is *swadharma* applied to one's immediate environment.

It is only when the doctrine of swadeshi is wrongly understood that mischief results, e.g., it would be a travesty of the doctrine of swadeshi, if to coddle my family I set about grabbing money by all means fair or foul. The law of swadeshi requires me no more than to discharge my legitimate obligations towards my family by just means, and the attempt to do so will reveal to me the Universal Code of Conduct. The practice of swadeshi can never do harm to anyone and if it does it is not *swadharma* but egotism that moves me.

There may come occasions when a votary of swadeshi may be called upon to sacrifice his family at the altar of universal service. Such an act of willing immolation will then constitute the highest service rendered to the family. 'Whosoever wants to save his life will lose it, and whosoever loses his life for the Lord's sake will find it,' holds good for the family group no less than the individual. Take another instance. Supposing there is an outbreak of the plague in my village and in trying to serve the victims of the epidemic I, my wife and children and all the rest of my family are wiped out of existence, then in inducing those dearest and nearest to join me I will not have acted as the destroyer of my family but on the contrary as its truest friend. In swadeshi there is no room for selfishness, or if there is selfishness in it, it is of the highest type which is not different from the highest altruism. Swadeshi in its purest form is the acme of universal service.

It was by following this line of argument that I hit upon khadi as a necessary and the most important corollary of the principle of swadeshi in its application to society. 'What is the kind of service,' I asked myself, 'that the teeming millions of India most need at the present time, that can be easily understood and appreciated by all, that is easy to perform and will at the same time enable the crores of our semi-starved countrymen to live,' and the reply came that it is the universalization of khadi or the spinning-wheel alone that can fulfil these conditions.

Let no one suppose that the practice of swadeshi through khadi would harm the foreign mill-owners. A thief who is weaned from his vice or is made to return the property that he has stolen is not harmed thereby, on the contrary he is the gainer consciously in the one case, unconsciously in the other. Similarly if all the opium addicts or the drunkards in the world were to shake themselves free from their vice, the canteen keepers or the opium vendors who would be deprived of their customers could not be said to be losers. They would be the gainers in the truest sense of the word. The elimination of the 'wages of sin' is never a loss either to the individual concerned or to society; it is pure gain.

It is the greatest delusion to suppose that the duty of swadeshi begins and ends with merely spinning so much yarn anyhow and wearing khadi made from it. Khadi is the first indispensable step towards the discharge of swadeshi *dharma* towards society. One often meets men who wear khadi but in all other things indulge their taste for foreign manufactures with a vengeance. Such men cannot be said to be practising swadeshi. They are simply following the fashion. A votary of swadeshi will carefully study his environment and try to help his neighbours wherever possible by giving preference to local manufactures even if they are of an inferior grade or dearer in price than thing manufactured elsewhere. He will try to remedy their defects but will not give them up because of their defects and take to foreign manufactures.

But even swadeshi like any other good thing can be ridden to death if it is made a fetish. That is a danger that must be guarded against. To reject foreign manufactures merely because they are foreign and to go on wasting national time and money to promote manufactures in one's country for which it is not suited would be criminal folly and a negation of the swadeshi spirit. A true votary of swadeshi will never harbour ill-will towards the foreigner, he will not be moved by antagonism towards anybody on earth. Swadeshism is not a cult of hatred. It is a doctrine of selfless service that has its roots in the purest ahimsa, i.e., love.

Enlightened Anarchy [January 1939]

Political power, in my opinion, cannot be our ultimate aim. It is one of the means used by men for their all-round advancement. The power to control national life through national representatives is called political power. Representatives will become unnecessary if the national life becomes so perfect as to be self-controlled. It will then be a state of enlightened anarchy in which each person will become his own ruler. He will conduct himself in such a way that his behaviour will not hamper the well-being of his neighbours. In an ideal State there will be no political institution and therefore no political power. That is why Thoreau has said in his classic statement that that government is the best which governs the least.

Question Box [18 July 1942]

Sevagram,
July 18, 1942

My idea of village swaraj is that it is a complete republic, independent of its neighbours for its own vital wants, and yet interdependent for many others in which dependence is a necessity. Thus every village's first concern will be to grow its own food crops and cotton for its cloth. It should have a reserve for its cattle, recreation and playground for adults and children. Then if there is more land available, it will grow *useful* money crops, thus excluding *ganja*, tobacco, opium and the like. The village will maintain a village theatre, school and public hall. It will have its own waterworks, ensuring clean water supply. This can be done through controlled wells or tanks. Education will be compulsory up to the final basic course. As far as possible every activity will be conducted on the co-operative basis. There will be no castes such as we have today with their graded untouchability. Non-violence with its technique of satyagraha and non-co-operation will be the sanction of the village community. There will be a compulsory service of village guards who will be selected by rotation from the register maintained by the village.

The government of the village will be conducted by a Panchayat of five persons annually elected by the adult villagers, male and female, possessing minimum prescribed qualifications. These will have all the authority and jurisdiction required. Since there will be no system of punishments in the accepted sense, this Panchayat will be the legislature, judiciary and executive combined to operate for its year of office. Any village can become such a republic today without much interference even from the present Government whose sole effective connection with the villages is the exaction of the village revenue. I have not examined here the question of relations with the neighbouring villages and the centre if any. My purpose is to present an outline of village government. Here there is perfect democracy based upon individual freedom. The individual is the architect of his own government. The law of non-violence rules him and his government. He and his village are able to defy the might of a world. For the law governing every villager is that he will suffer death in the defence of his and his village's honour[...]

Speech at a Prayer Meeting
[22 December 1945]

We do not want to live on the mercy of anybody except God. Gita teaches us to be fearless. If you could learn that, nobody would be able to keep you down. If anybody asks me to bow down my head—I am an old man and anybody can push me or knock me down—but if I say, 'I won't,' the utmost he can do is to kill me. This fearlessness is swaraj. If everybody acts in the same way or feels in the same spirit, swaraj is there. It, however, does not mean that Government will go away today but it means that no power can make us bow down our head. We would not achieve independence by simply repeating the word like a parrot. Our deeds must be on the same line.

Independence [29 April 1946]

New Delhi,
April 29, 1946

Friends have repeatedly challenged me to define independence. At the risk of repetition, I must say that the independence of my dream means Ramarajya, i.e., the Kingdom of God on Earth. I do not know what it will be like in Heaven. I have no desire to know the distant scene. If the present is attractive enough, the future cannot be very unlike.

In concrete terms, then, the independence should be political, economic and moral.

'Political' necessarily means the removal of the control of the British army in every shape and form.

'Economic' means entire freedom from British capitalists and capital, as also their Indian counterparts. In other words, the humblest must feel equal to the tallest. This can take place only by capital or capitalists sharing their skill and capital with the lowliest and the least.

'Moral' means freedom from armed defence forces. My conception of Ramarajya excludes replacement of the British army by a national army of occupation. A country that is governed by even its national army can never be morally free and, therefore, its so-called weakest member can never rise to his full moral height [...]

Independence [21 July 1946]

Q. You have said in your article in the *Harijan* of July 15, under the caption 'The Real Danger', that Congressmen in general certainly do not know the kind of independence they want. Would you kindly give them a broad but comprehensive picture of the Independent India of your own conception?

A. I do not know that I have not, from time to time, given my idea of Indian independence. Since, however, this question is part of a series, it is better to answer it even at the risk of repetition.

Independence of India should mean independence of the whole of India including what is called India of the States and the other foreign powers, French and Portuguese, who are there, I presume, by British sufferance. Independence must mean that of the people of India, not of those who are today ruling over them. The rulers should depend on the will of those who are under their heels. Thus, they have to be servants of the people, ready to do their will.

Independence must begin at the bottom. Thus, every village will be a republic or Panchayat having full powers. It follows, therefore, that every village has to be self-sustained and capable of managing its affairs even to the extent of defending itself against the whole world. It will be trained and prepared to perish in the attempt to defend itself against any onslaught from without. Thus, ultimately, it is the individual who is the unit. This does not exclude dependence on and willing help from neighbours or from the world. It will be free and voluntary play of mutual forces. Such a society is necessarily highly cultured in which every man and woman knows what he or she wants and, what is more, knows that no one should want anything that others cannot have with equal labour.

This society must naturally be based on truth and non-violence which, in my opinion, are not possible without a living belief in God, meaning a self-existent, all-knowing living Force which inheres every other force known to the world and which depends on none and which will live when all other forces may conceivably perish or cease to act. I am unable to account for my life without belief in this all-embracing living Light.

In this structure composed of innumerable villages, there will be ever-widening, never-ascending circles. Life will not be a pyramid with the apex sustained by the bottom. But it will be an oceanic circle whose centre will be the individual always ready to perish for the village, the latter ready to perish for the circle of villages, till at last the whole becomes one life composed of individuals, never aggressive in their arrogance but ever humble, sharing the majesty of the oceanic circle of which they are integral units.

Therefore the outermost circumference will not wield power to crush the inner circle but will give strength to all within and derive its own strength from it. I may be taunted with the retort that this is all Utopian and, therefore, not worth a single thought. If Euclid's point, though incapable of being drawn by human agency, has an imperishable value, my picture has its own for mankind to live. Let India live for this true picture, though never realizable in its completeness. We must have a proper picture of what we want, before we can have something approaching it. If there ever is to be a republic in every village of India, then I claim verity for my picture in which the last is equal to the first or, in other words, no one is to be the first and none the last.

In this picture every religion has its full and equal place. We are all leaves of a majestic tree whose trunk cannot be shaken off its roots which are deep down in the bowels of the earth. The mightiest wind cannot move it.

In this there is no room for machines that would displace human labour and that would concentrate power in a few hands. Labour has its unique place in a cultured human family. Every machine that helps every individual has a place. But I must confess that I have never sat down to think out what that machine can be. I have thought of Singer's sewing machine. But even that is perfunctory. I do not need it to fill in my picture.

Q. Do you believe that the proposed Constituent Assembly could be used for the realization of your picture?

A. The Constituent Assembly has all the possibilities of the realization of my picture. Yet I cannot hope for much, not because the State Paper holds no such possibilities but because the document, being wholly of a voluntary nature, requires the common consent of the many parties to it. These have no common goal. Congressmen themselves are not of one mind even on the contents of Independence. I do not know how many swear by non-violence or the charkha or, believing in decentralization, regard the village as the nucleus. I know on the contrary that many would have India become a first-class military power and wish for India to have a strong centre and build the whole structure round it. In the medley of these conflicts I know that if India is to be the leader in clean action based on clean thought, God will confound the wisdom of these big men and will provide the villages with the power to express themselves as they should.

Q. If the Constituent Assembly fizzles out because of the 'danger from within', as you have remarked in an article, would you advise the Congress to accept the alternative of general country-wide strike and capture of power, either non-violently or with the use of necessary force? What is your alternative in that eventuality if the above is not approved by you?

A. I must not contemplate darkness before it stares me in the face. And in no case can I be party, irrespective of non-violence, to a universal strike and capture of power. Though, therefore, I do not know what I should do in the case of a breakdown, I know that the actuality will find me ready with an alternative. My sole reliance being on the living Power which we call God, He will put the alternative in my hands when the time has come, not a minute sooner.

Extract from a Speech at Prayer Meeting
[12 February 1947]

Independent India, as conceived by me, will have all Indians belonging to different religions living in perfect friendship. There need be no millionaires and no paupers; all would belong to the State, for the State belonged to them. I will die in the act of realizing this dream. I would not wish to live to see India torn asunder by civil strife.

Talk with Y.M. Dadoo and O.M. Naicker
[11 April 1947]

India is now on the threshold of independence. But this is not the independence I want. To my mind it will be no independence if India is partitioned and the minorities do not enjoy security, protection and equal treatment. Because the independence of my dreams is altogether different. The country is not yet completely independent. If what is happening today is an earnest of things to come after independence, it bodes no good for the future. We have a proverb saying that the cradle bespeaks the child's future. I, therefore, feel ill at ease. But I am content to leave the future in God's good hands.

Talk with Englishwomen
[19 April 1947]

The foreign power will be withdrawn before long, but for me real freedom will come only when we free ourselves of the domination of Western education, Western culture and Western way of living which have been ingrained in us, because this culture has made our living expensive and artificial, both for men and for women. Emancipation from this culture would mean real freedom for us.

Swadeshi [20 June 1947]

I am told that with the advent of swadeshi raj in the shape of swaraj, the spirit of swadeshi is fast disappearing from the land. The stock of khadi is perhaps at its lowest. It is no unusual sight to see what are called Gandhi topies worn by men who are otherwise clad in *paradeshi*. If that is true on any large scale, the dearly loved liberty, in my opinion, would be short-lived. Goodbye then to the hope of India becoming the Light of Asia, as by right it should be. *Paradeshi* goes side by side with luxury which a correspondent says is rampant everywhere. I fondly hope that whilst the tragic picture might be true of the cities of India, it is not so of the villages, if only because they were famishing.

Immediately after my return to India in 1915 I discovered that the centre of swadeshi lay in khadi. If khadi goes, I contended even then, there is no swadeshi. I have shown that the manufactures in Indian mills do not constitute swadeshi. To that belief I cling even today.

Think of the bonfire of foreign cloth we had during our first national struggle. Shri Sarojini Naidu and Pandit Motilal Nehru threw their fineries in it. Pandit Motilal Nehru later wrote from jail that he had found true happiness in the simplicity and purity of khadi. It is sad that that spirit does not exist today. The charkha is the centre of our tricolour flag. It is the symbol of unity and the non-violent strength of the millions. The yarn spun by the charkha I consider to be the cementing force which can bind those whom the three colours of the flag represent. That is why I have said that the whole fabric of swaraj hangs on a thread of the handspun yarn and have called the charkha our mightiest weapon. Where is that wheel today?

I have already reminded you that if you have the swadeshi spirit in you, you will refuse to look to the West for the supply of your major wants. I have no quarrel in this time of extreme scarcity if India imports foodstuffs and cloth from outside, provided it is proved that India is wholly unable to supply the two wants from within India. This is in no way proved. I have not hesitated to say and I would repeat that India is fully able to manufacture her own khadi and grow her own foodstuffs in her numerous villages. But alas! The people have become too lazy to look inward and insist on supplying these two wants from within India's borders. I will go even so far as to say that I will face starvation and nakedness rather than look to the West to supply the two needs. Without grim determination it is not possible to do the right thing.

Note [August 1947]

I will give you a talisman. Whenever you are in doubt, or when the self becomes too much with you, apply the following test. Recall the face of the poorest and the weakest man whom you may have seen, and ask yourself if the step you contemplate is going to be of any use to him. Will he gain anything by it? Will it restore him to a control over his own life and destiny? In other words, will it lead to swaraj for the hungry and spiritually starving millions?

Then you will find your doubts and yourself melting away.

The Creed Of Non-violence

On Ahimsa [October 1916]

[...] There seems to be no historical warrant for the belief that an exaggerated practice of ahimsa synchronized with our becoming bereft of many virtues. During the past fifteen hundred years, we have as a nation given ample proof of physical courage, but we have been torn by internal dissensions and have been dominated by love of self instead of love of country. We have, that is to say, been swayed by the spirit of irreligion rather than of religion.

I do not know how far the charge of unmanliness can be made good against the Jains. I hold no brief for them. By birth I am a Vaishnavite, and was taught ahimsa in my childhood. I have derived much religious benefit from Jain religious works, as I have from scriptures of the other great faiths of the world. I owe much to the living company of the deceased philosopher Raja Chand Kavi who was a Jain by birth. Thus though my views on ahimsa are a result of my study of most of the faiths of the world, they are now no longer dependent upon the authority of these works. They are a part of my life and if I suddenly discovered that the religious books read by me bore a different interpretation from the one I had learnt to give them, I should still hold to the view of ahimsa as I am about to set forth here.

Our Shastras seem to teach that a man who really practises ahimsa in its fullness has the world at his feet, he so affects his surroundings that even the snake and other venomous reptiles do him no harm. This is said to have been the experience of St. Francis of Assisi.

In its negative form, it means not injuring any living being, whether by body or mind. I may not therefore hurt the person of any wrong-doer, or bear any ill will to him and so cause him mental suffering. This statement does not cover suffering caused to the wrong-doer by natural acts of mine which do not proceed from ill will. It, therefore, does not prevent me from withdrawing from his presence a child whom he, we shall imagine, is about to strike. Indeed the proper practise of ahimsa required me to withdraw the intended victim from the wrong-doer, if I am in any way whatsoever the guardian of such a child. It was therefore most proper for the passive resisters of South Africa to have resisted the

evil that the Union Government sought to do to them. They bore no
ill will to it. They showed this by helping the Government whenever
it needed their help. Their resistance consisted of disobedience of
the orders of the Government, even to the extent of suffering death
at their hands. Ahimsa requires deliberate self-suffering, not a
deliberate injuring of the supposed wrong-doer.

In its positive form, ahimsa means the largest love, the greatest
charity. If I am a follower of ahimsa, I must love my enemy. I must
apply the same rule to the wrong-doer who is my enemy or a
stranger to me, as I would to my wrong-doing father or son. This
active ahimsa necessarily includes truth and fearlessness. A man
cannot deceive the loved ones; he does not fear or frighten him or
her. The gift of life is the greatest of all gifts. A man who gives it
in reality disarms all hostility. He has paved the way for an
honourable understanding. And none who is himself subject of fear
can bestow that gift. He must therefore be himself fearless. A man
cannot then practise ahimsa and be a coward at the same time. The
practice of ahimsa calls forth the greatest courage. It is the most
soldierly of a soldier's virtues. General Gordon has been represented
in a famous statue as bearing only a stick. This takes us far on the
road to ahimsa. But a soldier, who needs the protection of even a
stick, is to that extent so much the less a soldier. He is the true
soldier who knows how to die and stand his ground in the midst of
a hail of bullets. Such a one was Ambarish who stood his ground
without lifting a finger, though Durvasa did his worst. The Moors,
who were being powdered by the French gunners, rushed into the
guns' mouth with 'Allah' on their lips, showed much the same type
of courage. Only theirs was the courage of desperation. Ambarish's
was due to love. Yet the Moorish valour, readiness to die,
conquered the gunners. They frantically waved their hats, ceased
firing and greeted their erstwhile enemies as comrades. And so the
South African passive resisters in their thousands were ready to die
rather than sell their honour for a little personal ease. This was
ahimsa in its active form. It never barters away honour.

A helpless girl in the hands of a follower of ahimsa finds better
and surer protection than in the hands of one who is prepared to
defend her only to the point to which his weapons would carry him.
The tyrant, in the first instance, will have to walk to his victim over
the dead body of her defender, in the second, he has but to

overpower the defender, for it is assumed that the canon of propriety in the second instance will be satisfied when the defender has fought to the extent of his physical valour. In the first instance, as the defender has matched his very soul against the mere body of the tyrant, the odds are that the soul in the latter will be awakened, and the girl will stand an infinitely greater chance of her honour being protected than in any other conceivable circumstance—barring, of course, that of her own personal courage.

If we are unmanly today, we are so, not because we do not know how to strike, but because we fear to die. He is no follower of Mahavira, the apostle of Jainism, or of the Buddha or of the Vedas, who being afraid to die, takes flight before any danger, real or imaginary, all the while wishing that somebody else would remove the danger by destroying the person causing it. He is no follower of ahimsa (I agree with Lalaji) who does not care a straw if he kills a man by inches by deceiving him in a trade, or who will protect by force of arms a few cows and make away with the butcher, or who in order to do a supposed good to his country does not mind killing off a few officials. All these are actuated by hatred, cowardice and fear. Here love of the cow or the country is a vague thing intended to satisfy one's vanity or soothe a stinging conscience.

Ahimsa, truly understood, is, in my humble opinion, a panacea for all evils mundane and extra-mundane. We can never overdo it. Just at present, we are not doing it at all. Ahimsa does not displace the practice of other virtues, but renders their practice imperatively necessary before it can be practised even in its rudiments. Lalaji need not fear the ahimsa of his father's faith. Mahavira and the Buddha were soldiers, and so was Tolstoy. Only they saw deeper and truer in their profession, and found the secret of a true, happy, honourable and godly life. Let us be joint sharers with these teachers and this land of ours will once more be the abode of gods.

The Doctrine of the Sword
[11 August 1920]

In this age of the rule of brute-force, it is almost impossible for anyone to believe that anyone else could possibly reject the law of the final supremacy of brute-force. And so I receive anonymous letters advising me that I must not interfere with the progress of non-co-operation even though popular violence may break out. Others come to me and assuming that secretly I must be plotting violence, enquire when the happy moment for declaring open violence will arrive. They assure me that the English will never yield to anything but violence secret or open. Yet others, I am informed, believe that I am the most rascally person living in India because I never give out my real intention and that they have not a shadow of a doubt that I believe in violence just as much as most people do.

Such being the hold that the doctrine of the sword has on the majority of mankind, and as success of non-co-operation depends principally on absence of violence during its pendency and as my views in this matter affect the conduct of a large number of people, I am anxious to state them as clearly as possible.

I do believe that where there is only a choice between cowardice and violence I would advise violence. Thus when my eldest son asked me what he should have done, had he been present when I was almost fatally assaulted in 1908, whether he should have run away and seen me killed or whether he should have used his physical force which he could and wanted to use, and defended me, I told him that it was his duty to defend me even by using violence. Hence it was that I took part in the Boer War, the so-called Zulu rebellion and the late War. Hence also do I advocate training in arms for those who believe in the method of violence. I would rather have India resort to arms in order to defend her honour than that she should in a cowardly manner become or remain a helpless witness to her own dishonour.

But I believe that non-violence is infinitely superior to violence, forgiveness is more manly than punishment. *Kshama virasya bhushanam.* 'Forgiveness adorns a soldier.' But abstinence is

98

forgiveness only when there is the power to punish; it is meaningless when it pretends to proceed from a helpless creature. A mouse hardly forgives a cat when it allows itself to be torn to pieces by her. I, therefore, appreciate the sentiment of those who cry out for the condign punishment of General Dyer and his ilk. They would tear him to pieces if they could. But I do not believe India to be helpless. I do not believe myself to be a helpless creature. Only I want to use India's and my strength for a better purpose.

Let me not be misunderstood. Strength does not come from physical capacity. It comes from an indomitable will. An average Zulu is any way more than a match for an average Englishman in bodily capacity. But he flees from an English boy, because he fears the boy's revolver or those who will use it for him. He fears death and is nerveless in spite of his burly figure. We in India may in a moment realize that one hundred thousand Englishmen need not frighten three hundred million human beings. A definite forgiveness would therefore mean a definite recognition of our strength. With enlightened forgiveness must come a mighty wave of strength in us, which would make it impossible for a Dyer and a Frank Johnson to heap affront upon India's devoted head. It matters little to me that for the moment I do not drive my point home. We feel too downtrodden not to be angry and revengeful. But I must not refrain from saying that India can gain more by waiving the right of punishment. We have better work to do, a better mission to deliver to the world.

I am not a visionary. I claim to be a practical idealist. The religion of non-violence is not meant merely for the rishis and saints. It is meant for the common people as well. Non-violence is the law of our species as violence is the law of the brute. The spirit lies dormant in the brute and he knows no law but that of physical might. The dignity of man requires obedience to a higher law—to the strength of the spirit.

I have therefore ventured to place before India the ancient law of self-sacrifice. For satyagraha and its off-shoots, non-co-operation and civil resistance, are nothing but new names for the law of suffering. The rishis, who discovered the law of non-violence in the midst of violence, were greater geniuses than Newton. They were themselves greater warriors than Wellington. Having themselves known the use of arms, they realized their uselessness and taught a weary world that its salvation lay not through violence but through non-violence.

Non-violence in its dynamic condition means conscious suffering. It does not mean meek submission to the will of the evil-doer, but it means the putting of one's whole soul against the will of the tyrant. Working under this law of our being, it is possible for a single individual to defy the whole might of an unjust empire to save his honour, his religion, his soul and lay the foundation for that empire's fall or its regeneration.

And so I am not pleading for India to practise non-violence because it is weak. I want her to practise non-violence being conscious of her strength and power. No training in arms is required for realization of her strength. We seem to need it because we seem to think that we are but a lump of flesh. I want India to recognize that she has a soul that cannot perish and that can rise triumphant above every physical weakness and defy the physical combination of a whole world. What is the meaning of Rama, a mere human being, with his host of monkeys, pitting himself against the insolent strength of ten-headed Ravana surrounded in supposed safety by the raging waters on all sides of Lanka? Does it not mean the conquest of physical might by spiritual strength? However, being a practical man, I do not wait till India recognizes the practicability of the spiritual life in the political world. India considers herself to be powerless and paralyzed before the machine-guns, the tanks and the aeroplanes of the English. And she takes up non-co-operation out of her weakness. It must still serve the same purpose, namely, bring her delivery from the crushing weight of British injustice if a sufficient number of people practise it.

I isolate this non-co-operation from Sinn Feinism, for, it is so conceived as to be incapable of being offered side by side with violence. But I invite even the school of violence to give this peaceful non-co-operation a trial. It will not fail through its inherent weakness. It may fail because of poverty of response. Then will be the time for real danger. The high-souled men, who are unable to suffer national humiliation any longer, will want to vent their wrath. They will take to violence. So far as I know, they must perish without delivering themselves or their country from the wrong. If India takes up the doctrine of the sword, she may gain momentary victory. Then India will cease to be the pride of my heart. I am wedded to India because I owe my all to her. I believe absolutely that she has a mission for the world. She is not to copy Europe blindly. India's acceptance of the doctrine of the sword will be the hour of my trial. I hope I shall not be found wanting. My religion has no geographical limits. If I have a living faith in it, it will transcend my love for India herself. My life is dedicated to service of India through the religion of non-violence which I believe to be the root of Hinduism[...]

Non-violence [9 March 1922]

[...] That non-violence which only an individual can use is not of much use in terms of society. Man is a social being. His accomplishments to be of use must be such as any person with sufficient diligence can attain. That which can be exercised only among friends is of value only as a spark of non-violence. It cannot merit the appellation of ahimsa. 'Enmity vanishes before ahimsa' is a great aphorism. It means that the greatest enmity requires an equal measure of ahimsa for its abatement. Cultivation of this virtue may need long practice, even extending to several births. It does not become useless on that account. Travelling along the route, the pilgrim will meet richer experiences from day to day so that he may have a glimpse of the beauty he is destined to see at the top. This will add to his zest.

No one is entitled to infer from this that the path will be a continuous carpet of roses without thorns. A poet has sung that the way to reach God accrues only to the very brave, never to the faint-hearted. The atmosphere today is so much saturated with poison that one refuses to recollect the wisdom of the ancients and to perceive the varied little experience of ahimsa in action. 'A bad turn is neutralized by a good' is a wise saying of daily experience in practice. Why can we not see that if the sum total of the world's activities was destructive, it would have come to an end long ago? Love, otherwise ahimsa, sustains this planet of ours.

This much must be admitted. The precious grace of life has to be strenuously cultivated, naturally so because it is uplifting. Descent is easy, not so ascent. A large majority of us being not become divine when he personifies innocence in himself. Only then does he become truly man. In our present state, we are partly men and partly beasts and, in our ignorance and even arrogance, say that we truly fulfil the purpose of our species when we deliver blow for blow and develop the measure of anger required for the purpose. We pretend to believe that retaliation is the law of our being, whereas in every scripture we find that retaliation is nowhere obligatory but only permissible. It is restraint that is obligatory. Retaliation is indulgence requiring elaborate regulating. Restraint is the law of our being. For, highest perfection is unattainable without highest restraint. Suffering is thus the badge of the human tribe.

The goal ever recedes from us. The greater the progress, the greater the recognition of our unworthiness. Satisfaction lies in the effort, not in the attainment. Full effort is full victory.

Therefore, though I realize more than ever how far I am from that goal, for me the Law of complete Love is the law of my being. Each time I fail, my effort shall be all the more determined for my failure.

But I am *not* preaching this final law through the Congress or the Khilafat organization. I know my own limitations only too well. I know that any such attempt is foredoomed to failure. To expect a whole mass of men and women to obey that law all at once is not to know its working. But I do preach from the Congress platform the deductions of the law. What the Congress and the Khilafat organizations have accepted is but a fragment of the implications of that law. Given true workers, the limited measure of its application can be realized in respect of vast masses of people within a short time. But the little measure of it to be true must satisfy the same test as the whole. A drop of water must yield to the analyst the same results as a lakeful. The nature of my non-violence towards my brother cannot be different from that of my non-violence to the universe. When I extend the love for my brother to the whole universe, it must still satisfy the same test.

A particular practice is a policy when its application is limited to time or space. Highest policy is therefore fullest practice. But honesty as policy while it lasts is not anything different from honesty as a creed. A merchant believing in honesty as a policy will sell the same measure and quality of cloth to the yard as a merchant with honesty as a creed. The difference between the two is that the political merchant will leave his honesty when it does not pay, the believing one will continue it even though he should lose his all.

The political non-violence of the non-co-operator does not stand this test in the vast majority of cases. Hence the prolongation of the struggle. Let no one blame the unbending English nature. The hardest 'fibre' must melt in the fire of love. I cannot be dislodged from the position because I know it. When British or other nature does not respond, the fire is not strong enough, if it is there at all.

Our non-violence need not be of the strong, but it *has* to be of the truthful. We must not intend harm to the English or to our co-operating countrymen if and whilst we claim to be non-violent. But the majority of us *have* intended harm, and we have refrained from doing it because of our weakness or under the ignorant belief that mere refraining from physical hurt amounted to due fulfilment of our pledge. Our pledge of non-violence excludes the possibility of future retaliation. Some of us seem, unfortunately, to have merely postponed the date of revenge.

Let me not be misunderstood. I do not say that the policy of non-violence excludes the possibility of revenge when the policy is abandoned. But it does most emphatically exclude the possibility of future revenge after a successful termination of the struggle. Therefore, whilst we are pursuing the policy of non-violence, we are bound to be actively friendly to English administrators and their co-operators. I felt ashamed when I was told that in some parts of India it was not safe for Englishmen or well-known co-operators to move about safely. The disgraceful scenes that took place at a recent Madras meeting were a complete denial of non-violence. Those who howled down the Chairman, because he was supposed to have insulted me, disgraced themselves and their policy. They wounded the heart of their friend and helper, Mr Andrews. They injured their own cause. If the Chairman believed that I was a scoundrel, he had a perfect right to say so. Ignorance is no provocation. But a non-co-operator is pledged to put up with the gravest provocation. Provocation there would be, when I act scoundrel-like. I grant that it will be enough to absolve every non-co-operator from the pledge of non-violence and that any non-co-operator will be fully justified in taking my life for misleading him.

It may be that even cultivation of such limited non-violence is impossible in the majority of cases. It may be that we must not expect people even out of self-interest not to *intend* harm to the opponent whilst they are *doing* none. We must then, to be honest, clearly give up the use of the word 'non-violence' in connection with our struggle. The alternative need not be immediate resort to violence. But the people will not then be called upon to subject themselves to any discipline in non-violence. A person like me will not then feel called upon to shoulder the responsibility for Chauri Chaura. The school of limited non-violence will then still flourish in its obscurity, but without the terrible burden of responsibility it carries today.

But if non-violence is to remain the policy of the nation, for its fair name and that of humanity, we are bound to carry it out to the letter and in the spirit.

And if we intend to follow out the policy, if we believe in it, we must then quickly make up with the Englishmen and the co-operators. We must get their certificate that they feel absolutely safe in our midst and that they may regard us as friends although we belong to a radically different school of thought and politics. We must welcome them to our political platforms as honoured guests. We must meet them on neutral platforms as comrades. We must devise methods of such meeting. Our non-violence must not breed violence, hatred and ill-will. We stand like the rest of fellow-mortals to be judged by our works. A programme of non-violence for the attainment of swaraj necessarily means ability to conduct our affairs on non-violent lines. That means inculcation of a spirit of obedience. Mr Churchill, who understands only the gospel of force, is quite right in saying that the Irish problem is different in character from the Indian. He means in effect that the Irish, having fought their way to their swaraj through violence, will be well able to maintain it by violence, if need be. India, on the other hand, if she wins swaraj in reality by non-violence, must be able to maintain it chiefly by non-violent means. This Mr Churchill can hardly believe to be possible unless India proves her ability by an ocular demonstration of the principle. Such a demonstration is impossible unless non-violence has permeated society so that people in their *corporate,* i.e., political, life respond to non-violence, in other words, civil instead of military authority, as at present, gains predominance.

Swaraj by non-violent means can therefore never mean an interval of chaos and anarchy. Swaraj by non-violence must be a progressively peaceful revolution such that the transference of power from a close corporation to the people's representatives will be as natural as the dropping of a fully ripe fruit from a well-nurtured tree. I say again that such a thing may be quite impossible of attainment. But I know that nothing less is the implication of non-violence. And if the present workers do not believe in the probability of achieving such comparatively non-violent atmosphere, they should drop the non-violent programme and frame another which is wholly different in character. If we approach our programme with the mental reservation that, after all, we shall wrest the power from the British by force of arms, then we are untrue to our profession of non-violence. If we believe in our programme, we are bound to believe that the British people are not un-amenable to the force of affection as they are undoubtedly amenable to force of arms. For the unbelievers, the Councils are undoubtedly the school of learning with their heavy programme of humiliations spread over a few generations or a rapid but bloody revolution probably never witnessed before in the world. I have no desire to take part in such a revolution. I will not be a willing instrument for promoting it. The choice, in my opinion, lies between honest non-violence with non-co-operation as its necessary corollary or reversion to responsive co-operation, i.e., co-operation *cum* obstruction.

Problems of Non-violence
[9 August 1925]

People keep asking me which acts may be termed violent and which non-violent, and what is one's duty at a particular time. While some of these queries reveal the ignorance of the enquirers, others serve to bring out the difficult dilemmas involved. A Punjabi gentleman has put a question the answer to which is worth giving here. It is as follows:

> What should be done when tigers, wolves and other wild beasts come and carry away other animals or human beings? Or, what should be done about germs in water?

In my humble opinion the simple answer is that where there is danger from tigers, wolves and so on, then killing them becomes inevitable. The germs that water contains must also be inevitably destroyed. Violence which is inevitable does not therefore cease to be so and become non-violence. It has to be recognized as violence. I have no doubt that it would be best if we could contrive to survive without destroying tigers, wolves, etc. However, who could do so? Only he who is not afraid of these animals and can regard them as friends, he alone could do so. Anyone who refrains from violence because he is afraid, is nevertheless guilty of violence. The mouse is not non-violent towards the cat. At heart, he always has a feeling of violence towards the cat. He cannot kill the latter because he is weak. He alone has the power to practise the *dharma* of ahimsa who although fully capable of inflicting violence does not inflict it. He alone practises the ahimsa *dharma* who voluntarily and with love refrains from inflicting violence on anyone.

Non-violence implies love, compassion, forgiveness. The Shastras describe these as the virtues of the brave. This courage is not physical but mental. There have been instances of physically frail men having indulged in grave acts of violence with the help of others. There have also been cases where those as physically strong as Yudhishthira have granted pardon to such persons as King Virata. Hence, so long as one has not developed inner strength, one can never practise the *dharma* of ahimsa. The non-violence practised by the Banias today does not deserve the name; one finds in it cruelty sometimes and ignorance all the time.

It was because I know this weakness of ours that during the War I went all out to recruit soldiers in Kheda. And, it was for this very reason that I said at that time that perhaps the most brutal act of the British Government was to have disarmed and thus emasculated the Indian people. I hold the same view even today. If anyone afraid at heart cannot, while remaining unarmed, rid himself of that fear, he should certainly arm himself with a stick or an even more deadly weapon.

Ahimsa is a great vow; it is more difficult than walking on the edge of a sword. Complete adherence to it is almost impossible for one who has a physical form. Severe penance is required for its practice. Penance should be taken to mean renunciation and knowledge. Anyone who desires to possess land cannot practise ahimsa. A peasant necessarily has to protect his land. He must guard it against tigers and wolves. A peasant who is not prepared to punish these animals or thieves, etc., should always be prepared to abandon his field.

In order to be able to practise the *dharma* of ahimsa, man must abide by the limits laid down by the Shastras and custom. The Shastras do not enjoin violence. But they permit certain acts of violence by regarding them as unavoidable at particular times. For instance, it is believed that the *Manusmriti* permits the slaughter of certain animals. Such slaughter has not been ordained. Thereafter, with progress in thinking, it was decided that this would not be permitted in the *Kaliyuga*. Hence it is customary today to regard certain forms of violence as pardonable, while some of the forms of violence allowed by *Manusmriti* are forbidden. It is obviously wrong to argue that we can go beyond the concessions allowed by the Shastras. There is *dharma* in self-control and, *adharma* in indulgence. Anyone who does not make use of the latitude given by the Shastras deserves to be congratulated. Ahimsa knows no limits because there are none to self-control. The latter has been welcomed by all the scriptures of the world, while opinions differ widely regarding indulgence. A right angle is the same everywhere, while there is no end to the number of other angles. Non-violence and truth together form, as it were, the right angle of all religions. Conduct which does not fit into that angle should undoubtedly be given up. Imperfect conduct may, perhaps, be permitted. Anyone who practises the *dharma* of ahimsa should increase his inner strength by being always on the alert and progressively restricting the latitude that he has allowed for himself. There is certainly nothing religious about indulgence. Renouncing through knowledge the worldly life—this is the attainment of *moksha*. Such absolute renunciation is not to be found even on the peaks of the Himalayas. The true cave is the one in the heart. Man can hide himself within it and thus protected can remain untouched by the world even though living and moving freely in it, taking part in those activities which cannot be avoided.

Excerpt from a Letter to Narandas Gandhi
[28–31 July 1930]

[...] The commencement of this discourse is both comic and painful.
We two had a discussion on how to economize in the use of cloth-
lined envelopes and save the same envelopes for use again and
again. The question was whether to paste a blank sheet on the
whole side of the envelope or paste only slips over portions where
something was written. This was a futile discussion. We wasted on
it fifteen minutes of beautiful time after prayers, demonstrating our
foolishness thereby. In doing this we violated truth and ahimsa and
displayed lack of discrimination. Truth was violated, because the
discussion was not inspired by an ardent desire for its search.
Ahimsa was shamed, because I, who ought to give every moment of
my time to discover the sufferings of the people and in thinking
about the ways of ending them, wasted fifteen priceless minutes in
a futile discussion. We displayed lack of discrimination, because if
we had thought about the utility of the discussion, it would not have
lasted even a minute. After we had stolen fifteen minutes from
people's time, we realized our foolishness and thanked God for
opening our eyes.

I have purposely given this introduction.

The path of Truth is as narrow as it is straight. Even so is that
of ahimsa. It is like balancing oneself on the edge of a sword. By
concentration an acrobat can walk on a rope. But the concentration
required to tread the path of Truth and ahimsa is far greater. The
slightest inattention brings one tumbling to the ground. One can
realize Truth and ahimsa only by ceaseless striving.

But it is impossible for us to realize perfect truth so long as we
are imprisoned in this mortal frame. We can only visualize it in our
imagination. We cannot, through the instrumentality of this
ephemeral body, see face to face truth which is eternal. That is why
in the last resort we must depend on faith.

It appears that the impossibility of full realization of truth in
this mortal body led some ancient seeker after truth to the
appreciation of ahimsa. The question which confronted him was:
'Shall I bear with those who create difficulties for me, or shall I
destroy them?' The seeker realized that he who went on destroying

others did not make headway but simply stayed where he was, while the man who suffered those who created difficulties marched ahead and at times even took the others with him. The first act of destruction taught him that the truth which was the object of his quest was not outside himself but within. Hence the more he took to violence, the more he receded from truth. For in fighting the imagined enemy without, he neglected the enemy within.

We punish thieves because we think they harass us. They may leave us alone; but they will only transfer their attentions to another victim. This other victim, however, is also a human being, ourselves in a different form, and so we are caught in a vicious circle. The trouble from thieves continues to increase, as they think it is their business to steal. In the end we see that it is better to tolerate the thieves than to punish them. The forbearance may even bring them to their senses. By tolerating them we realize that thieves are not different from ourselves, they are our brethren, our friends, and may not be punished. But whilst we may bear with the thieves, we may not endure the infliction. That would only induce cowardice. So we realize a further duty. Since we regard the thieves as our kith and kin, they must be made to realize the kinship. And so we must take pains to devise ways and means of winning them over. This is the path of ahimsa. It may entail continuous suffering and the cultivating of endless patience. Given these two conditions, the thief is bound in the end to turn away from his evil ways and we shall get a clearer vision of truth. Thus step by step we learn how to make friends with all the world; we realize the greatness of God, of Truth. Our peace of mind increases in spite of suffering; we become braver and more enterprising; we understand more clearly the difference between what is everlasting and what is not; we learn how to distinguish between what is our duty and what is not. Our pride melts away and we become humble. Our worldly attachments diminish and likewise the evil within us diminishes from day to day.

Ahimsa is not the crude thing it has been made to appear. Not to hurt any living thing is no doubt a part of ahimsa. But it is its least expression. The principle of ahimsa is hurt by every evil thought, by undue haste, by lying, by hatred, by wishing ill of anybody. It is also violated by our holding on to what the world needs. But the world needs even what we eat day by day. In the place where we stand there are millions of micro-organisms to whom the place belongs and who are hurt by our presence there. What should we do then? Should we commit suicide? Even that is no solution, if we believe, as we do, that so long as the spirit is attached to the flesh, on every destruction of the body it weaves for itself another. The body will cease to be only when we give up all attachment to it. This freedom from all attachment is the realization of God as Truth. Such realization cannot be attained in a hurry. Realizing that this body does not belong to us, that it is a trust handed over to our charge, we should make the right use of it and progress towards our goal.

I wished to write something which would be easy for all to understand, but I find that I have written a difficult discourse. However, no one who has thought even a little about ahimsa should find any difficulty in understanding what I have written.

It is perhaps clear from the foregoing that without ahimsa it is not possible to seek and find Truth. Ahimsa and Truth are so intertwined that it is practically impossible to disentangle and separate them. They are like the two sides of a coin, or rather of a smooth unstamped metallic disc. Who can say which is the obverse and which is the reverse? Nevertheless, ahimsa is the means and Truth is the end. Means to be means must always be within our reach, and so ahimsa becomes our supreme duty and Truth becomes God for us. If we take care of the means, we are bound to reach the end sooner or later. If we resolve to do this, we shall have won the battle. Whatever difficulties we encounter, whatever apparent reverses we sustain, we should not lose faith but should ever repeat one mantra: 'Truth exists, it alone exists. It is the only God and there is but one way of realizing it; there is but one means and that is ahimsa. I will never give it up. May the God that is Truth, in whose name I have taken this pledge, give me the strength to keep it.'

Both Happy and Unhappy
[29 June 1940]

It was on the 18th instant that I expressed the following hope in *Harijan*:

> If my argument has gone home, is it not time for us to declare our changeless faith in non-violence of the strong and say we do not seek to defend our liberty with the force of arms but we will defend it with the force of non-violence?

On the 21st the Working Committee felt unable to enforce such faith in action when the time for it came.[1] For the Committee never before had an occasion to test their faith. At the last meeting they had to lay down a course of action for meeting impending anarchy within and danger of aggression from without.

I pleaded hard with the Committee: 'If you have faith in non-violence of the strong, now is the time to act up to it. It does not matter that many parties do not believe in non-violence whether of the strong or of the weak. Probably that is all the greater reason for Congressmen to meet the emergency by non-violent action. For if all were non-violent, there could be no anarchy and there would be no question of anybody arming for meeting aggression from without. It is because Congressmen represent a party of non-violence, in the midst of parties who do not believe in it, that it becomes imperative for Congressmen to show that they are well able to act up to their faith.'

But the members of the Working Committee felt that Congressmen would not be able to act up to it. It would be a new experience for them. They were never before called upon to deal with such a crisis. The attempt made by me to form peace brigades to deal with communal riots and the like had wholly failed. Therefore they could not hope for the action contemplated.

My position was different. With the Congress non-violence was always a policy. It was open to it to reject it if it failed. If it could not bring political and economic independence, it was of no use. For me non-violence is a creed. I must act up to it whether I am alone or have companions. Since propagation of non-violence is the mission of my life, I must pursue it in all weathers. I felt that now was the time for me to prove my faith before God and man. And so I asked for absolution from the Committee. Hitherto I have been responsible for guiding the general policy of the Congress. I could no longer do so when fundamental differences were discovered between them and me. They readily recognized the correctness of my attitude. And they gave me the absolution. Once more they have justified the trust imposed in them. They have been true to themselves. They had not the confidence, in themselves or those whom they represented, that they could express in their actions the required measure of non-violence. And so they made the only choice they could honestly make. It was a tremendous sacrifice they made—the sacrifice of the prestige that the Congress had gained in the world for unadulterated non-violence, and the dissolution of the unwritten and unspoken bond between them and me. But though it is a break in the common practice of a common ideal or policy, there is no break in the friendship of over twenty years' standing.

I am both happy and unhappy over the result. Happy because I have been able to bear the strain of the break and have been given the strength to stand alone. Unhappy because my word seemed to lose the power to carry with me those whom it was my proud privilege to carry all these many years which seem like yesterday. But I know that, if God shows me the way to demonstrate the efficacy of non-violence of the strong, the break will prove to have been temporary. If there is no way, they will have justified their wisdom in bearing the wrench of letting me go my way alone. If that tragic discovery of my impotence is in store for me, I hope still to retain the faith that has sustained me all these years and to have humility enough to realize that I was not a fit enough instrument to carry the torch of non-violence any further.

But this argument and doubt are based upon the assumption that the members of the Working Committee represent the feeling of the vast majority of Congressmen. They would wish and hope that the vast majority of Congressmen had in them the non-violence of the strong. No one would be more glad than they to discover that they had underrated Congressmen's strength. The probability, however, is that there is no majority but only a good minority which represents the non-violence of the strong. It should be remembered that the matter does not lend itself to argument. The members of the Working Committee had all the argument before them. But non-violence, which is a quality of the heart, cannot come by an appeal to the brain. Therefore what is required is a quiet but resolute demonstration of non-violent strength. The opportunity comes to everyone almost daily. There are communal clashes, there are dacoities, there are wordy duels. In all these things those who are truly non-violent can and will demonstrate it. If it is shown in an adequate measure, it will not fail to infect their surroundings. I am quite clear that there is not a single Congressman who disbelieves in the efficacy of non-violence out of sheer cussedness. Let the Congressmen who believe that the Congress should adhere to non-violence in dealing with internal disorders or external aggression, express it in their daily conduct.

Non-violence of the strong cannot be a mere policy. It must be a creed, or a passion, if 'creed' is objected to. A man with a passion expresses it in every little act of his. Therefore he who is possessed by non-violence will express it in the family circle, in his dealings with neighbours, in his business, in Congress meetings, in public meetings, and in his dealings with opponents. It is because it has not expressed itself in this way among Congressmen that the members of the Working Committee rightly concluded that Congressmen were not ready for non-violent treatment of internal disorders or external aggression. Embarrassment caused by non-violent action would move established authority to yield to popular will. But such action has obviously no play in the face of disorders. We have to court death without retaliation and with no malice or anger towards those who bring about disorder. It is easy enough to see that non-violence required here is of a wholly different type from what the Congress has known hitherto. But it is the only non-violence that is true and that can save the world from self-destruction. This is a certainty sooner or later, sooner rather than later, if India cannot deliver the message of true non-violence to a world which wants to be saved from the curse of wars and does not know how to find the deliverance.

The Best Field for Ahimsa
[15 July 1940]

Last week I wrote about three fields for the operation of ahimsa. I propose to invite attention today to the fourth and the best field for the operation of non-violence. This is the family field, in a wider sense than the ordinary. Thus members of an institution should be regarded as a family. Non-violence as between the members of such families should be easy to practise. If that fails, it means that we have not developed the capacity for pure non-violence. For the love we have to practise towards our relatives or colleagues in our family or institution, we have to practise towards our foes, dacoits, etc. If we fail in one case, success in the other is a chimera.

We have generally assumed that, though it may not be possible to exercise non-violence in the domestic fields, it is possible to do so in the political field. This has proved a pure delusion. We have chosen to describe our methods adopted so far as non-violence, and thus caricatured non-violence itself. If non-violence it was, it was such poor stuff that it proved useless at the critical moment. The alphabet of ahimsa is best learnt in the domestic school, and I can say from experience that, if we secure success there, we are sure to do so everywhere else. For a non-violent person the whole world is one family. He will thus fear none, nor will others fear him.

It will be retorted that those who satisfy such a test of non-violence will be few and far between. It is quite likely, but that is no reply to my proposition. Those who profess to believe in non-violence should know the implications of that belief. And if these scare them away, they are welcome to give up the belief. Now that the Congress Working Committee has made the position clear, it is necessary that those who claim to believe in non-violence should know what is expected of them. If, as a result, the ranks of the non-violent army thin down, it should not matter. An army, however small, of truly non-violent soldiers is likely some day to multiply itself. An army of those who are not truly non-violent is never likely to yield any use whether it increases or decreases.

Let no one understand from the foregoing that a non-violent army is open only to those who strictly enforce in their lives all the implications of non-violence. It is open to all those who accept the implications and make an ever-increasing endeavour to observe them. There never will be an army of perfectly non-violent people. It will be formed of those who will honestly endeavour to observe non-violence. For the last fifty years I have striven to make my life increasingly non-violent and to inspire my co-workers in the same direction, and I think I have had a fair amount of success. The growing darkness around, far from damping my zeal and dimming my faith, brightens them, and makes the implications of non-violence more clearly visible to me.

117

Is Non-violence Impossible
[11 August 1940]

The doubts and difficulties raised by this correspondent occur to others also, and I have on various occasions tried to solve them too. But when the Working Committee of the Congress has been instrumental in making of ahimsa a live issue, it seems necessary to deal with these doubts and difficulties at some length.

The correspondent doubts in substance the universal application of ahimsa, and asserts that society has made little progress towards it. Teachers like the Buddha arose and made some effort with some little success perhaps in their lifetime, but society is just where it was in spite of them. Ahimsa may be good enough to be the duty of an individual; for society it is good for nothing, and India too will have to take to violence for her freedom.

The argument is, I think, fundamentally wrong. The last statement is incorrect inasmuch as the Congress has adhered to non-violence as the means for the attainment of swaraj. It has indeed gone a step further. The question having been raised as to whether non-violence continues to be the weapon against all internal disturbances, the AICC clearly gave the answer in the affirmative. It is only for protection against outside aggression that the Congress has maintained that it would be necessary to have an army. And then even on this matter there was a considerable body of the members of the AICC who voted against the resolution. This dissent has got to be reckoned with when the question voted upon is one of principle. The Congress policy must always be decided by a majority vote, but it does not cancel the minority vote. It stands. Where there is no principle involved and there is a programme to be carried out, the minority has got to follow the majority. But where there is a principle involved, the dissent stands, and it is bound to express itself in practice when the occasion arises. That means that ahimsa for all occasions and all purposes has been recognized by a society, however small it may be, and that ahimsa as a remedy to be used by society has made fair strides. Whether it will make further strides or no is a different matter. The Working Committee's resolution, therefore, fails to lend any support to the correspondent's doubts. On the contrary it should in a certain degree dispel them.

Now for the argument that I am but a rare individual, and that what little society has done in the matter of ahimsa is due to my influence, and that it is sure to disappear with me. This is not right. The Congress has a number of leaders who can think for themselves. The Maulana is a great thinker of keen intellect and vast reading. Few can equal him in his Arabic and Persian scholarship. Experience has taught him that ahimsa alone can make India free. It was he who insisted on the resolution accepting ahimsa as a weapon against internal disturbances. Pandit Jawaharlal is not a man to stand in awe of anyone. His study of history and contemporary events is second to none. It is after mature thought that he has accepted ahimsa as a means for the attainment of swaraj. It is true that he has said that he would not hesitate to accept swaraj if non-violence failed and it could be won by means of violence. But that is not relevant to the present issue. There are not a few other big names in the Congress who believe in ahimsa as the only weapon at least for the attainment of swaraj. To think that all of them will give up the way of ahimsa as soon as I am gone, is to insult them and to insult human nature. We must believe that everyone can think for himself. Mutual respect to that extent is essential for progress. By crediting our companions with independent judgment we strengthen them and make it easy for them to be independent-minded even if they are proved to be weak.

I hope neither the correspondent nor anyone else believes that the Congress or many Congress leaders have bidden goodbye to ahimsa. To the limited extent that I have pointed out faith in ahimsa has been reiterated and made clear beyond any doubt by the Congress. I agree that the limit laid down by the Congress considerably narrows down the sphere of ahimsa and dims its splendour. But the limited ahimsa of the Congress is good enough for the purpose of our present argument. For I am trying to make out that the field of ahimsa is widening, and the limited acceptance of ahimsa by the Congress sufficiently supports my position.

If we turn our eyes to the time of which history has any record down to our own time, we shall find that man has been steadily progressing towards ahimsa. Our remote ancestors were cannibals. Then came a time when they were fed up with cannibalism and they began to live on chase. Next came a stage when man was ashamed of leading the life of a wandering hunter. He therefore took to agriculture and depended principally on mother earth for his food. Thus from being a nomad he settled down to civilized stable life, founded villages and towns, and from member of a family he became member of a community and a nation. All these are signs of progressive ahimsa and diminishing himsa. Had it been otherwise, the human species should have been extinct by now, even as many of the lower species have disappeared.

Prophets and avatars have also taught the lesson of ahimsa more or less. Not one of them has professed to teach himsa. And how should it be otherwise? *Himsa* does not need to be taught. Man as animal is violent, but as spirit is non-violent. The moment he awakes to the spirit within he cannot remain violent. Either he progresses towards ahimsa or rushes to his doom. That is why the prophet and avatars have taught the lessons of truth, harmony, brotherhood, justice, etc.—all attributes of ahimsa.

And yet violence seems to persist, even to the extent of thinking people like the correspondent regarding it as the final weapon. But as I have shown history and experience are against him.

If we believe that mankind has steadily progressed towards ahimsa, it follows that it has to progress towards it still further. Nothing in this world is static, everything is kinetic. If there is no progression, then there is inevitable retrogression. No one can remain without the eternal cycle, unless it be God Himself.

The present war is the saturation point in violence. It spells to my mind also its doom. Daily I have testimony of the fact that ahimsa was never before appreciated by mankind as it is today. All the testimony from the West that I continue to receive points in the same direction. The Congress has pledged itself to ahimsa however limited. I invite the correspondent and doubters like him to shed their doubts and plunge confidently into the sacred sacrificial fire of ahimsa. Then I have little doubt that the Congress will retrace its step. 'It is always willing.' Well has Pritam, our poet, sung:

> *Happiest are those that plunge in the fire.*
> *The lookers-on are all but scorched by flames.*

My Idea of a Police Force
[1 September 1940]

For one who has never seen the arctic regions an imaginary description of them, however elaborate, can convey but an inadequate idea of the reality. Even so is it with ahimsa. If all Congressmen had been true to their creed, we would not be vacillating between violence and non-violence as we are today. The fruits of ahimsa would be in evidence everywhere. There would be communal harmony, the demon of untouchability would have been cast out, and, generally speaking, we should have evolved an ordered society. But the reverse is the case just now. There is even definite hostility to the Congress in certain quarters. The word of Congressmen is not always relied on. The Muslim League and most of the princes have no faith in the Congress and are in fact inimical to it. If Congressmen had true ahimsa in them, there would be none of this distrust. In fact the Congress would be the beloved of all.

Therefore I can only place an imaginary picture before the votaries of ahimsa.

So long as we are not saturated with pure ahimsa we cannot possibly win swaraj through non-violence. We can come into power only when we are in a majority or, in other words, when the large majority of people are willing to abide by the law of ahimsa. When this happy state prevails, the spirit of violence will have all but vanished and internal disorder will have come under control.

Nevertheless I have conceded that even in a non-violent State a police force may be necessary. This, I admit, is a sign of my imperfect ahimsa. I have not the courage to declare that we can carry on without a police force as I have in respect of an army. Of course I can and do envisage a State where the police will not be necessary; but whether we shall succeed in realizing it, the future alone will show.

The police of my conception will, however, be of a wholly different pattern from the present-day force. Its ranks will be composed of believers in non-violence. They will be servants, not masters, of the people. The people will instinctively render them every help, and through mutual co-operation they will easily deal with the ever-decreasing disturbances. The police force will have some kind of arms, but they will be rarely used, if at all. In fact the policemen will be reformers. Their police work will be confined primarily to robbers and dacoits. Quarrels between labour and capital and strikes will be few and far between in a non-violent State, because the influence of the non-violent majority will be so great as to command the respect of the principal elements in society. Similarly there will be no room for communal disturbances. Then we must remember that when such a Congress Government comes into power the large majority of men and women of twenty-one years and over will have been enfranchized. The rigid and cramped Constitution of today has of course no place in this picture.

The Mass Movements

Satyagraha—Not Passive Resistance
[2 September 1917]

The force denoted by the term 'passive resistance' and translated into Hindi as *nishkriya pratirodha* is not very accurately described either by the original English phrase or by its Hindi rendering. Its correct description is 'satyagraha'. Satyagraha was born in South Africa in 1908. There was no word in any Indian language denoting the power which our countrymen in South Africa invoked for the redress of their grievances. There was an English equivalent, namely, 'passive resistance', and we carried on with it. However, the need for a word to describe this unique power came to be increasingly felt, and it was decided to award a prize to anyone who could think of an appropriate term. A Gujarati-speaking gentleman submitted the word 'satyagraha', and it was adjudged the best.

'Passive resistance' conveyed the idea of the Suffragette Movement in England. Burning of houses by these women was called 'passive resistance' and so also their fasting in prison. All such acts might very well be 'passive resistance' but they were no 'satyagraha'. It is said of 'passive resistance' that it is the weapon of the weak, but the power which is the subject of the article can be used only by the strong. This power is not 'passive' resistance; indeed it calls for intense activity. The movement in South Africa was not passive but active. The Indians of South Africa believed that Truth was their object, that Truth ever triumphs, and with this definiteness of purpose they persistently held on to Truth. They put up with all the suffering that this persistence implied. With the conviction that Truth is not to be renounced even unto death, they shed the fear of death. In the cause of Truth, the prison was a palace to them and its doors the gateway to freedom.

Satyagraha is not physical force. A satyagrahi does not inflict pain on the adversary; he does not seek his destruction. A satyagrahi never resorts to firearms. In the use of satyagraha, there is no ill-will whatever.

Satyagraha is pure soul-force. Truth is the very substance of the soul. That is why this force is called satyagraha. The soul is informed with knowledge. In it burns the flame of love. If someone gives us pain through ignorance, we shall win him through love.

125

'Non-violence is the supreme *dharma*' is the proof of this power of love. Non-violence is a dormant state. In the waking state, it is love. Ruled by love, the world goes on. In English there is a saying, 'Might is Right'. Then there is the doctrine of the survival of the fittest. Both these ideas are contradictory to the above principle. Neither is wholly true. If ill-will were the chief motive-force, the world would have been destroyed long ago; and neither would I have had the opportunity to write this article nor would the hopes of the readers be fulfilled. We are alive solely because of love. We are all ourselves the proof of this. Deluded by modern Western civilization, we have forgotten our ancient civilization and worship the might of arms.

We forget the principle of non-violence, which is the essence of all religions. The doctrine of arms stands for irreligion. It is due to the sway of that doctrine that a sanguinary war is raging in Europe.

In India also we find worship of arms. We see it even in that great work of Tulsidas. But it is seen in all the books that soul-force is the supreme power.

Rama stands for the soul and Ravana for the non-soul. The immense physical might of Ravana is as nothing compared to the soul-force of Rama. Ravana's ten heads are as straw to Rama. Rama is a *yogi*, he has conquered self and pride. He is 'placid equally in affluence and adversity', he has 'neither attachment, nor the intoxication of status'. This represents the ultimate in satyagraha. The banner of *satyagraha* can again fly in the Indian sky and it is our duty to raise it. If we take recourse to satyagraha, we can conquer our conquerors the English, make them bow before our tremendous soul-force, and the issue will be of benefit to the whole world.

It is certain that India cannot rival Britain or Europe in force of arms. The British worship the war-god and they can all of them become, as they are becoming, bearers of arms. The hundreds of millions in India can never carry arms. They have made the religion of non-violence their own. It is impossible for the *varnashrama* system to disappear from India.

The way of *varnashrama* is a necessary law of nature. India, by making a judicious use of it, derives much benefit. Even the Muslims and the English in India observe this system to some extent. Outside of India, too, people follow it without being aware of it. So long as this institution of *varnashrama* exists in India, everyone cannot bear arms here. The highest place in India is assigned to the *brahmana dharma*—which is soul-force. Even the armed warrior does obeisance to the Brahmin. So long as this custom prevails, it is vain for us to aspire for equality with the West in force of arms.

It is our Kamadhenu. It brings good both to the satyagrahi and his adversary. It is ever victorious. For instance, Harishchandra was a satyagrahi, Prahlad was a satyagrahi, Mirabai was a satyagrahi. Daniel, Socrates and those Arabs who hurled themselves on the fire of the French artillery were all satyagrahis. We see from these examples that a satyagrahi does not fear for his body, he does not give up what he thinks is Truth; the word 'defeat' is not to be found in his dictionary, he does not wish for the destruction of his antagonist, he does not vent anger on him; but has only compassion for him.

A satyagrahi does not wait for others, but throws himself into the fray, relying entirely on his own resources. He trusts that when the time comes, others will do likewise. His practice is his precept. Like air, satyagraha is all-pervading. It is infectious, which means that all people—big and small, men and women—can become satyagrahis. No one is kept out from the army of satyagrahis. A satyagrahi cannot perpetrate tyranny on anyone; he is not subdued through application of physical force; he does not strike at anyone. Just as anyone can resort to satyagraha, it can be resorted to in almost any situation.

People demand historical evidence in support of satyagraha. History is for the most part a record of armed activities. Natural activities find very little mention in it. Only uncommon activities strike us with wonder. Satyagraha has been used always and in all situations. The father and the son, the man and the wife are perpetually resorting to satyagraha, one towards the other. When a father gets angry and punishes the son, the son does not hit back with a weapon, he conquers his father's anger by submitting to him. The son refuses to be subdued by the unjust rule of his father but he puts up with the punishment that he may incur through disobeying the unjust father. We can similarly free ourselves of the unjust rule of the Government by defying the unjust rule and accepting the punishments that go with it. We do not bear malice towards the Government. When we set its fears at rest, when we do not desire to make armed assaults on the administrators, nor to unseat them from power, but only to get rid of their injustice, they will at once be subdued to our will.

The question is asked why we should call any rule unjust. In saying so, we ourselves assume the function of a judge. It is true. But in this world, we always have to act as judges for ourselves. That is why the satyagrahi does not strike his adversary with arms. If he has Truth on his side, he will win, and if his thought is faulty, he will suffer the consequences of his fault.

What is the good, they ask, of only one person opposing injustice; for he will be punished and destroyed, he will languish in prison or meet an untimely end through hanging. The objection is not valid. History shows that all reforms have begun with one person. Fruit is hard to come by without tapasya. The suffering that has to be undergone in satyagraha is tapasya in its purest form. Only when the tapasya is capable of bearing fruit do we have the fruit. This establishes the fact that when there is insufficient tapasya, the fruit is delayed. The tapasya of Jesus Christ, boundless though it was, was not sufficient for Europe's need. Europe has disapproved Christ. Through ignorance, it has disregarded Christ's pure way of life. Many Christs will have to offer themselves as sacrifice at the terrible altar of Europe, and only then will realization dawn on that continent. But Jesus will always be the first among these. He has been the sower of the seed and his will therefore be the credit for raising the harvest.

It is said that it is a very difficult, if not an altogether impossible, task to educate ignorant peasants in satyagraha and that it is full of perils, for it is a very arduous business to transform unlettered ignorant people from one condition into another. Both the arguments are just silly. The people of India are perfectly fit to receive the training of satyagraha. India has knowledge of *dharma,* and where there is knowledge of *dharma,* satyagraha is a very simple matter. The people of India have drunk of the nectar of devotion. This great people overflows with faith. It is no difficult matter to lead such a people on to the right path of satyagraha. Some have a fear that once people get involved in satyagraha, they may at a later stage take to arms. This fear is illusory. From the path of satyagraha [clinging to truth], a transition to the path of a-satyagraha [clinging to untruth] is impossible. It is possible of course that some people who believe in armed activity may mislead the satyagrahis by infiltrating into their ranks and later making them take to arms. This is possible in all enterprises. But as compared to other activities, it is less likely to happen in satyagraha, for their motives soon get exposed and when the people are not ready to take up arms, it becomes almost impossible to lead them on to that terrible path. The might of arms is directly opposed to the might of satyagraha. Just as darkness does not abide in light, soulless armed activity cannot enter the sunlike radiance of soul-force. Many Pathans took part in satyagraha in South Africa abiding by all the rules of satyagraha.

Then it is said that much suffering is involved in being a satyagrahi and that the entire people will not be willing to put up with this suffering. The objection is not valid. People in general always follow in the footsteps of the noble. There is no doubt that it is difficult to produce a satyagrahi leader. Our experience is that a satyagrahi needs many more virtues like self-control, fearlessness, etc., than are requisite for one who believes in armed action. The greatness of the man bearing arms does not lie in the superiority of the arms, nor does it lie in his physical prowess. It lies in his determination and fearlessness in face of death. General Gordon was a mighty warrior of the British Empire. In the statue that has been erected in his memory he has only a small baton in his hand. It goes to show that the strength of a warrior is not measured by reference to his weapons but by his firmness of mind. A satyagrahi needs millions of times more of such firmness than does a bearer of arms. The birth of such a man can bring about the salvation of India in no time. Not only India but the whole world awaits the advent of such a man. We may in the meanwhile prepare the ground as much as we can through satyagraha.

How can we make use of satyagraha in the present conditions? Why should we take to satyagraha in the fight for freedom? We are all guilty of killing manliness. So long as our learned Annie Besant is in detention, it is an insult to our manhood. How can we secure her release through satyagraha? It may be that the Government has acted in good faith, that it has sufficient grounds for keeping her under detention. But, at any rate, the people are unhappy at her being deprived of her freedom. Annie Besant cannot be freed through armed action. No Indian will approve of such an action. We cannot secure her freedom by submitting petitions and the like. Much time has passed. We can all humbly inform the Government that if Mrs Annie Besant is not released within the time limit prescribed by us, we will all be compelled to follow her path. It is possible that all of us do not like all her actions; but we find nothing in her actions which threatens the 'established Government' or the vested interests. Therefore we too by participating in her activities will ask for her lot, that is, we shall all court imprisonment. The members of our Legislative Assembly also can petition the Government and when the petition is not accepted, they can resign their membership. For swaraj also, satyagraha is the unfailing weapon. Satyagraha means that what we want is truth, that we deserve it and that we will work for it even unto death.

Nothing more need be said. Truth alone triumphs. There is no *dharma* higher than Truth. Truth always wins. We pray to God that in this sacred land we may bring about the reign of *dharma* by following satyagraha and that this our country may become an example for all to follow.

Fifteen Instructions to Volunteers
[17 April 1918]

- The volunteers must remember that, as this is a satyagraha campaign, they must abide by truth under all circumstances.
- In satyagraha, there can be no room for rancour; which means that a satyagrahi should utter no harsh word about anyone, from a Ravana to the Governor himself; if someone does so, it is the volunteer's duty to stop him.
- Rudeness has no place in *satyagraha*. Perfect courtesy must be shown even to those who may look upon us as their enemies and the villagers must be taught to do the same. Rudeness may harm our cause and the struggle may be unduly prolonged. The volunteers should give the most serious attention to this matter and think out in their minds as many examples as possible of the advantages accruing from courtesy and the disadvantages resulting from rudeness and explain them to the people.
- The volunteers must remember that this is a holy war. We embarked upon it because, had we not, we would have failed in our *dharma*. And so all the rules which are essential for living a religious life must be observed here too.
- We are opposing the intoxication of power, that is, the blind application of law, and not authority as such. The difference must never be lost sight of. It is, therefore, our duty to help the officers in their other work.
- We are to apply here the same principle that we follow in a domestic quarrel. We should think of the Government and the people as constituting a large family and act accordingly.
- We are not to boycott or treat with scorn those who hold different views from ours. It must be our resolve to win them over by courteous behaviour.

- We must not try to be clever. We must always be frank and straightforward.
- When they stay in villages, the volunteers should demand the fewest services from the village-folk. Wherever it is possible to reach a place on foot, they should avoid using a vehicle. We must insist on being served the simplest food. Restraining them from preparing dainties will add grace to the service we render.
- As they move about in villages, the volunteers should observe the economic condition of the people and the deficiencies in their education and try, in their spare time, to make them good.
- If they can, they should create opportunities when they may teach the village children.
- If they notice any violation of the rules of good health, they should draw the villagers' attention to the fact.
- If, at any place, they find people engaged in quarrelling among themselves, the volunteers should try to save them from their quarrels.
- They should read out to the people, when the latter are free, books which promote satyagraha. They may read out stories of Prahlad, Harishchandra and others. The people should also be made familiar with instances of pure satyagraha to be found in the West and in Islamic literature.
- At no time and under no circumstances is the use of arms permitted in satyagraha. It should never be forgotten that in this struggle the highest type of non-violence is to be maintained. Satyagraha means fighting oppression through voluntary suffering. There can be no question here of making anyone else suffer. Satyagraha is always successful; it can never meet with defeat; let every volunteer understand this himself and then explain it to the people.

Non-Co-operation [4 July 1920]

Since there is no reason to hope that, before 1 August, either the Khilafat issue will have been satisfactorily solved or a revision of the peace terms promised, we must get ready to start non-co-operation. The Committee is making preparations in this behalf. Meantime, the following can be done:

- Not to subscribe to new loans.
- Not to register one's name for recruitment in military or civil service.

The Government has no right to occupy Mesopotamia. Mandate is in fact nothing but occupation. Moreover, according to newspaper reports, the Arabs do not like even the sight of Indian soldiers there. Whether or not this is true, it is the duty of every Indian not to join such service. Those who go to Mesopotamia will be doing so merely for money. We must refuse to do this, if we do no more.

Not only can it never be our duty to rule by force over the Arabs, but we, who do not wish to remain in slavery, cannot wish to make others slaves.

Thus it behoves us not to subscribe to new loans and to refuse, from this very day, to offer ourselves as new recruits for service under the Government, especially for service which requires us to go to Mesopotamia.

In addition, it is hoped that the following things will be done from 1 August onwards:

- Titles and honorary positions will be renounced.
- Legislatures will be boycotted.
- Parents will withdraw their children from Government schools.
- Lawyers will give up practice and help people to settle their civil disputes among themselves.
- Invitations to Government functions, parties, etc., will be politely refused, non-co-operation being given as the sole reason for doing so.

133

It is likely that this programme will be adopted from 1 August, if the Khilafat question is not settled.

Lala Lajpat Rai has announced non-co-operation in the form of boycott of legislatures if justice is not done in the matter of the Punjab. So we can now take it that the Punjab too has joined the Khilafat agitation. Just as on this issue Muslims should take the lead, in the matter of the Punjab the Punjabis themselves should take the lead. If they do not adopt non-co-operation, one may say that the other part of India cannot do so either.

We shall hope that Lalaji will not stop with boycott of legislatures. Until we win, we shall have to go on extending the scope of non-co-operation, and be ready to take the four steps suggested earlier. I am convinced, however, that we would win if the whole nation joins in boycotting legislatures.

Three different views on the question of boycotting legislatures have been expressed:

- Not to start non-co-operation at all;
- to adopt non-co-operation after election to legislatures;
- to boycott legislatures from the very start.

The first position is entirely opposed to non-co-operation. The second alone needs to be examined. I am convinced that it will be a waste of effort to try to enter legislatures and then to refrain from attending their sessions. It is a waste of money and time alike. I do not at all see the point of doing this. What if unworthy people get elected because we do not come forward? If such people enter the legislatures, the Government will not be able to run the government of an awakened people and it will be laughed at. Moreover, if we join in the elections we shall not be able to show what real boycott can be. Our duty is so to educate public opinion—opinion of the voters—that it will be impossible for anybody to get elected to legislatures as their representatives. So long as there is lack of understanding between the king and the subjects, to attend the king's council is to strengthen his hands. A king cannot govern at all if he is not able to carry any section of his subjects with him. It follows from this that the fewer the subjects who co-operate with him, the less will be his authority. Hence, for those who accept non-co-operation, the total boycott of legislatures is the only right course. And so I hope that those who are busy trying to get elected to legislatures will give up the attempt for the present and address themselves to the more important work, that of educating public opinion on the Khilafat and the Punjab issues, and so serve the people that, when the time for entering legislatures comes, they will be better qualified in virtue of their service.

Now remain the other two suggestions which are likely to be severely criticized. The lawyers should, for the time being, give up practice and intending litigants or those who find themselves dragged into litigation should boycott the courts and get their disputes settled through arbitration boards. It is my confirmed belief that every Government masks its brute-force and maintains its control over the people through civil and criminal courts, for it is cheaper, simpler and more honourable for a ruler that, instead of his controlling the people through naked force, they themselves, lured into slavery through courts, etc., submit to him of their own accord. If people settle their civil disputes among themselves and the lawyers, unmindful of self-interest, boycott the courts in the interest of the people, the latter can advance in no time. I have believed for many years that every State tries to perpetuate its power through lawyers. Hence, though fully aware that I will be criticized for making this suggestion, I have no hesitation in putting it forward.

What is true of lawyers is true of schools. Even without such momentous issues as those of the Khilafat and the Punjab, I would certainly, if I could, see to it that the present schools were completely abandoned and would provide the right kind of education for children on whom the future of India rests. But my purpose at present in calling for a boycott of the schools is different; I want to show the Government by rendering the schools idle that, so long as justice is not done in regard to the Punjab and the Khilafat, co-operation with it is distasteful. I know that this suggestion will be visited with a good deal of ridicule. But, with the passing of time, people will realize that if they refused to crowd the Government schools, it would be impossible to run the administration. Look where we will all over the world, we shall find that the education imparted to the children is intended to facilitate smooth running of the Government. Where the Government is concerned solely with public welfare, so is the educational system; where the Government is of a mixed kind—as in India—the educational system is also calculated to confuse the intellect and is positively harmful. While making this suggestion I do not wish that the youth should be left altogether unprovided with education. Not for a moment do I wish people's education to stop. But I believe that, even when the schools have been deserted, we can look after people's education all right. I know that the suggestions I have made are quite serious and I do not expect to be able to convince readers all at once. I shall take up these subjects time and again and place my arguments before the public.

Democracy vs Mobocracy
[8 September 1920]

Looking at the surface there is but a thin dividing line between mob-law and the people's law. And yet the division is complete and will persist for all time.

India is today quickly passing through the mob-law stage. The use of the adverb signifies my hope. It may be our misfortune to have to pass through that process even in slow stages. But it is wisdom to adopt every means at our disposal to have done with that stage as quickly as possible.

There is much tendency on our part to yield to the rule of the mob. There was mob rule at Amritsar on 10 April 1919. There was mob rule at Ahmedabad on the same fateful day. It represented undisciplined destruction and therefore it was thoughtless, profitless, wicked and harmful. War is disciplined destruction, much more bloody than any yet committed by mobs. And yet war has been apostrophized, because we have been deceived by the temporary but brilliant results achieved by some wars. So, if India has to achieve her freedom by violence, it will have to be by disciplined and honourable (insofar as it is possible to associate honour with violence) violence, named war. It will then be an act not of mobocracy but democracy.

But my purpose today is not to write of mobocracy of the Ahmedabad type. I intend to deal with the type with which I am more familiar. The Congress is a demonstration for the mob and in that sense and that only. Though organized by thoughtful men and women it may be called a mob-demonstration. Our popular demonstrations are unquestionably mob-demonstrations. During the memorable tour of the Khilafat mission through the Punjab, Sind and Madras, I have had a surfeit of such demonstrations. I have been ashamed to witness at railway stations thoughtless though unwitting destruction of passengers' luggage by demonstrators who in their adoration of their heroes have ignored everything else and everybody else. They have made, much to the discomfort of their heroes, unmusical and harsh noises. They have trampled upon one another. They have elbowed out one another. All have shouted, all at the same time, in the holy name of order and peace. Ten volunteers have been heard to give the same order at the same time.

Volunteers often become demonstrators instead of remaining people's policemen. It is a task often dangerous, always uncomfortable, for the heroes to be escorted through a broken chain of volunteers from the platform to the coach intended for them. Often it is a process which, although it should occupy no more than five minutes, has occupied one hour. The crowd instead of pressing back, presses towards the heroes and who therefore require to be protected. The coach is taken possession of by anybody who dares, volunteers being the greatest sinners. The heroes and other lawful occupants have to reason with the intruders that they may not mount the footboards in that summary fashion. The hood of the coach is roughly handled by the processionists. It is not often that I have seen hoods of motors left undamaged by crowds. On the route instead of crowds lining the streets, they follow the coach. The result is confusion worse confounded.

Every moment there is danger of accidents. That there is rarely any accident at such demonstrations is not due to the skill of the organizers, but the crowd is determined to put up with all jostling and retain its perfect good humour. In spite of everyone jostling everyone else, one has not the slightest *wish* to inconvenience one's neighbour. To finish the picture, there is the meeting, an ever-growing cause of anxiety. You face nothing but disorder, din, pressing, yelling and shouting there. A good speaker arrests the attention of the audience and there is order such that you can hear a pin drop.

All the same this is mobocracy. You are at the mercy of the mob. So long as there is sympathy between you and the mob, everything goes well. Immediately that cord is broken, there is horror. An Ahmedabad episode now and then gives you the mob psychology.

We must then evolve order out of chaos. And I have no doubt that the best and the speediest method is to introduce the people's law instead of mob-law.

One great stumbling block is that we have neglected music. Music means rhythm, order. Its effect is electrical. It immediately soothes. I have seen, in European countries, a resourceful superintendent of police by starting a popular song controlling the mischievous tendencies of mobs. Unfortunately like our Shastras, music has been the prerogative of the few, either the barter of prostitutes or high class religious devotees. It has never become nationalized in the modern sense. If I had any influence with volunteer boy scouts and Seva Samiti organizations, I would make compulsory a proper singing in company of national songs. And to that end I should have great musicians attending every congress or conference and teaching mass music.

Much greater discipline, method and knowledge must be exacted from volunteers and no chance comer should be accepted as a full-fledged volunteer. He only hinders rather than helping. Imagine the consequence of the introduction of one untrained soldier finding his way into an army at war. He can disorganize it in a second. My greatest anxiety about non-co-operation is not the slow response of the leaders, certainly not the well-meant and even ill-meant criticism, never unadulterated repression. The movement will overcome these obstacles. It will gain even strength from them. But the greatest obstacle is that we have not yet emerged from the mobocratic stage. But my consolation lies in the fact that nothing is so easy as to train mobs, for the simple reason that they have no mind, no premeditation. They act in a frenzy. They repent quickly. Our organized Government does not repent of its fiendish crimes at Jallianwala, Lahore, Kasur, Akalgarh, Ram Nagar, etc. But I have drawn tears from repentant mobs at Gujranwala and everywhere a frank acknowledgement of repentance from those who formed the mob during that eventful month of April. Non-co-operation I am therefore now using in order to evolve democracy. And I respectfully invite all the doubting leaders to help by refusing to condemn, in anticipation of a process of national purification, training and sacrifice.

Next week I hope to give some illustrations of how in a moment order was evolved out of mob disorder. My faith in the people is boundless. Theirs is an amazingly responsive nature. Let not the leaders distrust them. This chorus of condemnation of non-co-operation when properly analysed means nothing less than distrust of the people's ability to control themselves. For the present I conclude this somewhat lengthy article by suggesting some rules for guidance and immediate execution.

- There should be no raw volunteers accepted for big demonstrations. Therefore none but the most experienced should be at the head.
- Volunteers should have a general instructions book on their persons.
- At the time of demonstrations there must be a review of volunteers at which special instructions should be given.
- At stations, volunteers should not all be centred at one point, namely, where the reception committee should be. But they should be posted at different points in the crowd.
- Large crowds should never enter the station. They cannot but inconvenience traffic. There is as much honour in staying out as in entering the station.
- The first duty of the volunteers should be to see that other passengers' luggage is not trampled upon.
- Demonstrators ought not to enter the station long before the notified time for arrival.
- There should be a clear passage left in front of the train for the passengers.
- There should be another passage if possible half way through the demonstrators for the heroes to pass.
- There should be no chain formed. It is humiliating.
- The demonstrators must not move till the heroes have reached their coach or till they receive a pre-arranged signal from an authorized volunteer.
- National cries must be fixed and must be raised not anyhow, at any time or all the time, but just on the arrival of the train, on the heroes reaching the coach and on the route at fair intervals. No objections need be raised to this on the score of the demonstration becoming mechanical and not spontaneous. The spontaneity will depend upon numbers, the response to the cries above all the general look of the demonstrators, not in the greatest number of noises or the loudest. It is the training that a nation receives which characterizes the nature of its demonstrations.

A Mohammedan silently worshipping in his mosque is no less demonstrative than a Hindu temple-goer making a noise either through his voice or his gong or both.

- On the route the crowd must line and not follow the carriages. If pedestrians form part of the moving procession, they must noiselessly and in an orderly manner take their places and not at their own will join or abstain.
- A crowd should never press towards the heroes but should move away from them.
- Those on the last line or the circumference should never press forward but give way when pressure is directed towards them.
- If there are women in the crowd they should be specially protected.
- Little children should never be brought out in the midst of crowds.
- At meetings volunteers should be dispersed among the crowd. They should learn flag and whistle signalling in order to pass instructions from one to another when it is impossible for the voice to carry.
- It is not part of the audience to preserve order. They do so by keeping motionless and silent.
- Above all, everyone should obey volunteers' instructions without question.

This list does not pretend to be exhaustive. It is merely illustrative and designed to stimulate thought and discussion. I hope that all the vernacular papers will translate this article.

Civil Disobedience [4 August 1921]

Civil disobedience was on the lips of every one of the members of the All-India Congress Committee. Not having really ever tried it, everyone appeared to be enamoured of it from a mistaken belief in it as a sovereign remedy for our present-day ills. I feel sure that it can be made such if we can produce the necessary atmosphere for it. For individuals there always is that atmosphere except when their civil disobedience is certain to lead to bloodshed. I discovered this exception during the satyagraha days. But even so, a call may come which one dare not neglect, cost what it may. I can clearly see the time coming to me when I *must* refuse obedience to every single State-made law, even though there may be a certainty of bloodshed. When neglect of the call means a denial of God, civil disobedience becomes a peremptory duty.

Mass civil disobedience stands on a different footing. It can only be tried in a calm atmosphere. It must be the calmness of strength not weakness, of knowledge not ignorance. Individual civil disobedience may be and often is vicarious. Mass civil disobedience may be and often is selfish in the sense that individuals expect personal gain from their disobedience. Thus, in South Africa, Kallenbach and Polak offered vicarious civil disobedience. They had nothing to gain. Thousands offered it because they expected personal gain also in the shape, say, of the removal of the annual poll-tax levied upon exindentured men and their wives and grown-up children. It is sufficient in mass civil disobedience if the resisters understand the working of the doctrine.

It was in a practically uninhabited tract of country that I was arrested in South Africa when I was marching into a prohibited area with over two to three thousand men and some women. The company included several Pathans and others who were able-bodied men. It was the greatest testimony of merit the Government of South Africa gave to the movement. They knew that we were as harmless as we were determined. It was easy enough for that body of men to cut to pieces those who arrested me. It would have not only been a most cowardly thing to do, but it would have been a treacherous breach of their own pledge, and it would have meant ruin to the struggle of freedom and the forcible deportation of every

Indian from South Africa. But the men were no rabble. They were disciplined soldiers and all the better for being unarmed. Though I was torn from them, they did not disperse, nor did they turn back. They marched on to their destination till they were, every one of them, arrested and imprisoned. So far as I am aware, this was an instance of discipline and non-violence for which there is no parallel in history. Without such restraint I see no hope of successful mass civil disobedience here.

We must dismiss the idea of overawing the Government by huge demonstrations every time someone is arrested. On the contrary we must treat arrest as the normal condition of the life of a non-co-operator. For we must seek arrest and imprisonment, as a soldier who goes to battle seeks death. We expect to bear down the opposition of the Government by courting and not by avoiding imprisonment, even though it be by showing our supposed readiness to be arrested and imprisoned *en masse*. Civil disobedience then emphatically means our desire to surrender to a single unarmed policeman. Our triumph consists in thousands being led to the prisons like lambs to the slaughter-house. If the lambs of the world had been willingly led, they would have long ago saved themselves from the butcher's knife. Our triumph consists again in being imprisoned for no wrong whatsoever. The greater our innocence, the greater our strength and the swifter our victory.

As it is, this Government is cowardly, we are afraid of imprisonment. The Government takes advantage of our fear of jails. If only our men and women welcome jails as health resorts, we will cease to worry about the dear ones put in jails which our countrymen in South Africa used to nickname His Majesty's Hotels.

We have too long been mentally disobedient to the laws of the State and have too often surreptitiously evaded them to be fit all of a sudden for civil disobedience. Disobedience to be civil has to be open and non-violent.

Complete civil disobedience is a state of peaceful rebellion—a refusal to obey every single State-made law. It is certainly more dangerous than an armed rebellion. For it can never be put down if the civil resisters are prepared to face extreme hardships. It is based upon an implicit belief in the absolute efficiency of innocent suffering. By noiselessly going to prison a civil resister ensures a calm atmosphere. The wrong-doer wearies of wrong-doing in the absence of resistance. All pleasure is lost when the victim betrays no resistance. A full grasp of the conditions of successful civil resistance is necessary at least on the part of the representatives of the people before we can launch out on an enterprise of such magnitude. The quickest remedies are always fraught with the greatest danger and require the utmost skill in handling them. It is my firm conviction that, if we bring about a successful boycott of foreign cloth, we shall have produced an atmosphere that would enable us to inaugurate civil disobedience on a scale that no Government can resist. I would therefore urge patience and determined concentration on swadeshi upon those who are impatient to embark on mass civil disobedience.

The Momentous Issue
[10 November 1921]

The next few weeks should see civil disobedience in full working order in some part of India. With illustrations of partial and individual civil disobedience the country has become familiar. Complete civil disobedience is rebellion without the element of violence in it. An out and out civil resister simply ignores the authority of the State. He becomes an outlaw claiming to disregard every unmoral State law. Thus, for instance, he may refuse to pay taxes, he may refuse to recognize the authority of the State in his daily intercourse. He may refuse to obey the law of trespass and claim to enter military barracks in order to speak to the soldiers, he may refuse to submit to limitations upon the manner of picketing and may picket within the prescribed area. In doing all this he never uses force and never resists force when it is used against him. In fact, he invites imprisonment and other uses of force against himself. This he does because and when he finds the bodily freedom he seemingly enjoys to be an intolerable burden. He argues to himself that a State allows personal freedom only in so far as the citizen submits to its regulations.

Submission to the State law is the price a citizen pays for his personal liberty. Submission, therefore, to a State wholly or largely unjust is an immoral barter for liberty. A citizen who thus realizes the evil nature of a State is not satisfied to live on its sufferance, and therefore appears to the others who do not share his belief to be a nuisance to society whilst he is endeavouring to compel the State without committing a moral breach to arrest him. Thus considered, civil resistance is a most powerful expression of a soul's anguish and an eloquent protest against the continuance of an evil State. Is not this the history of all reform? Have not reformers, much to the disgust of their fellows, discarded even innocent symbols associated with an evil practice?

When a body of men disown the state under which they have hitherto lived, they nearly establish their own government. I say nearly, for they do not go to the point of using force when they are resisted by the state. Their 'business' as of the individual is to be locked up or shot by the state, unless it recognizes their separate existence, in other words bows to their will. Thus three thousand Indians in South Africa after due notice to the Government of the Transvaal crossed the Transvaal border in 1914 in defiance of the Transvaal immigration law and compelled the Government to arrest them. When it failed to provoke them to violence or to coerce them into submission, it yielded to their demand. A body of civil resisters is, therefore, like an army subject to all the discipline of a soldier, only harder because of want of excitement of an ordinary soldier's life. And as a civil resistance army is or ought to be free from passion because free from the spirit of retaliation, it requires the fewest number of soldiers. Indeed one PERFECT civil resister is enough to win the battle of Right against Wrong.

Though, therefore, the All-India Congress Committee has authorized civil disobedience by Provincial Congress Committees on their own responsibility, I hope they will put due emphasis on the word 'responsibility' and not start civil disobedience with a light heart. Every condition must be given its full effect. The mention of Hindu-Muslim unity, non-violence, swadeshi and removal of untouchability means that they have not yet become an integral part of our national life. If an individual or a mass have still misgivings about Hindu-Muslim unity, if they have still any doubt about the necessity of non-violence for the attainment of our triple goal, if they have not yet enforced swadeshi in its completeness, if the Hindus among that mass have still the poison of untouchability in them, that mass or that individual are not ready for civil disobedience. Indeed it would be best to watch and wait whilst the experiment is being carried on in one area. Reverting to the analogy of the army, those divisions that watch and wait are just as much co-operating actively as the division that is actually fighting.

The only time, whilst the experiment is going on, that individual civil disobedience may be resorted to simultaneously is when the Government obstruct even the silent prosecution of swadeshi. Thus if an order of prohibition is served upon an expert spinner going to teach or organize spinning, that order should be summarily disregarded and the teacher should court imprisonment. But in all other respects, is so far as I can judge at present, it will be best for every other part of India scrupulously to respect all orders and instructions whilst one part is deliberately taking the offensive and committing a deliberate breach of all the unmoral state laws it possibly can. Needless to add that any outbreak of violence in any other part of India must necessarily injure and may even stop the experiment. The other parts will be expected to remain immovable and unperturbed, even though the people within the area of experiment may be imprisoned, riddled with bullets or otherwise ill-treated by the authorities. We must expect them to give a good account of themselves in every conceivable circumstance.

The Immediate Issue
[5 January 1922]

Swaraj, the Khilafat, the Punjab occupy a subordinate place to the issue sprung upon the country by the Government. We must first make good the right of free speech and free association before we can make any further progress towards our goal. The Government would kill us if they could by a flank attack. To accept defeat in the matter of free speech and free association is to court disaster. If the Government is allowed to destroy non-violent activities in the country, however dangerous they may be to its existence, even the Moderates' work must come to a standstill. In the general interest, therefore, we must defend these elementary rights with our lives. We cannot be coerced into welcoming the Prince nor can we be coerced into disbanding volunteer associations or giving up any other activities which we may deem desirable for our growth.

The safest and the quickest way to defend these rights is to ignore the restriction. We must speak the Truth under a shower of bullets. We must band together in the face of bayonets. No cost is too great for purchasing these fundamental rights. And on this there can be no compromise, no parleying, no conference. Withdrawal of notifications of disbandment and prohibition orders and discharge of all who are imprisoned for non-violent activities must precede any conference or settlement. We must be content to die, if we cannot live as free men and women.

I wish I could persuade everybody that civil disobedience is the inherent right of a citizen. He dare not give it up without ceasing to be a man. Civil disobedience is never followed by anarchy. Criminal disobedience can lead to it. Every State puts down criminal disobedience by force. It perishes, if it does not. But to put down civil disobedience is to attempt to imprison conscience. Civil disobedience can only lead to strength and purity. A civil resister never uses arms and hence he is harmless to a State that is at all willing to listen to the voice of public opinion. He is dangerous for an autocratic State, for he brings about its fall by engaging public opinion upon the matter for which he resists the State. Civil disobedience, therefore, becomes a sacred duty when the State has become lawless, or which is the same thing, corrupt. And a citizen that barters with such a State shares its corruption or lawlessness.

It is, therefore, possible to question the wisdom of applying civil disobedience in respect of a particular act or law; it is possible to advice delay and caution. But the right itself cannot be allowed to be questioned. It is a birthright that cannot be surrendered without surrender of one's self-respect.

At the same time that the right of civil disobedience is insisted upon, its use must be guarded by all conceivable restrictions. Every possible provision should be made against an outbreak of violence or general lawlessness. Its area as well as its scope should also be limited to the barest necessity of the case. In the present case, therefore, aggressive civil disobedience should be confined to a vindication of the right of free speech and free association. In other words, non-co-operation, so long as it remains non-violent, must be allowed to continue without let or hindrance. When that position is attained it is time for a representative conference to be summoned for the settlement of Khilafat, the Punjab and swaraj but not till then.

The Crime of Chauri Chaura
[16 February 1922]

God has been abundantly kind to me. He has warned me the third time that there is not as yet in India that truthful and non-violent atmosphere which and which alone can justify mass disobedience which can be at all described as civil, which means gentle, truthful, humble, knowing, wilful yet loving, never criminal and hateful.

He warned me in 1919 when the Rowlatt Act agitation was started. Ahmedabad, Viramgam, and Kheda erred; Amritsar and Kasur erred. I retraced my steps, called it a Himalayan miscalculation, humbled myself before God and man, and stopped not merely mass civil disobedience but even my own which I knew was intended to be civil and non-violent.

The next time it was through the events of Bombay that God gave a terrific warning. He made me eyewitness of the deeds of the Bombay mob on 17 November. The mob acted in the interest of non-co-operation. I announced my intention to stop the mass civil disobedience which was to be immediately started in Bardoli. The humiliation was greater than in 1919. But it did me good. I am sure that the nation gained by the stopping. India stood for truth and non-violence by the suspension.

But the bitterest humiliation was still to come. Madras did give the warning, but I heeded it not. But God spoke clearly through Chauri Chaura. I understand that the constables who were so brutally hacked to death had given much provocation. They had even gone back upon the word just given by the Inspector that they would not be molested, but when the procession had passed the stragglers were interfered with and abused by the constables. The former cried out for help. The mob returned. The constables opened fire. The little ammunition they had was exhausted and they retired to the *Thana* for safety. The mob, my informant tells me, therefore set fire to the *Thana*. The self-imprisoned constables had to come out for dear life and as they did so, they were hacked to pieces and the mangled remains were thrown into the raging flames.

It is claimed that no non-co-operation volunteer had a hand in the brutality and that the mob had not only the immediate provocation but they had also general knowledge of the high-handed tyranny of the police in that district. No provocation can possibly justify the brutal murder of men who had been rendered defenceless and who had virtually thrown themselves on the mercy of the mob. And when India claims to be non-violent and hopes to mount the throne of Liberty through non-violent means, mob-violence even in answer to grave provocation is a bad augury. Suppose the "non-violent" disobedience of Bardoli was permitted by God to succeed, the Government had abdicated in favour of the victors of Bardoli, who would control the unruly element that must be expected to perpetrate inhumanity upon due provocation? Non-violent attainment of self-government presupposes a non-violent control over the violent elements in the country. Non-violent non-co-operators can only succeed when they have succeeded in attaining control over the hooligans of India, in other words, when the latter also have learnt patriotically or religiously to refrain from their violent activities at least whilst the campaign of non-co-operation is going on. The tragedy at Chauri Chaura, therefore, roused me thoroughly.

'But what about your manifesto to the Viceroy and your rejoinder to his reply?' spoke the voice of Satan. It was the bitterest cup of humiliation to drink. 'Surely it is cowardly to withdraw the next day after pompous threats to the Government and promises to the people of Bardoli.' Thus Satan's invitation was to deny Truth and therefore Religion, to deny God Himself. I put my doubts and troubles before the Working Committee and other associates whom I found near me. They did not all agree with me at first. Some of them probably do not even now agree with me. But never has a man been blessed, perhaps, with colleagues and associates so considerate and forgiving as I have. They understood my difficulty and patiently followed my argument. The result is before the public in the shape of the resolutions of the Working Committee. The drastic reversal of practically the whole of the aggressive programme may be politically unsound and unwise, but there is no doubt that it is religiously sound, and I venture to assure the doubters that the country will have gained by my humiliation and confession of error.

The only virtue I want to claim is Truth and Non-violence. I lay no claim to superhuman powers. I want none. I wear the same corruptible flesh that the weakest of my fellow beings wears and am therefore as liable to err as any. My services have many limitations, but God has upto now blessed them in spite of the imperfections.

For, confession of error is like a broom that sweeps away dirt and leaves the surface cleaner than before, I feel stronger for my confession. And the cause must prosper for the retracing. Never has man reached his destination by persistence in deviation from the straight path.

It has been urged that Chauri Chaura cannot affect Bardoli. There is danger, it is argued, only if Bardoli is weak enough to be swayed by Chauri Chaura and is betrayed into violence. I have no doubt whatsoever on that account. The people of Bardoli are in my opinion the most peaceful in India. But Bardoli is but a speck on the map of India. Its effort cannot succeed unless there is perfect co-operation from the other parts. Bardoli's disobedience will be civil only when the other parts of India remain non-violent. Just as the addition of a grain of arsenic to a pot of milk renders it unfit as food so will the civility of Bardoli prove unacceptable by the addition of the deadly poison from Chauri Chaura. The latter represents India as much as Bardoli.

Chauri Chaura is after all an aggravated symptom. I have never imagined that there has been no violence, mental or physical, in the places where repression is going on. Only I have believed, I still believe and the pages of *Young India* amply prove, that the repression is out of all proportion to the insignificant popular violence in the areas of repression. The determined holding of meetings in prohibited areas I do not call violence. The violence I am referring to is the throwing of brickbats or intimidation and coercion practised in stray cases. As a matter of fact in civil disobedience there should be no excitement. Civil disobedience is a preparation for mute suffering. Its effect is marvellous though unperceived and gentle. But I regarded a certain amount of excitement as inevitable, certain amount of unintended violence even pardonable, i.e., I did not consider civil disobedience impossible in somewhat imperfect conditions. Under perfect conditions disobedience when civil is hardly felt. But the present movement is admittedly a dangerous experiment under fairly adverse conditions.

The tragedy of Chauri Chaura is really the index finger. It shows the way India may easily go if drastic precautions be not taken. If we are not to evolve violence out of non-violence, it is quite clear that we must hastily retrace our steps and re-establish an atmosphere of peace, re-arrange our programme and not think of starting mass civil disobedience until we are sure of peace being retained in spite of mass civil disobedience being started and in spite of Government provocation. We must be sure of unauthorized portions not starting mass civil disobedience.

As it is, the Congress organization is still imperfect and its instructions are still perfunctorily carried out. We have not established Congress Committees in every one of the villages. Where we have, they are not perfectly amenable to our instructions. We have not probably more than one crore of members on the roll. We are in the middle of February, yet not many have paid the annual four-anna subscription for the current year. Volunteers are indifferently enrolled. They do not conform to all the conditions of their pledge. They do not even wear hand-spun and hand-woven khaddar. All the Hindu volunteers have not yet purged themselves of the sin of untouchability. All are not free from the taint of violence. Not by their imprisonment are we going to win swaraj or serve the holy cause of the Khilafat or attain the ability to stop payment to faithless servants. Some of us err in spite of ourselves. But some others among us sin wilfully. They join Volunteer Corps well knowing that they are not and do not intend to remain non-violent. We are thus untruthful even as we hold the Government to be untruthful. We dare not enter the kingdom of Liberty with mere lip homage to Truth and Non-violence.

Suspension of mass civil disobedience and subsidence of excitement are necessary for further progress, indeed indispensable to prevent further retrogression. I hope, therefore, that by suspension every Congressman or woman will not only not feel disappointed but he or she will feel relieved of the burden of unreality and of national sin.

Let the opponent glory in our humiliation or so-called defeat. It is better to be charged with cowardice and weakness than to be guilty of denial of our oath and sin against God. It is a million times better to *appear* untrue before the world than to *be* untrue to ourselves.

And so, for me the suspension of mass civil disobedience and other minor activities that were calculated to keep up excitement is not enough penance for my having been the instrument, however involuntary, of the brutal violence by the people at Chauri Chaura.

I must undergo personal cleansing. I must become a fitter instrument able to register the slightest variation in the moral atmosphere about me. My prayers must have much deeper truth and humility about them than they evidence. And for me there is nothing so helpful and cleansing as a fast accompanied by the necessary mental co-operation.

I know that the mental attitude is everything. Just as a prayer may be merely a mechanical intonation as of a bird, so may a fast be a mere mechanical torture of the flesh. Such mechanical contrivances are valueless for the purpose intended. Again, just as a mechanical chant may result in the modulation of voice, a mechanical fast may result in purifying the body. Neither will touch the soul within.

But a fast undertaken for fuller self-expression, for attainment of the spirit's supremacy over the flesh, is a most powerful factor in one's evolution. After deep consideration, therefore, I am imposing on myself a five days' continuous fast, permitting myself water. It commenced on Sunday evening; it ends on Friday evening. This is the least I must do.

I have taken into consideration the All-India Congress Committee meeting in front of me. I have in mind the anxious pain even the five days' fast will cause many friends; but I can no longer postpone the penance nor lessen it.

I urge co-workers not to copy my example. The motive in their case will be lacking. They are not the originators of civil disobedience. I am in the unhappy position of a surgeon proved skilless to deal with an admittedly dangerous case. I must either abdicate or acquire greater skill. Whilst the personal penance is not only necessary but obligatory on me, the exemplary self-restraint prescribed by the Working Committee is surely sufficient penance for everyone else. It is no small penance and, if sincerely carried out, it can become infinitely more real and better than fasting. What can be richer and more fruitful than a greater fulfilment of the vow of non-violence in thought, word, and deed or the spread of that spirit? It will be more than food for me during the week to observe that comrades are all, silently and without idle discussion, engaged in fulfilling the constructive programme sketched by the Working

Committee, in enlisting Congress members after making sure that they understand the Congress creed of truth and non-violence for the attainment of swaraj, in daily and religiously spinning for a fixed time, in introducing the wheel of prosperity and freedom in every home, in visiting "untouchable" homes and finding out their wants, in inducing national schools to receive "untouchable" children, in organizing social service specially designed to find a common platform for every variety of man and woman, and in visiting the homes which the drink curse is desolating, in establishing real *panchayats* and in organizing national schools on a proper footing. The workers will be better engaged in these activities than in fasting. I hope, therefore, that no one will join me in fasting, either through false sympathy or an ignorant conception of the spiritual value of fasting.

All fasting and all penance must as far as possible be secret. But my fasting is both a penance and a punishment, and a punishment has to be public. It is penance for me and punishment for those whom I try to serve, for whom I love to live and would equally love to die. They have unintentionally sinned against the laws of the Congress though they were sympathizers if not actually connected with it. Probably they hacked the constables—their countrymen and fellow beings—with my name on their lips. The only way love punishes is by suffering. I cannot even wish them to be arrested. But I would let them know that I would suffer for their breach of the Congress creed. I would advise those who feel guilty and repentant to hand themselves voluntarily to the Government for punishment and make a clean confession. I hope that the workers in the Gorakhpur district will leave no stone unturned to find out the evil-doers and urge them to deliver themselves into custody. But whether the murderers accept my advice or not, I would like them to know that they have seriously interfered with swaraj operations, that in being the cause of the postponement of the movement in Bardoli, they have injured the very cause they probably intended to serve. I would like them to know, too, that this movement is not a cloak or a preparation for violence. I would, at any rate, suffer every humiliation, every torture, absolute ostracism and death itself to prevent the movement from becoming violent or a precursor of violence. I make my penance public also because I am now denying myself the opportunity of sharing their lot with the prisoners. The immediate issue has again shifted. We can no longer press for the withdrawal of notifications or discharge of prisoners. They and we must suffer for the crime of Chauri Chaura. The incident proves, whether we wish it or not, the unity of life. All, including even the administrators, must suffer. Chauri Chaura must stiffen the Government, must still further corrupt the police, and the reprisals that will follow must further demoralize the people. The suspension and the penance will take us back to the position we occupied before the tragedy. By strict discipline and purification we regain the moral confidence required for demanding the withdrawal of notifications and the discharge of prisoners.

If we learn the full lesson of the tragedy, we can turn the curse into a blessing. By becoming truthful and non-violent, both in spirit and deed, and by making the swadeshi i.e., the khaddar programme complete, we can establish full swaraj and redress the Khilafat and the Punjab wrongs without a single person having to offer civil disobedience.

Some Rules of Satyagraha
[27 February 1930]

RULES FOR SATYAGRAHIS

Satyagraha literally means insistence on truth. This insistence arms the votary with matchless power. This power or force is connoted by the word satyagraha. Satyagraha, to be genuine, may be offered against one's wife or one's children, against fellow-citizens, even against the whole world.

Such a universal force necessarily makes no distinction between kinsmen and strangers, young and old, man and woman, friend and foe. The force to be so applied can never be physical. There is in it no room for violence. The only force of universal application can, therefore, be that of ahimsa or love. In other words, it is soul-force.

Love does not burn others, it burns itself. Therefore, a satyagrahi, i.e., a civil resister, will joyfully suffer even unto death.

It follows, therefore, that a civil resister, whilst he will strain every nerve to compass the end of the existing rule, will do no intentional injury in thought, word or deed to the person of a single Englishman. This necessarily brief explanation of satyagraha will perhaps enable the reader to understand and appreciate the following rules:

AS AN INDIVIDUAL

- A satyagrahi, i.e., a civil resister, will harbour no anger.
- He will suffer the anger of the opponent.
- In so doing he will put up with assaults from the opponent, never retaliate; but he will not submit, out of fear of punishment or the like, to any order given in anger.
- When any person in authority seeks to arrest a civil resister, he will voluntarily submit to the arrest, and he will not resist the attachment or removal of his

157

own property, if any, when it is sought to be confiscated by authorities.

- If a civil resister has any property in his possession as a trustee, he will refuse to surrender it, even though in defending it he might lose his life. He will, however, never retaliate.
- Non-retaliation excludes swearing and cursing.
- Therefore a civil resister will never insult his opponent, and therefore also not take part in many of the newly coined cries which are contrary to the spirit of ahimsa.
- A civil resister will not salute the Union Jack, nor will he insult it or officials, English or Indian.
- In the course of the struggle if anyone insults an official or commits an assault upon him, a civil resister will protect such official or officials from the insult or attack even at the risk of his life.

AS A PRISONER

- As a prisoner, a civil resister will behave courteously towards prison officials, and will observe all such discipline of the prison as is not contrary to self-respect; as for instance, whilst he will salaam officials in the usual manner, he will not perform any humiliating gyrations and refuse to shout 'Victory to *Sarkar*' or the like. He will take cleanly cooked and cleanly served food, which is not contrary to his religion, and will refuse to take food insultingly served or served in unclean vessels.
- A civil resister will make no distinction between an ordinary prisoner and himself, will in no way regard himself as superior to the rest, nor will he ask for any conveniences that may not be necessary for keeping his body in good health and condition. He is entitled to ask for such conveniences as may be required for his physical or spiritual well-being.

- A civil resister may not fast for want of conveniences whose deprivation does not involve any injury to one's self-respect.

AS A UNIT

- A civil resister will joyfully obey all the orders issued by the leader of the corps, whether they please him or not.
- He will carry out orders in the first instance even though they appear to him insulting, inimical or foolish, and then appeal to higher authority. He is free before joining to determine the fitness of the corps to satisfy him, but after he has joined it, it becomes a duty to submit to its discipline, irksome or otherwise. If the sum total of the energy of the corps appears to a member to be improper or immoral, he has a right to sever his connection but being within it, he has no right to commit a breach of its discipline.
- No civil resister is to expect maintenance for his dependents. It would be an accident if any such provision is made. A civil resister entrusts his dependents to the care of God. Even in ordinary warfare wherein hundreds of thousands give themselves up to it, they are able to make no previous provision. How much more, then, should such be the case in satyagraha? It is the universal experience that in such times hardly anybody is left to starve.

IN COMMUNAL FIGHTS

- No civil resister will intentionally become a cause of communal quarrels.
- In the event of any such outbreak, he will not take sides, but he will assist only that party which is demonstrably in the right. Being a Hindu he will be generous towards Musalmans and others, and will sacrifice himself in the attempt to save non-Hindus

from a Hindu attack. And if the attack is from the other side, he will not participate in any retaliation but will give his life in protecting Hindus.

- He will, to the best of his ability, avoid every occasion that may give rise to communal quarrels.
- If there is a procession of satyagrahis they will do nothing that would wound the religious susceptibilities of any community, and they will not take part in other processions that are likely to wound such susceptibilities.

A New Orientation
[12 March 1930]

The discussion that has raged round the eleven points mentioned in my article on the Viceregal address to the Assembly and my reference to some of them in my letter to the Viceroy shows how necessary it was to bring them out. Critics have said that these points fall far below even Dominion Status, not to speak of Independence. They could not have carefully read my article or my letter. If they will re-read them, they will find it stated therein that the conceding of those points was a preliminary to a conference about Independence.

Whilst therefore there is no substance in the criticism levelled against my presentation of the case, I am free to admit that I have endeavoured to give a new orientation to the national demand. Just as it was necessary in 1921 to keep the Khilafat and the Punjab wrongs separate from swaraj and I used to say then that for me to have their redress purely through our effort was tantamount to swaraj, so has it become necessary for me on the eve of battle to lay stress on the eleven points and even to say that they are swaraj. For if they are not included in swaraj, it can have no meaning for the nation; and if we generated sufficient strength to gain those points, we have strength enough to gain an Independence Constitution.

Let me illustrate my point. There is the proposal for protecting the mill industry and at the same time of Imperial Preference. I call this a dangerous trap, especially when the expression Dominion Status is being bandied about in connection with the proposed Round Table Conference. If against the grant of Dominion Status or even Independence a stipulation is made that there should always be preference for British cloth, Dominion Status or Independence will have no meaning either for the millions or for the indigenous mills. There can never be preference for things British when India is capable of manufacturing them to the full extent of the demand thereof within her own borders. She may share foreign trade with others; she dare not share her inland trade with anybody so long as she is able to cope with it herself. Indeed she is entitled and it is her duty to protect growing industries against even a friendly England or any other friendly power. It would be wrong and unpatriotic for the mill-owners to fall into the trap laid for them. They should stoutly refuse to have anything to do with Imperial Preference for British cloth, even if they gain a prohibitive tariff against all other foreign cloth.

But to revert to my point. The new orientation consists in familiarizing the nation with the contents of Independence. It must know what it is to mean for the masses. There was much meaning in the circular letter of a Youth League recently criticized in these pages. The masses should know both what Independence will and will not mean for them. If the main features are not constantly kept in view and public opinion formulated, when the time comes, they are likely to be overlooked or even deliberately sacrificed. The controversy over public debt has now made it impossible, I hope, for any representative to bind the nation to its payment without being satisfied that it was all incurred in the national interest. It is, I hope, impossible similarly to bind the nation in any future constitution to the high cost of civil and military expenditure. And so it may be mentioned by me.

The plan therefore I have in mind is to concentrate the national attention on all these points one after another or simultaneously and demand relief preparatory to Independence.

This is the most expeditious plan, if Independence is to be achieved through peaceful means. Satyagraha works only in this manner. It arms people with power not to seize power but to convert the usurper to their own view till at last the usurper retires or sheds the vices of a usurper and becomes a mere instrument of service to those whom he has wronged. The mission of satyagrahis ends when they have shown the way to the nation to become conscious of the power lying latent in it.

Speech at AICC Meeting
[8 August 1942]

I congratulate you on the resolution that you have just passed. I also congratulate the three comrades on the courage they have shown in pressing their amendments to a division, even though they knew that there was an overwhelming majority in favour of the resolution, and I congratulate the thirteen friends who voted against the resolution. In doing so, they had nothing to be ashamed of. For the last twenty years we have tried to learn not to lose courage even when we are in a hopeless minority and are laughed at. We have learned to hold on to our beliefs in the confidence that we are in the right. It behoves us to cultivate this courage of conviction, for it ennobles man and rises his moral stature. I was, therefore, glad to see that these friends had imbibed the principle which I have tried to follow for the last fifty years and more.

Having congratulated them on their courage, let me say that what they asked this Committee to accept through their amendments was not the correct representation of the situation. These friends ought to have pondered over the appeal made to them by the Maulana to withdraw their amendments; they should have carefully followed the explanations given by Jawaharlal. Had they done so, it would have been clear to them that the right which they now want the Congress to concede has already been conceded by the Congress.

Time was when every Mussalman claimed the whole of India as his motherland. During the years that the Ali Brothers were with me, the assumption underlying all their talks and discussions was that India belonged as much to the Mussalmans as to the Hindus. I can testify to the fact that this was their innermost conviction and not a mask; I lived with them for years. I spent days and nights in their company. And I make bold to say that their utterances were the honest expression of their beliefs. I know there are some who say that I take things too readily at their face value, that I am gullible. I do not think I am such a simpleton, nor am I so gullible as these friends take me to be. But their criticism does not hurt me. I should prefer to be considered gullible rather than deceitful.

What these Communist friends proposed through their amendments is nothing new. It has been repeated from thousands of platforms. Thousands of Mussalmans have told me that if the Hindu-Muslim question was to be solved satisfactorily, it must be done in my lifetime. I should feel flattered at this; but how can I agree to a proposal which does not appeal to my reason? Hindu-Muslim unity is not a new thing. Millions of Hindus and Mussalmans have sought after it. I consciously strove for its achievement from my boyhood. While at school, I made it a point to cultivate the friendship of Muslim and Parsi fellow students. I believed even at that tender age that the Hindus in India, if they wished to live in peace and amity with the other communities, should assiduously cultivate the virtue of [good] neighbourliness. It did not matter, I felt if I made no special effort to cultivate the friendship with Hindus, but I must make friends with at least a few Mussalmans. It was as counsel for a Mussalman merchant that I went to South Africa. I made friends with other Mussalmans there, even with the opponents of my client, and gained a reputation for integrity and good faith. I had among my friends and co-workers Muslims as well as Parsis. I captured their hearts and when I left finally for India, I left them sad and shedding tears of grief at the separation.

In India, too, I continued my efforts and left no stone unturned to achieve that unity. If was my life-long aspiration for it that made me offer my fullest co-operation to the Mussalmans in the Khilafat movement. Muslims throughout the country accepted me as their true friend.

How then is it that I have now come to be regarded as so evil and detestable? Had I any axe to grind in supporting the Khilafat movement? True, I did in my heart of hearts cherish a hope that it might enable me to save the cow. I am a worshipper of the cow. I believe the cow and myself to be the creation of the same God, and I am prepared to sacrifice my life in order to save the cow. But, whatever my philosophy of life and my ultimate hopes, I joined the movement in no spirit of bargain. I co-operated in the struggle for the Khilafat solely in order to discharge my obligation to my neighbour who, I saw, was in distress. The Ali Brothers, had they been alive today, would have testified to the truth of this assertion. And so would many others bear me out in that it was not a bargain on my part for saving the cow. The cow, like the Khilafat, stood on her own merits. As an honest man, a true neighbour and a faithful friend, it was incumbent on me to stand by the Mussalmans in the hour of their trial.

In those days I shocked the Hindus by dining with the Mussalmans, though with the passage of time they have now got used to it. Maulana Bari told me, however, that though he would insist on having me as his guest, he would not allow me to dine with him, lest some day he should be accused of a sinister motive. And, so, whenever I had occasion to stay with him, he called a Brahmin cook and made special arrangements for separate cooking. Firangi Mahal, his residence, was an old-styled structure with limited accommodation; yet he cheerfully bore all hardships and carried out his resolve from which I could not dislodge him. It was the spirit of courtesy, dignity and nobility that inspired us in those days. The members of each community vied with one another in accommodating members of sister communities. They respected one another's religious feelings, and considered it a privilege to do so. Not a trace of suspicion lurked in anybody's heart. Where has all that dignity, that nobility of spirit, disappeared now? I should ask all Mussalmans, including Qaid-e-Azam Jinnah, to recall those glorious days and to find out what has brought us to the present impasse. Qaid-e-Azam Jinnah himself was at one time a Congressman. If today the Congress has incurred his wrath, it is because the canker of suspicion has entered his heart. May God bless him with long life, but when I am gone, he will realize and admit that I had no designs on Mussalmans and that I had never betrayed their interests. Where is the escape for me if I injure their cause or betray their interests? My life is entirely at their disposal. They are free to put an end to it, whenever they wish to do so. Assaults have been made on my life in the past, but God has spared me till now, and the assailants have repented for their action. But if someone were to shoot me in the belief that he was getting rid of a rascal, he would kill not the real Gandhi, but the one that appeared to him a rascal.

To those who have been indulging in a campaign of abuse and vilification I would say, 'Islam enjoins you not to revile even an enemy. The Prophet treated even enemies with kindness and tried to win them over by his fairness and generosity. Are you followers of that Islam or of any other? If you are followers of the true Islam, does it behove you to distrust the words of one who makes a public declaration of his faith? You may take it from me that one day you will regret the fact that you distrusted and killed one who was a true and devoted friend of yours.' It cuts me to the quick to see that the more I appeal and the more the Maulana importunes, the more intense does the campaign of vilification grow. To me, these abuses are like bullets. They can kill me, even as a bullet can put an end to my life. You may kill me. That will not hurt me. But what of those who indulge in abusing? They bring discredit to Islam. For the fair name of Islam, I appeal to you to resist this unceasing campaign of abuse and vilification.

Maulana Saheb is being made a target for the filthiest abuse. Why? Because he refuses to exert on me the pressure of his friendship. He realizes that it is a misuse of friendship to seek to compel a friend to accept as truth what he knows is an untruth.

To the Qaid-e-Azam I would say: 'Whatever is true and valid in the claim for Pakistan is already in your hands. What is wrong and untenable is in nobody's gift, so that it can be made over to you. Even if someone were to succeed in imposing an untruth on others, he would not be able to enjoy for long the fruits of such coercion. God dislikes pride and keeps away from it. God would not tolerate a forcible imposition of an untruth.'

The Qaid-e-Azam says that he is compelled to say bitter things but that he cannot help giving expression to his thoughts and his feelings. Similarly I would say: I consider myself a friend of the Mussalmans. Why should I then not give expression to the things nearest to my heart, even at the cost of displeasing them? How can I conceal my innermost thoughts from them? I should congratulate the Qaid-e-Azam on his frankness in giving expression to his thoughts and feelings, even if they sound bitter to his hearers. But even so why should the Mussalmans sitting here be reviled, if they do not see eye to eye with him? If millions of Mussalmans are with you, can you not afford to ignore the handful of Mussalmans who may appear to you to be misguided? Why should one with the following of several millions be afraid of a majority community, or of the minority being swamped by the majority? How did the Prophet work among the Arabs and Mussalmans? How did he propagate Islam? Did he say he would propagate Islam only when he commanded a majority? I, therefore, appeal to you for the sake of Islam to ponder over what I say. There is neither fair play nor justice in saying that the Congress must accept a thing even if it does not believe in it and even if it goes counter to principles it holds dear.

Rajaji said: 'I do not believe in Pakistan. But Mussalmans ask for it, Mr Jinnah asks for it, and it has become an obsession with them. Why not then say 'yes' to them just now? The same Mr Jinnah will later on realize the disadvantages of Pakistan and will forgo the demand.' I said: 'It is not fair to accept as true a thing which I hold to be untrue and ask others to do so in the belief that the demand will not be pressed when the time comes for settling it finally. If I hold the demand to be just, I should concede it this very day. I should not agree to it merely in order to placate Jinnah Saheb. Many friends have come and asked me to agree to it for the time being to placate Mr Jinnah, disarm his suspicions and to see how he reacts to it. But I cannot be party to a course of action with a false promise. At any rate, it is not my method.'

The Congress has no sanction but the moral one for enforcing its decisions. It believes that true democracy can only be the outcome of non-violence. The structure of a world federation can be raised only on a foundation of non-violence, and violence will have to be totally abjured from world affairs. If this is true, the solution of the Hindu-Muslim question, too, cannot be achieved by resort to violence. If the Hindus tyrannize over the Mussalmans, with what face will they talk of a world federation? It is for the same reason that I do not believe in the possibility of establishing world peace through violence as the English and American statesmen propose to do. The Congress has agreed to submitting all the differences to an impartial international tribunal and to abide by its decisions. If even this fairest of proposals is unacceptable, the only course that remains open is that of the sword, of violence. How can I persuade myself to agree to an impossibility? To demand the vivisection of a living organism is to ask for its very life. It is a call to war. The Congress cannot be party to such a fratricidal war. Those Hindus who, like Dr Moonje and Shri Savarkar, believe in the doctrine of the sword may seek to keep the Mussalmans under Hindu domination. I do not represent that section. I represent the Congress. You want to kill the Congress which is the goose that lays golden eggs. If you distrust the Congress, you may rest assured that there is to be a perpetual war between the Hindus and the Mussalmans, and the country will be doomed to continue warfare and bloodshed. If such warfare is to be our lot, I shall not live to witness it.

It is for that reason that I say to Jinnah Saheb, 'You may take it from me that whatever in your demand for Pakistan accords with considerations of justice and equity is lying in your pocket; whatever in the demand is contrary to justice and equity you can take only by the sword and in no other manner.'

There is much in my heart that I would like to pour out before this assembly. One thing which was uppermost in my heart I have already dealt with. You may take it from me that it is with me a matter of life and death. If we Hindus and Mussalmans mean to achieve a heart unity, without the slightest mental reservation on the part of either, we must first unite in the effort to be free from the shackles of this Empire. If Pakistan after all is to be a portion of India, what objection can there be for Mussalmans against joining this struggle for India's freedom? The Hindus and Mussalmans must, therefore, unite in the first instance on the issue of fighting for freedom. Jinnah Saheb thinks the war will last long. I do not agree with him. If the war goes on for six months more, how shall we be able to save China?

I, therefore, want freedom immediately, this very night, before dawn, if it can be had. Freedom cannot now wait for the realization of communal unity. If that unity is not achieved, sacrifices necessary for it will have to be much greater than would have otherwise sufficed. But the Congress must win freedom or be wiped out in the effort. And forget not that the freedom which the Congress is struggling to achieve will not be for the Congressmen alone but for all the forty crores of the Indian people. Congressmen must forever remain humble servants of the people.

The Qaid-e-Azam has said that the Muslim League is prepared to take over the rule from the Britishers if they are prepared to hand it over to the Muslim League, for the British took over the Empire from the hands of the Muslims. This, however, will be Muslim raj. The offer made by Maulana Saheb and by me does not imply establishment of Muslim raj or Muslim domination. The Congress does not believe in the domination of any group or any community. It believes in democracy which includes in its orbit Muslims,

Hindus, Christians, Parsis, Jews—every one of the communities inhabiting this vast country. If Muslim raj is inevitable, then let it be; but how can we give it the stamp of our assent? How can we agree to the domination of one community over the others?

Millions of Mussalmans in this country come from Hindu stock. How can their homeland be any other than India? My eldest son embraced Islam some years back. What would his homeland be— Porbander or the Punjab? I ask the Mussalmans: 'If India is not your homeland, what other country do you belong to? In what separate homeland would you put my son who embraced Islam?' His mother wrote him a letter after his conversion, asking him if he had on embracing Islam given up drinking which Islam forbids to its followers. To those who gloated over the conversion, she wrote to say: 'I do not mind his becoming a Mussalman so much as his drinking. Will you, as pious Mussalmans, tolerate his drinking even after his conversion? He has reduced himself to the state of a rake by drinking. If you are going to make a man of him again, his conversion will have been turned to good account. You will, therefore, please see that he as a Mussalman abjures wine and women. If that change does not come about, his conversion goes in vain and our non-co-operation with him will have to continue.'

India is without doubt the homeland of all the Mussalmans inhabiting this country. Every Mussalman should therefore co-operate in the fight for India's freedom. The Congress does not belong to any one class or community; it belongs to the whole nation. It is open to Mussalmans to take possession of the Congress. They can, if they like, swamp the Congress by their numbers, and can steer it along the course which appeals to them. The Congress is fighting not on behalf of the Hindus but on behalf of the whole nation, including the minorities. It would hurt me to hear of a single instance of a Mussalman being killed by a Congressman. In the coming revolution, Congressmen will sacrifice their lives in order to protect the Mussalman against a Hindu's attack and *vice versa*. It is a part of their creed, and is one of the essentials of non-violence. You will be expected on occasions like these not to lose your heads. Every Congressman, whether a Hindu or a Mussalman, owes this duty to the organization to which he belongs. The Mussalman who will act in this manner will render a service to Islam. Mutual trust is essential for success in the final nationwide struggle that is to come.

I have said that much greater sacrifices will have to be made this time in the wake of our struggle because of the opposition from the Muslim League and from Englishmen. You have seen the secret circular issued by Sir Frederick Puckle. It is a suicidal course that he has taken. It contains an open incitement to organizations which crop up like mushrooms to combine to fight the Congress. We have thus to deal with an Empire whose ways are crooked. Ours is a straight path which we can tread even with our eyes closed. That is the beauty of satyagraha.

In satyagraha, there is no place for fraud or falsehood, or any kind of untruth. Fraud and untruth today are stalking the world. I cannot be a helpless witness to such a situation. I have travelled all over India as perhaps nobody in the present age has. The voiceless millions of the land saw in me their friend and representative, and I identified myself with them to an extent it was possible for a human being to do. I saw trust in their eyes, which I now want to turn to good account in fighting this Empire upheld on untruth and violence. However gigantic the preparations that the Empire has made, we must get out of its clutches. How can I remain silent at this supreme hour and hide my light under the bushel? Shall I ask the Japanese to tarry a while? If today I sit quiet and inactive, God will take me to task for not using up the treasure He had given me, in the midst of the conflagration that is enveloping the whole world. Had the condition been different, I should have asked you to wait yet awhile. But the situation now has become intolerable, and the Congress has no other course left for it.

Nevertheless, the actual struggle does not commence this moment. You have only placed all your powers in my hands. I will now wait upon the Viceroy and plead with him for the acceptance of the Congress demand. That process is likely to take two or three weeks. What would you do in the meanwhile? What is the programme, for the interval, in which all can participate? As you know, the spinning-wheel is the first thing that occurs to me. I made the same answer to the Maulana. He would have none of it, though he understood its import later. The fourteen-fold constructive programme is, of course, there for you to carry out. What more should you do? I will tell you. Every one of you should, from this moment onwards, consider yourself a free man or woman, and act as if you are free and are no longer under the heel of this imperialism.

It is not a make-believe that I am suggesting to you. It is the very essence of freedom. The bond of the slave is snapped the moment he considers himself to be a free being. He will plainly tell the master: 'I was your bondslave till this moment, but I am a slave no longer. You may kill me if you like, but if you keep me alive, I wish to tell you that if you release me from the bondage of your own accord, I will ask for nothing more from you. You used to feed and clothe me, though I could have provided food and clothing for myself by my labour. I hitherto depended on you instead of on God, for food and raiment. God has now inspired me with an urge for freedom and I am today a free man and will no longer depend on you.'

You may take it from me that I am not going to strike a bargain with the Viceroy for ministries and the like. I am not going to be satisfied with anything short of complete freedom. Maybe, he will propose the abolition of salt-tax, the drink evil, etc. But I will say: 'Nothing less than freedom.'

Here is a mantra, a short one, that I give you. You may imprint it on your hearts and let every breath of yours give expression to it. The mantra is: 'Do or Die.' We shall either free India or die in the attempt; we shall not live to see the perpetuation of our slavery. Every true Congressman or (Congress) woman will join the struggle with an inflexible determination not to remain alive to see the country in bondage and slavery. Let that be your pledge. Keep jails out of your consideration. If the Government keeps me free, I will spare you the trouble of filling the jails. I will not put on the Government the strain of maintaining a large number of prisoners at a time when it is in trouble. Let every man and woman live every moment of his or her life hereafter in the consciousness that he or she eats or lives for achieving freedom and will die, if need be, to attain that goal. Take a pledge with God and your own conscience as witness, that you will no longer rest till freedom is achieved and will be prepared to lay down your lives in the attempt to achieve it. He who loses his life will gain it; he who will seek to save it shall lose it. Freedom is not for the coward or the faint-hearted.

A word to the journalists. I congratulate you on the support you have hitherto given to the national demand. I know the restrictions and handicaps under which you have to labour. But I would now ask you to snap the chains that bind you. It should be the proud privilege of the newspapers to lead and set an example in laying down one's life for freedom. You have the pen which the Government can't suppress. I know you have large properties in the form of printing presses, etc., and you would be afraid lest the Government should attach them. I do not ask you to invite an attachment of the printing press voluntarily. For myself, I would not suppress my pen, even if the press was to be attached. As you know my press was attached in the past and returned later on. But I do not ask from you that final sacrifice. I suggest a middle way. You should now wind up your Standing Committee, and you may declare that you will give up writing under the present restrictions and take up the pen only when India has won her freedom. You may tell Sir Frederick Puckle that he can't expect from you a command performance, that his Press notes are full of untruth, and that you will refuse to publish them. You will openly declare that you are whole-heartedly with the Congress. If you do this, you will have changed the atmosphere before the fight actually begins.

From the princes I ask with all respect due to them a very small thing. I am a well-wisher of the princes. I was born in a State. My grandfather refused to salute with his right hand any prince other than his own. But he did not say to the prince, as I feel he ought to have said, that even his own master could not compel him, his minister, to act against his conscience. I have eaten the princes' salt and I would not be false to it. As a faithful servant, it is my duty to warn the princes that if they will act while I am still alive, the princes may come to occupy an honourable place in free India. In Jawaharlal's scheme of free India, no privileges or the privileged classes have a place. Jawaharlal considers all property to be State-owned. He wants planned economy. He wants to reconstruct India according to plan. He likes to fly; I do not. I have kept a place for the princes and the zamindars in India that I envisage. I would ask the princes in all humility to enjoy through renunciation. The princes may renounce ownership over their properties and become their trustees in the true sense of the term. I visualize God in the assemblage of people. The princes may say to their people: 'You are the owners and masters of the State and we are your servants.' I would ask the princes to become servants of the people and render to them an account of their own services. The Empire too bestows power on the princes, but they should prefer to derive power from their own people; and if they want to indulge in some innocent pleasures, they may seek to do so as servants of the people. I do not want the princes to live as paupers. But I would ask them: 'Do you want to remain slaves for all time? Why should you, instead of paying homage to a foreign power, not accept the sovereignty of your own people?' You may write to the Political Department: 'The people are now awake. How are we to withstand an avalanche before which even the large Empires are crumbling? We, therefore, shall belong to the people from today onwards. We shall sink or swim with them.' Believe me, there is nothing unconstitutional in the course I am suggesting. There are, so far as I know, no treaties enabling the Empire to coerce the princes. The people of the States will also declare that though they are the princes' subjects, they are part of the Indian nation and that they will accept the leadership of the princes, if the latter cast their lot with the People, but not otherwise. If this declaration enrages the princes and they choose to kill the people, the latter will meet death bravely and unflinchingly, but will not go back on their word.

Nothing, however, should be done secretly. This is an open rebellion. In this struggle secrecy is a sin. A free man would not engage in a secret movement. It is likely that when you gain freedom you will have a CID of your own, in spite of my advice to the contrary. But in the present struggle, we have to work openly and to receive the bullets on our chest, without taking to heels.

I have a word to say to the Government servants also. They may not, if they like, resign their posts yet. The late Justice Ranade did not resign his post, but he openly declared that he belonged to the Congress. He said to the Government that though he was a judge, he was a Congressman and would openly attend the sessions of the Congress, but that at the same time he would not let his political views warp his impartiality on the bench. He held Social Reform Conference in the very pandal of the Congress. I would ask all the Government servants to follow in the footsteps of Ranade and to declare their allegiance to the Congress as an answer to the secret circular issued by Sir Frederick Puckle.

This is all that I ask of you just now. I will now write to the

Viceroy. You will be able to read the correspondence not just now but when I publish it with the Viceroy's consent. But you are free to aver that you support the demand to be put forth in my letter. A judge came to me and said: 'We get secret circulars from high quarters. What are we to do?' I replied, 'If I were in your place, I would ignore the circulars. You may openly say to the Government: "I have received your secret circular. I am, however, with the Congress. Though I serve the Government for my livelihood, I am not going to obey these secret circulars or to employ underhand methods."'

Soldiers too are covered by the present programme. I do not ask them just now to resign their posts and leave the army. Soldiers come to me, Jawaharlal and to the Maulana and say: 'We are wholly with you. We are tired of the governmental tyranny.' To these soldiers I would say: 'You may say to the Government, "Our hearts are with the Congress. We are not going to leave our posts. We will serve you so long as we receive your salaries. We will obey your just orders, but will refuse to fire on our own people."'

To those who lack the courage to do this much I have nothing to say. They will go their own way. But if you can do this much, you may take it from me that the whole atmosphere will be electrified. Let the Government then shower bombs, if they like. But no power on earth will then be able to keep you in bondage any longer.

If the students want to join the struggle only to go back to their studies after a while, I would not invite them to it. For the present, however, till the time that I frame a programme for the struggle, I would ask the students to say to their professors: 'We belong to the Congress. Do you belong to the Congress or the Government? If you belong to the Congress, you need not vacate your posts. You will remain at your posts but teach us and lead us unto freedom.' In all fights for freedom, the world over, the students have made very large contributions.

If in the interval that is left to us before the actual fight begins, you do even the little I have suggested to you, you will have changed the atmosphere and will have prepared the ground for the next step.

There is much I should yet like to say. But my heart is heavy.

I have already taken up much of your time. I have yet to say a few words in English also. I thank you for the patience and attention with which you have listened to me even at this late hour. It is just what true soldiers would do. For the last twenty-two years, I have controlled my speech and pen and have stored up my energy. He is a true brahmachari who does not fritter away his energy. He will, therefore, always control his speech. That has been my conscious effort all these years. But today the occasion has come when I had to unburden my heart before you. I have done so, even though it meant putting a strain on your patience; and I do not regret having done it. I have given you my message and through you I have delivered it to the whole of India.

Message to the Country
[5 a.m., 9 August 1942]

Everyone is free to go the fullest length under ahimsa. Complete deadlock by strikes and other non-violent means. Satyagrahis must go out to die not to live. They must seek and face death. It is only when individuals go out to die that the nation will survive.

Karenge ya marenge.

Women And Sex

Women of Gujarat [15 January 1922]

[...] If it had been merely a matter of replacing one Government by another, I would never have advised women to come forward. I have seen that there is much sordid work in an effort to secure that. But, at the end of this struggle, we hope to establish Ramarajya and the poor hope to get protection, women to live in safety and the starving millions to see an end of hunger. When the struggle ends, we hope to see the resurrection of the spinning-wheel, decrease in the poison of communal discord, eradication of the practice of untouchability so that the so-called untouchables may look forward to being treated as our brothers, the closing of the liquor shops and the disappearance of the drink habit, the preservation of the Khilafat and the protection of the cow, the healing of the Punjab wounds, the restoration of our traditional culture to its rightful place and the introduction, in every home, of the spinning-wheel to take its place along with the oven.

How can women stand aside from a movement which is inspired by such great hopes? I have, therefore, been requesting women to come forward and take part in it. It is these hopes, I think, which have roused women throughout the country.

But should I, trusting to this enthusiasm, advise women to go to jail? I feel that I cannot do otherwise. If I did not encourage them to do so, that would be a reflection on my faith in them. A *yajna* is incomplete without women taking part in it. Fearlessness is just as essential for women as it is for men. I thought, therefore, that it would be good if women give their signatures and get used to the idea of going to jail. It also occurred to me that if women ceased being frightened by the thought of jail, it would be easier for men to court arrest.

But just as I have a responsibility, so also have these sisters who have made a beginning. Having given their signatures, they should start work. Women can picket liquor shops. Customers will surely be put to shame by their presence. If any women want to take up this work, they will have to carry wooden plates round their necks, like Abbas Saheb. They will also have to find out the homes of drink-addicts and persuade them to abstain. I would first suggest to the women that they should postpone the picketing of liquor shops for the present and start going round to sell khadi. Pure khadi is not available in all khadi shops. Moreover, those who have not so far thought about swadeshi will not go to these shops and will wear khadi only if it is taken to their doors. If women carry khadi with them, they can display it and thus tempt even those who wear foreign cloth or mill-made cloth to buy it. They should go from house to house and sell khadi. They should also keep a stock of khadi caps and sell these. As they go about doing this, they will lose their fear and the Government then will feel impelled to arrest them. As long as the work does not affect the Government's revenues nor increase the people's strength in any way, it will not arrest women. Besides, it will be more fitting if women think of going to jail after they have developed capacity for organized work.

I also hope that women will fulfil the conditions of the pledge they have taken. I believe that they will remain peaceful and bear love for Hindus, Muslims and all others. But will they wear pure khadi even in their homes? Will they regard *Dheds* and *Bhangis* as brothers? Will they stop giving left-over and rotten food to them and cease to regard themselves as defiled by contact with them? The women who have given their signatures belong to all communities. If these women can fulfil their pledge in this true spirit, then the 140 will soon become 1,400 and this number will rise to 14,00,000.

It is in this hope and faith that I give the sacred names of these women.

Speech at Women's Conference, Sojitra
[16 January 1925]

To women I talk about Ramarajya. Ramarajya is more than swarajya. Let me therefore talk about what Ramarajya will be like— not about swaraj. Ramarajya can come about only when there is likelihood of a Sita arising. Among the many *shlokas* recited by Hindus, one is on women. It enumerates women who are worthy of being remembered prayerfully early in the morning. Who are these women by taking whose names men and women become sanctified? Among such virtuous women Sita's name is bound to figure. We never say Rama-Sita but Sita-Rama, not Krishna-Radha, but Radha-Krishna. It is thus that we tutor even the parrot. The reason why we think of Sita's name first is that, without virtuous women, there can be no virtuous men. A child will take after the mother, not the father. It is the mother who holds its reins. The father's concerns lie outside the home and that is why I keep saying that, as long as the women of India do not take part in public life, there can be no salvation for the country. Only those can take part in public life who are pure in body and mind. As long as women whose body and mind tend in one direction—i.e., towards the path of virtue—do not come into public life and purify it, we are not likely to attain Ramarajya or swaraj. Even if we did, I would have no use for that kind of swaraj to which such women have not made their full contribution. One could well stretch oneself on the ground in obeisance to a woman of purity of mind and heart. I should like such women to take part in public life.

Who shall we say is a woman of this kind? It is said that a virtuous woman can be recognized by the grace on her face. Must we then accept all the prostitutes in India as virtuous? For it is their trade to deck themselves up. Not at all. The thing needed for grace is not beauty of face but purity of heart. A woman who is pure of heart and mind is ever fit to be worshipped. It is a law of nature that our outward appearance reflects what we really are within. If inwardly we are sallied, so shall we appear without. The eyes and the voice are external signs. The discerning can recognize virtue by voice.

Then what does it mean to be virtuous? What is the sign of virtue? I accept khadi as the symbol of virtue. I do not suggest that anyone who wears khadi has become sanctified for that reason alone.

I ask you to participate in public life. What does it mean to participate in public life? Public work does not mean attendance at meetings, but wearing khadi—the symbol of purity—and serving the men and women of India. After all, what service can we render to the Rajas and Maharajas? If we try to approach the Maharajas, the sentry at the gate may not even let us in. Likewise, we do not have to wait on millionaires: to serve India therefore is to serve its poor. God we cannot see with our eyes; it would do if we serve those whom we can see. The object of our public life is to serve the visible God, that is, the poor. If you want to serve them, take the name of God, go amidst them and ply the spinning-wheel.

To take part in public life is to serve your poor sisters. Their lot is wretched. I met them on the banks of the Ganga where Janaka lived, where Sitaji lived. They were in a pitiful state. They had scanty clothes, but I could not give them saris because I had not found the charkha then. Indian women remain naked even if they have clothes, because as long as one Indian woman has to go naked it must be said that all are naked. Or even if a woman is adorned in a variety of ways but is of unworthy soul, she would still be naked. We have to think of ways of making them spin, weave and thus covering themselves truly.

At present when people go to the villages to render service, the villagers imagine that they have come to exact *chauth*. Why do they imagine this? You must realize that you go to the villages to give and not to take.

Were our mothers mad that they used to spin? Now when I ask you to spin, I must appear mad to you. But it is not Gandhi who is mad; it is yourself who are so. You do not have any compassion for the poor. Even so you try to convince yourself that India has become prosperous and sing of that prosperity. If you want to enter public life, render public service, then spin on the charkha, wear khadi. If your body and mind are pure you will become truly swadeshi. Spin in the name of God. To spin for your sisters is to worship God. Giving in charity to the poor means an offering to God. That alone is charity by which the poor become happy. If you give in charity to whomsoever you please, it would be said that you indulge your whims. If you give in charity to those who have a pair of hands, a pair of legs and good health, it would be said that you were out to impoverish them. Do not give alms to a Brahmin because he is a Brahmin. Make him spin and give him a handful of *jowar* or rice. The finest sign of purity of mind is to go and work for khadi amidst such people.

The second sign of virtue is service to *Antyajas*. Brahmins and gurus of today regard touching an *Antyaja* as sinful. I say that it is a meritorious act, not a sin. I do not ask you to eat and drink with them, but to mix with them in order to render service. It is meritorious to serve sick *Antyaja* boys who are worthy of service. *Antyajas* eat, drink, stand and sit, and so do we all. It is not that doing this is either sinful or meritorious. My mother used to become *Antyaja* for some time and then she would not allow anyone to touch her. My wife similarly used to become an *Antyaja*. At this time she became an untouchable. Our *Bhangis* also become untouchable when they do their work. As long as they do not bathe, one can understand not touching them. But if you would not touch them even when they have bathed and tidied up, for whose sake do they bathe then? They have no God even. They think others have the same kind of nose and eyes and yet the latter despise them. What then should they do? Think of this: did Ramachandraji despise the *Antyajas*? He ate berries already savoured by Shabari and he hugged the king of Nishadas, and they were both untouchables. You can see for yourselves that there is no untouchability in the Hindu religion.

The third sign of virtue is furtherance of friendship with the Muslims. If someone tells you that 'they are Mias' or 'Mia and Mahadev cannot get on', then tell him that you cannot harbour enmity towards the Muslims.

If you do these three things, you will be said to have taken full part in public life. By doing so you will become worthy of being prayerfully remembered early in the morning; and it would be said that you have worked for India's salvation. I beseech you to become thus worthy.

Reply to Women's Address, Noakhali [14 May 1925]

Who says that woman is dependent on others? The Shastras say nothing of the sort. Sita was Rama's better half and enjoyed empire over his heart. Neither was Damayanti dependent. Who will say, after reading the *Mahabharata*, that Draupadi was dependent on others? Who will call Draupadi dependent, Draupadi who, when the Pandavas failed to protect her, saved herself by an appeal to Lord Krishna? We cherish as sacred the names of seven women as chaste and virtuous wives. Were they dependent? A woman who has the strength to preserve her purity, to defend her virtue—to call such a woman dependent is to murder language and violate *dharma*.

What Women Should Do in a Difficult Situation
[4 September 1932]

Touching upon non-violence, if some maniac should try to assault a woman, and if another man should happen to be present, should he not protect her honour with the use of a weapon? Should not women train themselves in the use of weapons and learn to protect themselves? I have given my opinion. Use of weapons would certainly imply violence but I have never permitted anyone to draw from this the inference that a man or woman who happens to be present should not run to the rescue of the woman and should tolerate an outrage on her modesty. On the contrary, I have said that the man who allows the modesty of a woman to be thus outraged will be regarded as a coward. He will be a partner in violence because violence is implicit in cowardice. It is my firm opinion that heroic violence is less sinful than cowardly violence. A heroic man or woman can learn the lesson of non-violence, it is pretty nearly impossible for a coward to learn it. I have not begun this article in order to repeat all this. One will find these ideas in many other places in my writings.

But there is one thing which I think I have not remarked upon anywhere else which I wish to put down. I have dissuaded the Ashram women from learning the tricks of *jamaiya*, etc. The woman who depends on a *jamaiya* (dagger-like weapon) or a *gothi* (name of a weapon) to guard her honour may some day fail to do so. When someone snatches away the *jamaiya* or the *gothi* from her, she will become defenceless, so that there is a possibility of her falling into the hands of a maniac....Sita had no weapons. But she had soul-force. Hence her consent was necessary before Ravana could so much as touch her. Our sisters should have self-confidence of this kind. Hence we have introduced Draupadi's prayer specially for women. But we were discussing an ideal. When a woman is faced by a maniac, what is she to do? If she truly has courage in her and also compassion, instead of becoming panicky she will melt him with the radiance of her compassion. But if that emotion has not arisen in her, she will certainly become enraged. In her rage she will slap him and raise such a row that he will run away from the scene. Or he will fall at her feet then and there. That is to say, the woman will use all her physical strength. Will that not constitute violence? If that is to be so, why not carry a weapon? My opinion is that there is violence in carrying and learning to use a weapon. But in a situation like the above, slapping or scratching, if the occasion demands it, does not constitute violence. If there is violence in a mouse biting a cat, the conduct of a woman in such a situation would also constitute violence. The trust of a woman who slaps is not in the slap, her trust is in God. Only compassion has not awakened her, while anyone can become enraged. Her rage will indicate her opposition. When a lecherous man approaches a woman, he does so in the belief that he will be able to subdue her, that is to say, that desire will also ultimately possess her. How is the woman to show that this cannot happen? Either by calm but immense compassion or by shouting and struggling. Slapping and so on is like the struggling of a mouse against a cat. The woman's slap certainly cannot cause any injury to the lecher. This will be evident, if we go deeper into it. Here I do not have in mind women of a giant's strength. Such a woman will be blinded by the consciousness of her strength. She may be faced by a man of greater strength and she may then surrender herself to him. Here I have in mind Ashram girls or women without physical strength who repose their trust in soul-force. Their slap is not an expression of violence, only of their opposition. Their cry will render that lustful man meek, because crime itself has no strength and he who has come to commit an offence knows it. This belief of mine implies that the woman will not even till death surrender herself to the man. Her anger, her alarm, proclaims for herself as well as for the man her preparedness to die. For what I have pictured may not happen and the maniac instead of becoming meek at the woman's anger, may hit her and determine to throw her on the ground. If at that time the woman is defeated, if she does not think of God, if she loses her self-confidence, she will be trembling, so that it will not occur to her to die. Even if it occurs to her to die, she will not know how to die. Fear,...self-confidence become utterly weak. And enthusiasm in her....This is merely to warn women. It is quite possible for her to be in a state where she may think: 'I do not have such faith in God that I shall be able to get rid of the maniac by my purity alone. Bapu has said that one must not use a weapon; for that will be violence. One may then not use even one's hands. What, O God, am I to do! Oh! I am dying.' Such a thought is intolerable to me. This instruction of mine is not meant only for one man or woman. There is no question of my instruction rendering anyone weak. If anyone becomes so, it will be due to their own misunderstanding. The above suggestion is to clarify my thought. Women should just forget that they are the weaker sex. She who has the desire and the strength to die can never be regarded as weak. There is danger to the body, not to the soul. The soul which has attenuated its relation to the body, has made it absolutely insignificant like a blade of grass, cannot be harassed or defeated even by all the maniacs of the world. This lesson should be learnt by every boy and girl who is of an age to understand it. It is to impart this lesson that I have made the above observation. Instead of feeling helpless and scared, she should say to herself: 'I shall offer up my body and life, but shall not become a coward.' Her slap or scratching indicates this resolve. It is in itself an act of non-violence. She has no strength to cause harm. Hence her act is not violence; but it has power to move a lecherous mind and to awaken the woman who administers the slap.

Interview to Margaret Sanger
[3/4 December 1935]

Gandhiji poured his whole being into his conversation. He revealed himself inside out, giving Mrs Sanger an intimate glimpse of his own private life. He also declared to her his own limitations, especially the stupendous limitation of his own philosophy of life—a philosophy that seeks self-realization through self-control, and said that from him there could be one solution and one alone:

[*G.*] I could not recommend the remedy of birth-control to a woman who wanted my approval. I should simply say to her: My remedy is of no use to you. You must go to others for advice.

Both seemed to be agreed that woman should be emancipated, that woman should be the arbiter of her destiny. But Mrs Sanger would have Gandhiji work for woman's emancipation through her pet device, just as believers in violence want Gandhiji to win India's freedom through violence, since they seem to be sure that non-violence can never succeed.

She forgets this fundamental difference in her impatience to prove that Gandhiji does not know the women of India. And she claims to prove this on the ground that he makes an impossible appeal to the women of India— the appeal to resist their husbands. Well, this is what he said:

My wife I made the orbit of all women. In her I studied all women. I came in contact with many European women in South Africa, and I knew practically every Indian woman there. I worked with them. I tried to show them they were not slaves either to their husbands or parents, not only in the political field but in the domestic as well. But the trouble was that some could not resist their husbands. The remedy is in the hands of women themselves. The struggle is difficult for them, and I do not blame them. I blame

188

the men. Men have legislated against them. Man has regarded woman as his tool. She has learned to be his tool and in the end found it easy and pleasurable to be such, because when one drags another in his fall the descent is easy.... I have felt that during the years still left to me if I can drive home to women's minds the truth that they are free, we will have no birth-control problem in India. If they will only learn to say 'no' to their husbands when they approach them carnally! I do not suppose all husbands are brutes and if women only know how to resist them, all will be well. I have been able to teach women who have come in contact with me how to resist their husbands. The real problem is that many do not want to resist them... No resistance bordering upon bitterness will be necessary in ninety-nine out of a hundred cases. If a wife says to her husband, 'No, I do not want it,' he will make no trouble. But she hasn't been taught. Her parents in most cases won't teach it to her. There are some cases, I know, in which parents have appealed to their daughters' husbands not to force motherhood on their daughters. And I have come across amenable husbands too. I want woman to learn the primary right of resistance. She thinks now that she has not got it....

> Mrs Sanger raises the phantasmagoria of "irritations, disputes, and thwarted longings that Gandhiji's advice would bring into the home.".....She cited cases of great nervous and mental breakdowns as a result of the practice of self-control. Gandhiji spoke from a knowledge of the numerous letters he receives every mail, when he said to her:

The evidence is all based on examination of imbeciles. The conclusions are not drawn from the practice of healthy-minded people. The people they take for examples have not lived a life of even tolerable continence. These neurologists assume that people are expected to exercise self-restraint while they continue to lead the same ill-regulated life. The consequence is that they do not exercise self-restraint but become lunatics. I carry on correspondence with many of these people and they describe their own ailments to me. I simply say that if I were to present them with this method of birth-control they would lead far worse lives.

He told her that when she went to Calcutta she would be told by those who knew what havoc contraceptives had worked among unmarried young men and women. But evidently for the purpose of the conversation, at any rate, Mrs Sanger confined herself to propagation of knowledge of birth-control among married couples only....The distinction that Gandhiji drew between love and lust will be evident from the following excerpts from the conversation:

When both want to satisfy animal passion without having to suffer the consequences of their act it is not love, it is lust. But if love is pure, it will transcend animal passion and will regulate itself. We have not had enough education of the passions. When a husband says, 'Let us not have children, but let us have relations,' what is that but animal passion? If they do not want to have more children they should simply refuse to unite. Love becomes lust the moment you make it a means for the satisfaction of animal needs. It is just the same with food. If food is taken only for pleasure it is lust. You do not take chocolates for the sake of satisfying your hunger. You take them for pleasure and then ask the doctor for an antidote. Perhaps you tell the doctor that whisky befogs your brain and he gives you an antidote. Would it not be better not to take chocolates or whisky?

[*Mrs S.*] No, I do not accept the analogy.

[*G.*] Of course you will not accept the analogy because you think this sex expression without desire for children is a need of the soul, a contention I do not endorse.

[*Mrs S.*] Yes, sex expression is a spiritual need and I claim that the quality of this expression is more important than the result, for the quality of the relationship is there regardless of results. We all know that the great majority of children are born as an accident, without the parents having any desire for conception. Seldom are two people drawn together in the sex act by their desire to have children....Do you think it possible for two people who are in love, who are happy together, to regulate their sex act only once in two years, so that relationship would only take place when they wanted a child? Do you think it possible?

[*G.*] I had the honour of doing that very thing and I am not the only one.

> Mrs Sanger thought it was illogical to contend that sex union for the purpose of having children would be love and union for the satisfaction of the sexual appetite was lust, for the same act was involved in both. Gandhiji immediately capitulated and said he was ready to describe all sexual union as partaking of the nature of lust.

I know, from my own experience that as long as I looked upon my wife carnally, we had no real understanding. Our love did not reach a high plane. There was affection between us always, but we came closer and closer the more we or rather I became restrained. There never was want of restraint on the part of my wife. Very often she would show restraint, but she rarely resisted me although she showed disinclination very often. All the time I wanted carnal pleasure I could not serve her. The moment I bade goodbye to a life of carnal pleasure our whole relationship became spiritual. Lust died and love reigned instead....

> Mrs Sanger is so impatient to prove that Gandhiji is a visionary that she forgets the practical ways and means that Gandhiji suggested to her. She asked:
> Must the sexual union take place only three or four times in an entire lifetime?

[*G.*] Why should people not be taught that it is immoral to have more than three or four children and that after they have had that number they should sleep separately? If they are taught this it would harden into custom. And if social reformers cannot impress this idea upon the people, why not a law? If husband and wife have four children, they would have had sufficient animal enjoyment. Their love may then be lifted to a higher plane. Their bodies have met. After they have had the children they wanted, their love transforms itself into a spiritual relationship. If these children die and they want more, then they may meet again. Why must people be slaves of this passion when they are not of others? When you give them education in birth-control, you tell them it is a duty. You say to them that if they do not do this thing they will interrupt their spiritual evolution. You do not even talk of regulation. After giving them education in birth-control, you do not say to them, 'thus far and no further'. You ask people to drink temperately, as though it was possible to remain temperate. I know these temperate people....

And yet as Mrs Sanger was so dreadfully in earnest Gandhiji did mention a remedy which could conceivably appeal to him. That method was the avoidance of sexual union during unsafe periods confining it to the "safe" period of about ten days during the month. That had at least an element of self-control which had to be exercised during the unsafe period. Whether this appealed to Mrs Sanger or not I do not know. But therein spoke Gandhiji the truth-seeker. Mrs Sanger has not referred to it anywhere in her interviews or her *Illustrated Weekly* article. Perhaps if birth-controllers were to be satisfied with this simple method, the birth-control clinics and propagandists would find their trade gone....

Message to the All-India Women's Conference
[23 December 1936]

I have grown old but will give a message still, if you need one from me. I can only say that until women establish their womanhood, the progress of India in all directions is impossible. When woman whom we call *abala* becomes *sabala,* all those who are helpless will become powerful.

What is Woman's Role?
[12 February 1940]

With certain omissions I quote below the following from a highly educated sister:

> You have shown the world, through ahimsa and satyagraha, the dignity of the soul.... But just as there is need for ahimsa and brahmacharya for a man to get rid of his aggressive spirit, lust..., etc., there is for a woman need of certain principles that would enable her to get rid of her baser qualities, which are different from men's and commonly said to belong by nature to her. The natural qualities for her sex, the upbringing meted out to her because of her sex, and her environment which is created because of her sex, all are against her. And in her work these things, namely, her nature, upbringing and surroundings always get in the way and hinder her and give occasion for the hackneyed phrase, 'She is only a woman, after all'....I think that, if we only possess the correct solution, the correct method of improving ourselves, we could make our natural qualities, such as sympathy and tenderness, a help instead of a hindrance. The improvement, just as your solution in the case of men and children, must come from within us...
>
> Your advice to me was to read *Harijan*. I do so eagerly. But so far I have not come across, well, the advice for the inner spirit. Spinning and fighting for the national freedom are only some aspects of the training. They do not seem to contain the whole solution. For I have seen women who do spin and do try to work out the Congress ideals and still commit blunders which are attributed to the fact of their being women.
> ...Tell us, please, how to make the best use of our qualities, how to turn our disadvantages into advantages...

I had flattered myself that my contribution to the woman's cause definitely began with the discovery of satyagraha. But the writer of the letter is of the opinion that the fair sex requires treatment different from men. If it is so, I do not think any man will find the correct solution. No matter how much he tries, he must fail because nature has made him different from woman. Only the toad under the harrow knows where it pinches him. Therefore ultimately woman will have to determine with authority what she needs. My own opinion is that, just as fundamentally man and woman are one, their problem must be one in essence. The soul in both is the same. The two live the same life, have the same feelings. Each is a complement of the other. The one cannot live without the other's active help.

But somehow or other man has dominated woman from ages past, and so woman has developed an inferiority complex. She has believed in the truth of man's interested teaching that she is inferior to him. But the seers among men have recognized her equal status.

Nevertheless, there is no doubt that at some point there is bifurcation. Whilst both are fundamentally one, it is also equally true that in the form there is a vital difference between the two. Hence the vocations of the two must also be different. The duty of motherhood, which the vast majority of women will always undertake, requires qualities which man need not possess. She is passive, he is active. She is essentially the mistress of the house. He is the bread-winner, she is the keeper and distributor of the bread. She is the caretaker in every sense of the term. The art of bringing up the infants of the race is her special and sole prerogative. Without her care the race must become extinct.

In my opinion it is degrading both for man and woman that women should be called upon or induced to forsake the hearth and shoulder the rifle for the protection of that hearth. It is a reversion to barbarity and the beginning of the end. In trying to ride the horse that man rides, she brings herself and him down. The sin will be on man's head for tempting or compelling his companion to desert her special calling. There is as much bravery in keeping one's home in good order and condition as there is in defending it against attack from without.

As I have watched millions of peasants in their natural

surroundings and as I watch them daily in little Segaon, the natural division of spheres of work has forced itself on my attention. There are no women blacksmiths and carpenters. But men and women work on the fields, the heaviest work being done by the males. The women keep and manage the homes. They supplement the meagre resources of the family, but man remains the main bread-winner.

The division of the spheres of work being recognized, the general qualities and culture required are practically the same for both the sexes.

My contribution to the great problem lies in my presenting for acceptance truth and ahimsa in every walk of life, whether for individuals or nations. I have hugged the hope that in this woman will be the unquestioned leader and, having thus found her place in human evolution, will shed her inferiority complex. If she is able to do this successfully, she must resolutely refuse to believe in the modern teaching that everything is determined and regulated by the sex impulse. I fear I have put the proposition rather clumsily. But I hope my meaning is clear. I do not know that the millions of men who are taking an active part in the war are obsessed by the sex spectre. Nor are the peasants working together in their fields worried or dominated by it. This is not to say or suggest that they are free from the instinct implanted in man and woman. But it most certainly does not dominate their lives as it seems to dominate the lives of those who are saturated with the modern sex literature. Neither man nor woman has time for such things when he or she is faced with the hard fact of living life in its grim reality.

I have suggested in these columns that woman is the incarnation of ahimsa. Ahimsa means infinite love, which again means infinite capacity for suffering. Who but woman, the mother of man, shows this capacity in the largest measure? She shows it as she carries the infant and feeds it during nine months and derives joy in the suffering involved. What can beat the suffering caused by the pangs of labour? But she forgets them in the joy of creation. Who again suffers daily so that her babe may wax from day to day? Let her transfer that love to the whole of humanity, let her forget she ever was or can be the object of man's lust. And she will occupy her proud position by the side of man as his mother, maker and silent leader. It is given to her to teach the art of peace to the warring world thirsting for that nectar. She can become the leader in satyagraha which does not require the learning that books give but does require the stout heart that comes from suffering and faith.

My good nurse in the Sassoon Hospital, Poona, as I was lying on a sick bed years ago, told me the story of a woman who refused to take chloroform because she would not risk the life of the babe she was carrying. She had to undergo a painful operation. The only anaesthetic she had was her love for the babe, to save whom no suffering was too great. Let not women, who can count many such heroines among them, ever despise their sex or deplore that they were not born men. The contemplation of that heroine often makes me envy woman the status that is hers, if she only knew. There is as much reason for man to wish that he was born a woman as for woman to do otherwise. But the wish is fruitless. Let us be happy in the state to which we are born and do the duty for which nature has destined us.

Message to Chinese Women
[18 July 1947]

If only the women of the world would come together they could display such heroic non-violence as to kick away the atom bomb like a mere ball. Women have been so gifted by God. If an ancestral treasure lying buried in a corner of the house unknown to the members of the family were suddenly discovered, what a celebration it would occasion. Similarly, women's marvellous power is lying dormant. If the women of Asia wake up, they will dazzle the world. My experiment in non-violence would be instantly successful if I could secure women's help.

Brahmacharya or Chastity[1]

This observance does not give rise to ever so many problems and dilemmas as ahimsa does. Its meaning is generally well understood; but understanding it is one thing, practising it is quite another thing and calls forth all our powers. Many of us put forth a great effort but without making any progress. Some of us even lost ground previously won. None has reached perfection. But everyone realizes its supreme importance. My striving in this direction began before 1906 when I took the vow. There were many ups and downs. It was only after I had burnt my fingers at times that I realized the deeper meaning of brahmacharya. And then I found that expositions made in books cannot be understood without actual experience, and wear a fresh aspect in the light of it. Even in the case of a simple machine like the spinning-wheel, it is one thing to read the directions for plying it, and it is another thing to put the directions into practice. New light dawns upon us as soon as we commence our practice. And what is true of simple tangible things like the wheel is still more true of spiritual states.

A brahmachari is one who controls his organs of sense in thought, word and deed. The meaning of this definition became somewhat clear after I had kept the observance for some time, but it is not quite clear even now, for I do not claim to be a perfect brahmachari, evil thoughts having been held in restraint but not eradicated. When they are eradicated, I will discover further implications of the definition.

Ordinary brahmacharya is not so difficult as it is supposed to be. We have made it difficult by understanding the term in a narrow sense. Many of us play with brahmacharya like fools who put their hands in the fire and still expect to escape being burnt. Very few realize that a brahmachari has to control not one but all the organs of sense. He is no brahmachari who thinks that mere control of animal passion is the be-all and end-all of brahmacharya. No wonder if he finds it very difficult. He who attempts to control only one organ and allows all the others free play must not expect to achieve success. He might as well deliberately descend into a well and expect to keep his body dry. Those who would achieve an easy conquest of animal passion must give up all unnecessary things which stimulate it. They must control their palate and cease to read suggestive literature and to enjoy all luxuries. I have not the shadow of a doubt that they will find brahmacharya easy enough after such renunciation.

Some people think that is is not a breach of brahmacharya to cast a lascivious look at one's own or another's wife or to touch her in the same manner; but nothing could be farther from the truth. Such behaviour constitutes a direct breach of brahmacharya in the grosser sense of the term. Men and women who indulge in it deceive themselves and the world, and growing weaker day by day, make themselves easily susceptible to disease. If they stop short of a full satisfaction of desire, the credit for it is due to circumstances and not to themselves. They are bound to fall at the very first opportunity.

In brahmacharya as conceived by the Ashram those who are married behave as if they were not married. Married people do well to renounce gratification outside the marital bond; theirs is a limited brahmacharya. But to look upon them as brahmacharis is to do violence to that glorious term.

Such is the complete Ashram definition of brahmacharya. However there are men as well as women in the Ashram who enjoy considerable freedom in meeting one another. The ideal is that one Ashramite should have the same freedom in meeting another as is enjoyed by a son in meeting his mother or by a brother in meeting his sister. That is to say, the restrictions that are generally imposed for the protection of brahmacharya are lifted in the Satyagraha Ashram, where we believe that brahmacharya which ever stands in need of such adventitious support is no brahmacharya at all. The restrictions may be necessary at first but must wither away in time. Their disappearance does not mean that a brahmachari goes about seeking the company of women, but it does mean that if there is an occasion for him to minister to a woman, he may not refuse such ministry under the impression that it is forbidden to him.

Woman for a brahmachari is not the 'doorkeeper of hell' but is an incarnation of our Mother who is in Heaven. He is no brahmachari at all whose mind is disturbed if he happens to see a woman or if he has to touch her in order to render service. A brahmachari's reaction to a living image and to a bronze statue is one and the same. But a man who is perturbed at the very mention of woman and who is desirous of observing brahmacharya must fly even from a figurine made of metal.

An ashram, where men and women thus live and work together, serve one another and try to observe brahmacharya, is exposed to many perils. Its arrangements involve to a certain extent a deliberate imitation of life in the West. I have grave doubts about my competence to undertake such an experiment. But this applies to all my experiments. It is on account of these doubts that I do not look upon anyone else as my disciple. Those who have joined the Ashram after due deliberation have joined me as co-workers, fully conscious of all the risks involved therein. As for the young boys and girls, I look upon them as my own children, and as such they are automatically drawn within the pale of my experiments. These experiments are undertaken in the name of the God of Truth. He is the Master Potter while we are mere clay in His all-powerful hands.

My experience of the Ashram so far has taught me that there is no ground for disappointment as regards the results of this pursuit of brahmacharya under difficulties. Men as well as women have on the whole derived benefit from it, but the greatest benefit has in my opinion accrued to women. Some of us have fallen, some have risen after sustaining a fall. The possibility of stumbling is implicit in all such experimentation. Where there is cent per cent success, it is not an experiment but a characteristic of omniscience.

I now come to a point of vital importance which I have reserved for treatment towards the end of the discussion. We are told in the Bhagavad Gita (II. 59) that 'when a man starves his senses, the objects of those senses disappear from him, but not the yearning for them; the yearning too departs when he beholds the Supreme,' that is to say, the Truth or Brahman (God). The whole truth of the matter has here been set forth by the experienced Krishna. Fasting and all other forms of discipline are ineffective without the grace of God. What is the vision of the Truth or God? It does not mean seeing something with the physical eye or witnessing a miracle. Seeing God means realization of the fact that God abides in one's heart. The yearning must persist until one has attained this realization, and will vanish upon realization. It is with this end in view that we keep observances, and engage ourselves in spiritual endeavour at the Ashram. Realization is the final fruit of constant effort. The human lover sacrifices his all for his beloved, but this sacrifice is fruitless inasmuch as it is offered for the sake of momentary pleasure. But the quest of Truth calls for even greater concentration than that of the human beloved. There is joy ineffable in store for the aspirant at the end of the quest. Still very few of us are as earnest as even the human lover. Such being the facts of the case, what is the use of complaining that the quest of truth is an uphill task? The human beloved may be at a distance of several thousand miles; God is there in the tabernacle of the human heart, nearer to us than the finger nails are to the fingers. But what is to be done with a man who wanders all over the wide world in search of treasure which as a matter of fact is buried under his very feet?

The brahmacharya observed by a self-restraining person is not something to be despised. It certainly serves to weaken the force of the yearning for the 'flesh-pots of Egypt.' One may keep fasts or adopt various other methods of mortifying the flesh, but the objects of sense must be compelled to disappear. The yearning will get itself in readiness to go as this process is on. Then the seeker will have the beatific vision, and that will be the signal for the yearning to make its final exit. The treasure supposed to be lost will be recovered. He who has not put all his strength into his effort has no right to complain that he has not 'seen' Brahman. Observing brahmacharya is one of the means to the end which is seeing Brahman. Without brahmacharya no one may expect to see Him, and without seeing Him one cannot observe brahmacharya to perfection. The verse therefore does not rule out self-discipline but only indicates its limitations.

All members of the Ashram, young as well as old, married as well as unmarried, try to observe brahmacharya, but only a few will observe it for life. When the young people come to years of discretion, they are told that they are not bound to observe brahmacharya any longer against their will, and that whoever feels that he is unable to put forth the requisite effort has a right to marry. And when he makes the request the Ashram helps him in finding out a suitable partner in life. This position is very well understood, and the results have been uniformly good. The young men have persisted in larger numbers. The girls too have done pretty well. None of them married before she was fifteen, and many married only after they were nineteen.

Those who wish to marry with Ashram assistance must rest

satisfied with the simplest of religious ceremonies. There are no dinners, no guests invited from outside, no beating of drums. Both bride and bridegroom are dressed in hand-spun and hand-woven khadi. There are no ornaments in gold or silver. There is no marriage settlement and no dowry except a few clothes and a spinning-wheel. The function hardly costs even ten rupees, and takes not more than one hour. The bride and bridegroom recite in their own language the mantras (Vedic verses) of the *saptapadi* the purport of which has already been explained to them. On the day fixed for the marriage, the bride and bridegroom keep a fast, water trees, clean the cowshed and the Ashram well and read the Gita before the ceremony. Those who give away the bride also fast until they have made the gift. We now insist that the Ashram will not help to arrange a marriage between members of the same subcaste, and everyone is encouraged to seek his mate outside his own subcaste. The profound truth upon which this observance is based is that God never creates more than that is strictly needed for the moment. Therefore whoever appropriates more than the minimum that is really necessary for him is guilty of theft.

Caste And Untouchability

Speech at Tanjore [16 September 1927]

I had hoped on coming to Tanjore today to discuss the Brahmin-non-Brahmin question here and I had the pleasure of having a brief discussion with some of the friends this afternoon. I am not free nor is it necessary for me to discuss and place before you the contents of our discussion. But I was exceedingly glad of this discussion. I now understand the movement perhaps a little better than I did before the discussion. I have placed my humble view before those friends, of which they are at liberty to make what use they like. But throughout the discussion I saw a note of one thing which seemed to oppress these friends. They seemed to think that I had identified myself with the notion of inherited superiority and inferiority. I assured them that nothing was farther from my thought and told them that I would gladly explain my meaning of *varnashrama* more fully than I have done in order to remove the slightest misunderstanding as to this question of superiority. In my opinion there is no such thing as inherited or acquired superiority. I believe in the rock-bottom doctrine of Advaita and my interpretation of Advaita excludes totally any idea of superiority at any stage whatsoever. I believe implicitly that all men are born equal. All—whether born in India or in England or America or in any circumstances whatsoever—have the same soul as any other. And it is because I believe in this inherent equality of all men that I fight the doctrine of superiority which many of our rulers arrogate to themselves. I have fought this doctrine of superiority in South Africa inch by inch, and it is because of that inherent belief that I delight in calling myself a scavenger, a spinner, a weaver, a farmer and a labourer. And I have fought against the Brahmins themselves wherever they have claimed any superiority for themselves either by reason of their birth or by reason of their subsequently acquired knowledge. I *consider that it is unmanly for any person to claim superiority over a fellow-being.* And there is the amplest warrant for the belief that I am enunciating in the Bhagavad Gita, and I am therefore through and through with every non-Brahmin when he fights this monster of superiority, whether it is claimed by a Brahmin or by anybody else. He who claims superiority at once forfeits his claim to be called a man. That is my opinion.

But in spite of all my beliefs that I have explained to you, I still believe in *varnashrama dharma*. *Varnashrama dharma* to my mind is a law which, however much you and I may deny, cannot be abrogated. To admit the working of that law is to free ourselves for the only pursuit in life for which we are born. *Varnashrama dharma* is humility. Whilst I have said that all men and women are born equal, I do not wish therefore to suggest that qualities are not inherited, but on the contrary I believe that just as everyone inherits a particular form so does he inherit the particular characteristics and qualities of his progenitors, and to make this admission is to conserve one's energy. That frank admission, if we will act up to it, would put a legitimate curb upon our material ambitions, and thereby our energy is set free for extending the field of spiritual research and spiritual evolution. It is this doctrine of *varnashrama dharma* which I have always accepted. You would be entitled to say that this is not how *varnashrama* is understood in these days. I have myself said time without number that *varnashrama* as it is at present understood and practised is a monstrous parody of the original, but in order to demolish this distortion let us not seek to demolish the original. And if you say that the idealistic *varnashrama* which I have placed before you is quite all right you have admitted all that I like you to admit. I would also urge on you to believe with me that no nation, no individual, can possibly live without proper ideals. And if you believe with me in the idealistic *varnashrama* you will also strive with me to reach that ideal so far as may be. As a matter of fact the world has not anywhere been able to fight against this law. What has happened and what must happen in fighting against the law is to hurt ourselves and to engage in a vain effort; and I suggest to you that your fight will be all the more successful if you understand all that our forefathers have bequeathed to us and engage in fighting all the evil excrescences that have grown round this great bequest. And if you accept what I have ventured to suggest to you, you will find that the solution of the Brahmin and non-Brahmin question also, in so far as it is concerned with the religious aspect, becomes very easy. As a non-Brahmin I would seek to purify Brahminism in so far as a non-Brahmin can, but not to destroy it. I would dislodge the Brahmin from the arrogation of superiority or from places of profit. Immediately a Brahmin becomes a profiteering agency he ceases to be a Brahmin. But I would not touch his great learning wherever I see it. And whilst he may not claim superiority by reason of learning I myself must not withhold that meed of homage that learning, wherever it resides, always commands. But I must not go deeper into the subject before a large audience of this kind.

After all I must fall upon one sovereign remedy which I think is applicable for all the ills of life. And that is, in whatever fight we engage, the fight should be clean and straight, there should not be the slightest departure from truth and ahimsa. And if we will keep our carriage safely on these two rails you will find that our fight even though we may commit a thousand blunders will always smell clean and will be easier fought. And even as a train that is derailed comes to a disastrous end, so shall we, if we be derailed off these two rails, come to a disaster. A man who is truthful and does not mean ill even to his adversary will be slow to believe charges even against his foes. He will, however, try to understand the viewpoints of his opponents and will always keep an open mind and seek every opportunity of serving his opponents. I have endeavoured to apply this law in my relations with Englishmen and Europeans in general in South Africa as well as here and not without some success. How much more then should we apply this law in our homes, in our relations, in our domestic affairs, in connection with our own kith and kin?

Excerpt from a Speech at Trivandrum
[17 September 1927]

[...] One question was put to me arising out of this question this morning, and that was what was the bearing of *varnashrama dharma* upon untouchability. That means that I should say a few words about my conception of *varnashrama dharma*. So far as I know anything at all about Hinduism, the meaning of *varna* is incredibly simple. It simply means the following on the part of us all the hereditary and traditional calling of our forefathers, in so far as that traditional calling is not inconsistent with fundamental ethics, and this only for the purpose of earning one's livelihood. I regard this as the law of our being, if we would accept the definition of man given in all religions. Of all the animal creation of God, man is the only animal who has been created in order that he may know his Maker. Man's aim in life is not therefore to add from day to day to his material prospects and to his material possessions but his predominant calling is from day to day to come nearer his own Maker, and from this definition it was that the rishis of old discovered this law of our being. You will realize that if all of us follow this law of *varna* we would limit our material ambition, and our energy would be set free for exploring those vast fields whereby and wherethrough we can know God. You will at once then see that nine-tenths of the activities that are today going on throughout the world and which are engrossing our attention would fall into disuse. You will then be entitled to say that *varna* as we observe it today is a travesty of the *varna* that I have described to you. And so it undoubtedly is, but just as we do not hate truth because untruth parades itself as truth, but we sift untruth from truth and cling to the latter, so also we can destroy the distortion that passes as *varna* and purify the state to which the Hindu society has been reduced today.

Ashrama is a necessary corollary to what I have stated to you, and if *varna* today has become distorted, ashrama has altogether disappeared. *Ashrama* means the four stages in one's life, and I wish the students who have kindly presented their purses to me—the Arts and Science students and the Law College students—were able to assure me that they were living according to the laws of the first

ashrama and that they were brahmacharis in thought, word and deed.
The *brahmacharyashrama* enjoins that only those who live the life
of a brahmachari, at least up to twenty-five years, are entitled to
enter upon the second *ashrama*, i.e., the *grihasthashrama*. And
because the whole conception of Hinduism is to make man better
than he is and draw him nearer to his Maker, the rishis set a limit
even to the *grihasthashrama* stage and imposed on us the obligation
of *vanaprastha* and sannyasa. But today you will vainly search
throughout the length and breadth of India for a true brahmachari,
for a true *grihastha*, not to talk of a *vanaprastha* and a sannyasi.
We may, in our elongated wisdom, laugh at this scheme of life, if
we wish to. But I have no doubt whatsoever that this is the secret
of the great success of Hinduism. The Hindu civilization has
survived the Egyptian, the Assyrian and the Babylonian. The
Christian is but two thousand years old. The Islamic is but of
yesterday. Great as both these they are still in my opinion in the
making. Christian Europe is not at all Christian, but is groping, and
so in my opinion is Islam still groping for its great secret, and there
is today a competition, healthy as also extremely unhealthy and
ugly, between these three great religions. As years go by, the
conviction is daily growing upon me that *varna* is the law of man's
being and therefore as necessary for Christianity and Islam as it has
been necessary for Hinduism and has been its saving. I refuse,
therefore, to believe that *varnashrama* has been the curse of
Hinduism, as it is the fashion nowadays in the South on the part of
some Hindus to say. But that does not mean that you and I may
tolerate for one moment or be gentle towards the hideous travesty of
varnashrama that we see about us today. There is nothing in
common between *varnashrama* and caste. Caste, if you will, is
undoubtedly a drag upon Hindu progress, and untouchability is, as I
have already called it or described it, an excrescence upon
varnashrama. It is a weedy growth fit only to be weeded out, as we
weed out the weeds that we see growing in wheat fields or rice
fields. In this conception of *varna*, there is absolutely no idea of
superiority and inferiority. If I again interpret the Hindu spirit
rightly, all life is absolutely equal and one. It is therefore an
arrogant assumption on the part of the Brahmin when he says: 'I am
superior to the other three *varnas*.' That is not what the Brahmins of
old said. They commanded homage not because they claimed

superiority, but because they claimed the right of service through and through, without the slightest expectation of a reward. The priests, who today arrogate to themselves the function of the Brahmin and distort religion, are no custodians of Hinduism or Brahminism. Consciously or unconsciously they are laying the axe at the root of the very tree on which they are sitting, and when they tell you that Shastras enjoin untouchability and when they talk of pollution distance, I have no hesitation in saying that they are belying their creed and they are misinterpreting the spirit of Hinduism. You will now perhaps understand why it is absolutely necessary for you Hindus who are here and listening to me to energize yourselves and rid yourselves of this curse. You should take pride in leading the way of reform, belonging as you do to an ancient Hindu State. So far as I can read the atmosphere around you here, the moment is certainly propitious for you if you will sincerely and energetically undertake this reform.

Varnadharma and Duty of Labour
[13 February 1930]

Q. Is not the division of labour under *varnashrama dharma* sufficient for the development and welfare of humanity? Which do you value more—*varnadharma* or duty of labour?

A. The purport of this question is that *varnadharma* and duty of labour are incompatible obligations. In fact they are not. Both are concurrent and imperative. *Varnadharma* pertains to the society and duty of labour pertains to the individual. The sages divided society into four sections for its welfare and thereby attempted to root out rivalry which is fatal to society. Therefore they made one *varna* responsible for the growth of knowledge in society, the second responsible for the protection of life and property in society, the third for trade in society, and the fourth for service to society. All the four functions were and are equally essential; therefore there was no reason to consider one high and the other low. Adverting to the equilibrium of scales Maharshi Vyas has indeed said that each individual by performing the duties of his own *varna* acquires fitness for salvation; whereas mutual rivalry and distinctions of high and low bring about ruin. *Varnadharma* does not in the least imply that any *varna* is exempt from manual labour. The duty of labour is incumbent on every person belonging to every *varna*. The Brahmin also had to approach his guru with firewood in his hands, that is to say, he also had to go into the forest and glean firewood and tend cattle. This work he did for himself and his family, not for society. Only children and cripples were exempt from such manual work.

The doctrine of manual labour for a living which Tolstoy has expounded is a corollary of the duty of labour. Tolstoy felt that if everyone had to do manual work then it means that man must earn his bread by manual labour, never by mental work. In *varnadharma* the work of each *varna* was for the welfare of society. Livelihood was not the motive. Gain or no gain, the Kshatriya had to defend the people. The Brahmin had to impart knowledge whether he received alms or not. The Vaishya had to farm and tend cattle whether he earned money or not. But Tolstoy's doctrine that every person must do manual work for a living is perfectly true. We come across distressing disparities in the world today because this universal duty has been neglected or forgotten. Disparities will always be there, but like the several leaves of a tree they will look beautiful and pleasant. In the pure *varnadharma* disparity is no doubt there, and when it was in its pure form, it was pleasing, peaceful and pretty. But when several people use their talents for amassing wealth, distressing disparities are created. Just as, if a teacher (Brahmin), a soldier (Kshatriya), a businessman (Vaishya) and a carpenter (Shudra) follow their professions for amassing wealth, not for the welfare of society, then *varnadharma* is destroyed. Because in matters of duty there can be no room whatever for amassing wealth. In society there is need for teachers, lawyers, doctors, soldiers and others. But when they work for selfish ends they no longer are protectors of society but become parasites on society.

The Gita, III. 10, has expounded a great principle where it says: 'Together with sacrifice did the Lord of beings create, of old, mankind, declaring: By this shall ye increase; may this be to you the giver of all your desires.'

Now we can clearly comprehend the etymology of the word *yajna*. The meaning of *yajna* is manual work and this is the first and foremost act of worship of God. He has given us bodies. Without food the body cannot exist and without labour food cannot be produced. That is why manual labour has become a universal duty. This duty of labour is not Tolstoy's alone but of the whole world. Ignorance of this great *yajna* has led to the worship of Mammon in the world and intelligent people have used their talents to exploit others. It is clear that God is not covetous. Being all-powerful, He creates every day only as much food as is sufficient for every human being or living creature. Not knowing this great truth, several people indulge in all kinds of luxuries and thereby starve many others. If they could give up this greed and work for their living, and eat enough to meet their needs, the poverty that we find today will vanish. I hope the interrogator would now see that *varnadharma* and duty of labour are concurrent, complementary and essential.

Introduction to Varnavyavastha
[23 September 1934]

This booklet is a collection of all my writings on *varnadharma*. Its printing was complete some or perhaps many months ago but it remained unpublished in the absence of an introduction. I had agreed to write the introduction but could not do so till now on account of my *Harijan* tour.

I

I should have loved to go through all my speeches and writings on *varnashrama* during the past fifteen years before writing this introduction, but it was physically impossible. Perhaps it is well that I cannot do so. I have never made a fetish of consistency. I am a votary of truth and I must say what I feel and think at a given moment on the question, without regard to what I may have said before on it. The publisher too wants this. It is for the reader to find out how far my present views coincide with those formerly expressed. Wherever he finds that what I have said or written before runs contrary to what I am writing now, he should without hesitation reject the former. I do not claim omniscience. I claim to be a votary of truth and to follow to the best of my ability what seems to be the truth at a given time. As my vision gets clearer, my views must grow clearer with daily practice. Where I have deliberately altered an opinion, the change should be obvious, only a careful eye would notice a gradual and imperceptible evolution.

Varnashramadharma is a compound word known to all our vernaculars, and, though the word *dharma* (law) is related to both the components, *varna* and *ashrama*, the words are rarely used in separation. Hinduism is but another and imperfect name for *varnashramadharma*. The word 'Hindu' was apparently coined by foreigners and has more geographical than any other content. The *dharma* (religion or law) that Hindus have professed to observe is *varnashramadharma*. To say that the *dharma* of the Hindus is Aryan does not carry us very far. It simply means that the Hindus, or those who lived in the east of the Indus or believed in the Vedic *dharma*, called themselves Aryas and others non-Aryas. To give our *dharma* this kind of ethnic label is in my opinion misleading. It should have a name that declares its predominant characteristic, and everyone will admit that Hinduism is nothing without the law of *varna* and ashrama. It would be impossible to find any *smriti* of which a large part was not devoted to *varnashramadharma*. This law of *varna* and ashrama is to be traced to our most ancient scriptures—the Vedas, and so no one who calls himself a Hindu may ignore it. It is his duty to study it in all its bearings, and to reject it if it is an excrescence, and to foster it and restore it to its pristine purity, if it represents a universal law.

So far as the law of ashrama is concerned, it is extinct, alike in profession and observance. Hinduism lays down four ashramas or stages—the life of a brahmachari (continent student), the life of a *grihastha* (householder), the life of a *vanaprastha* (who has retired) and the life of a sannyasi (renunciator)—through which every Hindu has to pass to fulfil his purpose in life. But the first and the third are practically non-existent today, the fourth may be said to be observed in name to a small extent. The second is professed to be observed by all today, but it is observed in name, not in spirit. *Grihasthas* or householders of a kind we all are, inasmuch as we eat and drink and propagate our kind, like all created beings. But in doing so, we fulfil the law of the flesh and not of the spirit. Only those married couples who fulfil the law of the spirit can be said to observe the law of *grihasthashrama*. Those who live the mere animal life do not observe the law. The life of householders of today is one of indulgence. And as the four stages represent a ladder of growth and are interdependent, one cannot leap to the stage of a *vanaprastha* or a sannyasi, unless he or she fulfilled the law of the first two ashramas—brahmacharya and *grihastha*. The law of the ashrama, therefore, is a dead letter today. It can be revived only if the law of *varna*, with which it is intimately interlinked, is revived.

That brings us to a consideration of the law of *varna*. *Varna* can certainly be said to exist, though in a distorted form. There are four *varnas*, but the distortion that passes as *varna* today is divided into countless castes. All the four *varnas* are divided into numerous castes and sub-castes, but whilst those who belong to the first three are not ashamed to declare that they belong to them, those who belong to the fourth, viz., Shudra, prefer to declare the sub-caste as their label rather than their *varna*, which they regard as a badge of humiliation.

But labels never reveal a man's character, nor does the fact that a man clings to a label show that he deserves it. A black man will not be red, no matter how repeatedly he calls himself red. In the same way, one does not become a Brahmin by calling oneself a Brahmin. Not until a man reveals in his life the attributes of a Brahmin can he deserve that name. Considered in this light, *varna* may be said to be extinct. If we may, indeed, claim a label, we can call ourselves Shudras, though really we are not entitled to that name either, inasmuch as we do not observe the law of that *varna*. This law is the law of one's being, which one has to fulfil. The fulfilment should be spontaneous and no matter of honour or shame. How many are there who are fulfilling the law as law, i.e., spontaneously? We fulfil it because we cannot help it, we are all serfs, whether we will it or not. Let no one contend that *varna* exists today, because all the functions of the different *varnas* are being performed by someone or the other and somehow or the other. *Varna* is intimately, if not indissolubly, connected with birth, and the observance of the law of *varna* means the following on the part of us all the hereditary and traditional calling of our forefathers in a spirit of duty. Those who thus fulfil the law of their *varna* can be counted on one's fingers' ends. This performance of one's hereditary function is done as a matter of duty, though it naturally carries with it the earning of one's livelihood. Thus, the function of a Brahmin is to study and to teach the science of Brahman (or spiritual truth). He performs the function, as he cannot do otherwise, as it is the law of his being. That secures him his livelihood, but he will take it as a gift from God. A Kshatriya will perform the function of protecting the people in the same spirit, accepting for his livelihood whatever the people can afford to give him. A Vaishya will pursue wealth-producing occupations for the welfare of the community, keeping for himself enough for his own maintenance and rendering the balance to the community in one shape or another. A Shudra will perform physical labour in the same spirit of service.

Varna is determined by birth, but can be retained only by observing its obligations. One born of Brahmin parents will be called a Brahmin, but if his life fails to reveal the attributes of a Brahmin when he comes of age, he cannot be called a Brahmin. He will have fallen from Brahminhood. On the other hand, one who is born not a Brahmin will be regarded as a Brahmin, though he will himself disclaim the label.

Varna thus conceived is no man-made institution by the law of life universally governing the human family. Fulfilment of the law would make life livable, would spread peace and content, end all clashes and conflicts, put an end to starvation and pauperization, solve the problem of population and even end disease and suffering.

But if *varna* reveals the law of one's being and thus the duty one has to perform, it confers no right, and the idea of superiority or inferiority is wholly repugnant to it. All *varnas* are equal, for the community depends no less on one than on another. Today *varna* means gradations of high and low. It is a hideous travesty of the original. The law of *varna* was discovered by our ancestors by stern austerities. They sought to live up to the law to the best of their capacity. We have distorted it today and have made ourselves the laughing-stock of the world. No wonder that we have today amongst the Hindus a section which is bending its energies to a destruction of the institution which in their opinion spells the ruin of the Hindus. And certainly one need have no mercy for the hideous distortion, which means nothing but destruction of Hinduism.

II

I do not for a moment suggest that there should be no restrictions about food and drink or about marital relations. I do not myself regard it a duty to eat whatever is offered and in whatever company I should chance to be, and I regard it as nothing short of self-indulgence to marry according to one's fancy. Strict restraint is the law of life and must, therefore, govern these relations no less than others. I hold that there are rules about diet. Man is not an omnivorous animal, nor may he pick up his mate wherever he likes. But restrictions on marital or social relations have nothing to do with *varnadharma,* which is a different thing altogether. I can conceive blameless marital relations between different *varnas*, and people of different *varnas* seated together to eat food permissible to all. There is evidence enough to show that in ancient times there were no watertight compartments between *varnas*, so far as marital and social relations went, and I have no doubt that, in making *varna* a mere matter of restrictions about food and drink and marriage, we have done Hinduism grave harm.

Though the law of *varna* is a special discovery of some Hindu seer, it has universal application. Every religion has some distinguishing characteristic, but if it expresses a principle or law, it ought to have universal application. That is how I look at the law of *varna*. The world may ignore it today but it will have to accept it in the time to come.

I would define the law briefly thus: the law of *varna* means that everyone shall follow as a matter of *dharma*—duty—the hereditary calling of his forefathers, in so far as it is not inconsistent with fundamental ethics. He will earn his livelihood by following that calling. He may not hoard riches, but devote the balance for the good of the people.

The four *varnas* have been compared in the Vedas to the four members of the body, and no simile could be happier. If they are members of one body, how can one be superior or inferior to another? If the members of the body had the power of expression and each of them were to say that it was higher and better than the rest, the body would go to pieces. Even so our body politic, the body of humanity, would go to pieces, if it were to perpetuate the canker of superiority or inferiority. It is this canker that is at the root of the various ills of our time, especially class-wars and civil strife. It should not be difficult for even the meanest understanding to see that these wars and strife could not be ended except by the observance of the law of *varna*. For it ordains that everyone shall fulfil the law of one's being by doing in a spirit of duty and service that to which one is born. Earning of livelihood is the necessary result. But the law has to be fulfilled for its own sake. Its due observance by a large part of mankind will end the conflicting inequalities and give place to an equality in diversity. All callings would be equally reputable—whether that of the minister or of the lawyer, of the doctor or the leather-worker, of the carpenter or the scavenger, of the soldier or the trader, of the farmer or the spiritual teacher. In this ideal state of things, there would be no room for the monstrous anomaly of the three *varnas* lording it over the Shudra, or of the Kshatriya and the Vaishya enjoying themselves in their palaces and the Brahmin contenting himself with a cottage and the Shudra toiling for the rest and living in a hovel. This chaotic state of things indicates that the law of *varna* has become a dead letter.

When, if ever, the ideal state of things, as indicated above, had been reached in India, I do not know. But I do hold that it is the only ideal state that is easy enough to approach and that it is not only for the Hindus but for the whole of humanity.

Under such dispensation, all property will be held by its respective holders in trust for the community. No one will claim it as his own. The king will hold his palace in trust for his people and will collect the taxes only to be used for the benefit of the people. He has the right to have no more than is enough to keep him; the rest belongs to, and shall be spent only for, the people. Indeed, he will, by virtue of his resourcefulness as a ruler, add to what he collects from the people and return it to them manifold. The Vaishya likewise is such a trustee. The Shudra is made so. Indeed, if one may have preference, the Shudra, who performs body-labour in a spirit of service and duty, who has nothing to call his own and who has no desire for ownership, is worthy of the world's homage; he is the lord of all because he is the greatest servant. The dutiful Shudra will, of course, repudiate any such claim, but the gods will shower their choicest blessings on him. One may not say this of the proletariat of the present day. They certainly own nothing, but I expect they covet ownership. The calling of labour and service is no pleasant duty to them. It is a painful task, for it does not satisfy even the cravings of the flesh. My praise is for the ideal labourer. It is the estate I have longed to attain.

But this duty of labour cannot be imposed on anybody. In fact, the panegyric may be uttered only by those of the three *varnas* who fulfil the law themselves, viz., the law of regarding and behaving themselves as the servants of the community and holding all the property in trust for it. The three *varnas* exist today only in name, they are supposed to invest one with a higher status than that of the Shudras and have ceased to imply any duty to be performed. There is nothing, therefore, to be surprised at, nor to be sorry for, when in such a state of things the Shudras should be jealous of the other's possessions and their estate and seek to share them. When the law of *varna* was discovered, there could be no compulsion from without. The world can only be sustained by a willing and dutiful observance of it.

In an age where competition is held to be the law of life, and possession in the largest measure of the world's goods the *summum bonum*, and when everyone counts oneself free to follow any calling one likes, this attempt to hold up *varna* as the law of life may well be regarded as an idle dream, and an attempt to revive it as childish folly. Be that as it may, it is my firm conviction that it is true socialism. In the language of the Gita, it is equality of the spirit, without which no other equality is possible. The performance of it, no matter how slight, bodes well both for him who performs it and for the rest of mankind.

I may add that, though the *varnas* are to be four, the numbers is not, in my opinion, unalterable. In the future reconstruction, the number may be more or even less than four. What is essential is that one must seek one's livelihood, and no more, from following the vocation to which one is born.

Caste Has to Go [16 November 1935]

My own position has been often stated in these columns. It may be summed up as follows:

- I believe in *varnashrama* of the Vedas which in my opinion is based on absolute equality of status, notwithstanding passages to the contrary in the *smritis* and elsewhere.

- Every word of the printed works passing muster as 'Shastras' is not, in my opinion, a revelation.

- The interpretation of accepted texts has undergone evolution, and is capable of indefinite evolution, even as the human intellect and heart are.

- Nothing in the Shastras which is manifestly contrary to universal truths and morals can stand.

- Nothing in the Shastras which is capable of being reasoned can stand if it is in conflict with reason.

- *Varnashrama* of the Shastras is today non-existent in practice.

- The present caste system is the very antithesis of *varnashrama*. The sooner public opinion abolishes it the better.

- In *varnashrama* there was and should be no prohibition of intermarriage or interdining. Prohibition there is of change of one's hereditary occupation for purposes of gain. The existing practice is, therefore, doubly wrong in that it has set up cruel restrictions about interdining and intermarriage and tolerates anarchy about choice of occupation.

- Though there is in *varnashrama* no prohibition against intermarriage and interdining, there can be no compulsion. It must be left to the unfettered choice of the individual as to where he or she will marry or dine. If the law of *varnashrama* was observed there would naturally be a tendency, so far as marriage is concerned, for people to restrict the marital relations to their own *varna*.

- As I have repeatedly said there is no such thing as untouchability by birth in the Shastras. I hold the present practice to be a sin and the greatest blot on Hinduism. I feel more than ever that if untouchability lives, Hinduism dies.

- The most effective, quickest and the most unobtrusive way to destroy caste is for reformers to begin the practice with themselves and where necessary take the consequences of social boycott. The reform will not come by reviling the orthodox. The change will be gradual and imperceptible. The so-called higher classes will have to descend from their pedestal before they can make any impression upon the so-called lower classes. Day-to-day experience of village work shows how difficult the task is of bridging the gulf that exists between the city-dwellers and the villagers, the higher classes and the lower classes. The two are not synonymous terms. For the class distinction exists both in the cities and the villages.

Caste and Varna [28 November 1935]

A gentleman writes that I advocate the abolition of castes and maintain that the *varnas* are and ought to be enduring. He wants me to explain this with illustrations.

Castes are numerous. They are man-made. They undergo constant change. The older ones die and new ones spring up. Castes based on occupations are to be found all over the world. It is only in India that there are restrictions, as regards intermarriage and inter-dining, which defy reason. This is very harmful. It stands in the way of the community's progress. It has nothing to do with religion.

Varnas are just four and not numerous. They have been sanctioned by the Shastras. Whether or not people are conscious of them, they do exist all over the world as we see. There are everywhere these four classes: one to impart knowledge of god for the welfare of the world, another to protect the people against manifold dangers, a third one to carry on the work of farming, etc., to sustain the community and one class to work for these three classes. There is no feeling of high and low in this division. But since this is not understood as a great law of nature, there has been confusion in it, that is, these four functions are no more confined to the respective *varnas*. Instead men have been taking up any occupation they choose with a view to achieving their selfish ends. At one time in India people used to consciously follow this law and thus lived in peace. One accepted the calling of one's own *varna* and was satisfied in its pursuit for general welfare. There was no unhealthy competition among people to jump from one *varna* to another for the sake of money or fame. At present this significance of the *varna* system seems to have disappeared even in India. Destructive competition is on the increase, everyone takes liberty of following any profession and the meaning of *varna* has been restricted to unnatural and meaningless restrictions on intermarriage and interdining. And that is why the country has stopped progressing. Hinduism will once again shine forth if such senseless restrictions are abolished, the pristine *varna* system is resurrected and the distinctions of high and low are banished. This would be to the good of India as well as the whole world.

Answers to Questions at Gandhi Sevak Sangh
[6 May 1939]

Today castes have become mongrelized. *Varnas* have disappeared. In such a situation how should those believing in the *varnas* proceed? This is what this question implies. Today there is only one *varna*. Call it the Shudra *varna*. We cannot say *Atishudra* since we do not believe in untouchability. We do not believe in a fifth *varna*. Hence only the fourth *varna*, that is, Shudra, is left. Let all of us consider that we are Shudras. Then there will be no feeling of high or low left. Envy and discrimination will automatically disappear. This is the only thing that would be fitting in the prevailing atmosphere. Brahmins are a rarity these days. Who possesses learning which is unique and will make for the welfare of the world? And where is the man who will expect nothing for that learning? As for the Kshatriyas there are none left in India. If there had been any, the country would not have lost its freedom. India would not remain in her present condition if great learning and great valour could be found here. So far as the Vaishyas are concerned, *Vaishyadharma* is a *varnadharma*. It is not merely an occupation to earn money. It is a duty, not a right. They should use their wealth for the benefit of society. Many of the occupations which the Banias follow are immoral. Earning too much money is also immoral. Many of these occupations cannot be included in *varnadharma*. This means that today even the Vaishyas are not there. Only some money-grubbing professional people are left. Three *varnas* have thus passed out.

That leaves us the Shudras. They possess no learning. They consider themselves slaves. They do not serve with knowledge. That is to say, there are not really even Shudras left in India. In other words, we cannot say that even one of the four *varnas* is still extant. Even so, since we believe in *varnadharma*, let us accept the *dharma* of service. Let us adopt *Shudradharma*. This does not mean that we should discard learning. We should acquire as much learning as we could. We should acquire as much valour, that is, fearlessness as we can. We must develop commerce and industries to the greatest possible extent. If we do all these things out of a sense of service and devotion, true Brahmins, Kshatriyas and

Vaishyas may be born amongst us. Then there would no feeling of high or low among them. If we do something like this something may happen in future. When such *varnadharma* prevails, all the bickerings that go on in the name of Communism, Socialism, Congressism, Gandhism, Casteism, etc., would be over.

Removal of Untouchability[1]

The Ashram was founded in order to serve and if necessary to die in the service of Truth. If therefore while holding that untouchability is a sinful thing, it did not do something positive in order to end it, it could hardly deserve the name of Satyagraha (adherence to truth) Ashram. Even in South Africa we recognized untouchability as a sin. When the Ashram therefore was founded in India, removal of untouchability easily became one of its major activities.

Within a month of the foundation of the Ashram, Dudabhai applied for admission along with his family. I had no idea that the testing time of the Ashram would arrive so soon. Dudabhai's application was supported by Shri Amritlal Thakkar. I felt bound to admit a family which was recommended by him.

The arrival of Dudabhai was the signal for a storm breaking upon the placid atmosphere of the Ashram. Kasturba, Maganlal Gandhi and Mrs Maganlal had each of them some scruples in living with so-called untouchables. Things came to such a pass that Kasturba should either observe Ashram rules or else leave the Ashram. But the argument that a woman in following in her husband's footsteps incurs no sin appealed to her and she quieted down. I do not hold that a wife is bound to follow her husband in what she considers sinful. But I welcomed my wife's attitude in the present case, because I looked upon the removal of untouchability as a meritorious thing. No one could uphold untouchability and still live in the Ashram. It would have been extremely painful to me if my wife had had to leave the Ashram, seeing that she had been my companion all these days at the cost of great suffering. It was hard to be separated from her, but one must put up with every hardship that comes his way in the discharge of his duty. I had therefore no hesitation in accepting my wife's renunciation of untouchability not as an independent person but only as a faithful wife[...]

The Ashram passed the test as regards its opposition to untouchability. 'Untouchable' families come to the Ashram freely and live in it. Dudabhai's daughter Lakshmi has become a full member of the family.

Three callings followed by the so-called untouchables are practised in the Ashram, and improved methods are devised in each.

Everyone in the Ashram has in turn to do sanitary service, which is looked upon not as a special calling but a universal duty. No outside labour is engaged for this work, which is carried on lines suggested by Dr Poore. Night-soil is buried in shallow trenches and is thus converted into manure in only a few days. Dr Poore says that the soil is living up to a depth of twelve inches. Millions of bacteria are there to clean up dirt. Sunlight and air penetrate the ground to that depth. Therefore night-soil buried in the upper layer readily combines with the earth.

Closets are so constructed that they are free from smell and there is no difficulty in cleaning them. Everyone who visits them covers the night-soil with plenty of dry earth, so that the top is always dry.

Then again we have handloom weaving. Coarse khadi was manufactured in Gujarat by Harijan weavers only. The industry was almost on the verge of destruction, and many weavers were compelled to take up scavenging for a living. But now there has been a revival of this handicraft.

Thirdly we have tanning. We shall deal with it in the chapter on the Ashram dairy.

The Ashram does not believe in subcastes. There are no restrictions on interdining and all Ashramites sit to dinner in the same line. But no propaganda in favour of interdining is carried on outside the Ashram, as it is unnecessary for the removal of untouchability, which implies the lifting of bans imposed on Harijans in public institutions and discarding the superstition that a man is polluted by the touch of certain persons by reason of their birth in a particular caste. This disability can also be removed by legislation. Interdining and intermarriage are reforms of a different type which cannot be promoted by legislation or social pressure. The Ashramites therefore feel themselves free to take permitted food with everyone else but do not carry on any such propaganda.

Schools are established and wells sunk for Harijans through the Ashram which chiefly finds the finance for such activities. The real anti-untouchability work carried on in the Ashram is the reformed conduct of the Ashramites. There is no room in the Ashram for any ideas of high and low.

However the Ashram believes that *varnas* and ashramas are

essential elements of Hinduism. Only it puts a different interpretation on these time-honoured terms. Four *varnas* and four ashramas are an arrangement not peculiar to Hinduism but capable of world-wide application, and a universal rule, the breach of which has involved humanity in numerous disasters. The four ashramas are brahmacharya, *grihastha, vanaprastha* and sannyasa. Brahmacharya is the stage during which men as well as women prosecute their studies, and should not only observe brahmacharya but should also be free from any other burden except that of studies. This lasts till at least the twenty-fifth year, when the student becomes a householder if he wishes. Almost all the students thus become householders. But this stage should close at the age of fifty. During that period the householder enjoys the pleasures of life, makes money, practises a profession and rears a family. From fifty to seventy-five wife and husband should live apart and wholly devote themselves to the service of the people. They must leave their families and try to look upon the world as a big family. During the last twenty-five years they should become sannyasis, live apart, set to the people an example of ideal religious life and maintain themselves with whatever the people choose to give them. It is clear that society as a whole would be elevated if many carried out this scheme in their lives.

So far as I am aware, the ashrama arrangement is unknown outside India, but even in India it has practically disappeared at present. There is no such thing now as brahmacharya, which is intended to be the foundation of life. For the rest we have sannyasis, most of them such only in name, with nothing of sannyasa about them except the orange robe. Many of them are ignorant, and some who have acquired learning are not knowers of Brahman but fanatics. There are some honourable exceptions but even these well-conducted monks lack the lustre we love to associate with sannyasa. It is possible that some real sannyasis lead a solitary life. But it is obvious that sannyasa as a stage in life has fallen into desuetude. A society which is served by able sannyasis would not be poor in spirit, unprovided even with the necessaries of life, and politically dependent, as Hindu society is at present. If sannyasa were with us a living thing, it would exert a powerful influence on neighbouring faiths, for the sannyasi is a servant not only of Hinduism, but of all the faiths of mankind.

But we can never hope to see such sannyasis unless brahmacharya is observed in the country. As for *vanaprastha*, there is no trace of it. The last stage we have to consider is that of the householder. But our householders are given to unregulated self-indulgence. Householders in the absence of the three other ashramas live like brutes. Self-restraint is the one thing which differentiates man from beast, but it is practised no longer.

The Ashram is engaged in the great endeavour to resuscitate the four ashramas. It is like an ant trying to lift a bag of sugar. This effort though apparently ridiculous is part of the Ashram's quest of truth. All the inmates of the Ashram therefore observe brahmacharya. Permanent members must observe it for life. All the inmates are not members in this sense. Only a few are members, the rest are students. If this effort is crowned with success, we may hope to see a revival of the ashrama scheme of life. The sixteen years during which the Ashram has functioned are not a sufficiently long period for the assessment of results. I have no idea of the time when such assessment will be possible. I can only say that there is nothing like dissatisfaction with the progress achieved up to date.

If the ashrama scheme has broken down, the plight of the *varnas* is equally bad. At first there were four *varnas*; but now there are innumerable sections or only one. If we take it that there are as many *varnas* as there are castes and subcastes, their name is Legion; on the other hand if, as I think, *varnas* have nothing to do with caste, there is only a single *varna* left and that is the Shudra. We are here not finding fault with anybody but only stating the facts of the case. Shudras are those who serve and are dependent upon others. India is a dependency; therefore every Indian is a Shudra. The cultivator does not own his land, the merchant his merchandize. There is hardly a Kshatriya or a Brahmin who possesses the virtues which the Shastras attribute to his *varna*.

My impression is that there was no idea of high and low when the *varna* system was discovered. No one is high and no one is low in this world; therefore he who thinks he belongs to a high class is never high-class, and he who believes himself to be low is merely the victim of ignorance. He has been taught by his masters that he is low. If a Brahmin has knowledge, those who are without it will respect him as a matter of course. But if he is puffed up by the respect thus shown to him and imagines himself to belong to a high class, he directly ceases to be a Brahmin. Virtue will always command respect, but when the man of virtue thinks much of himself, his virtue ceases to have any significance for the world. Talents of all kinds are a trust and must be utilized for the benefit of society. The individual has no right to live unto himself. Indeed it is impossible to live unto oneself. We fully live unto ourselves when we live unto society.

No matter what was the position in ancient times, no one can nowadays go through life claiming to belong to a high class. Society will not willingly admit any such claim to superiority, but only under duress. The world is now wide awake. This awakening has perhaps given rise to some licence, but even so public opinion is not prepared to accept any distinctions of high and low, which are being attacked on all sides. There is an ever-increasing realization that all are equal as human souls. The fact that we are all the creatures of one God rules out all ideas of high and low. When we say that no one is high-born or low-born, it does not mean that all have or ought to have equal talents. All have not equal talents, equal property or equal opportunities. Still all are equal like brothers and sisters of different dispositions, abilities and ages.

If therefore the *varna* system is a spiritual arrangement, there cannot be any place in it for high and low.

Thus there are four *varnas* all equal in status, and they are determined by birth. They can be changed by a person choosing another profession, but if *varnas* are not as a rule determined by birth, they tend to lose all meaning.

The *varna* system is ethical as well as economic. It recognizes the influence of previous lives and of heredity. All are not born with equal powers and similar tendencies. Neither the parents nor the State can measure the intelligence of each child. But there would be no difficulty if each child is prepared for the profession indicated by heredity, environment and the influence of former lives; no time would be lost in fruitless experimentation, there would be no soul-killing competition, a spirit of contentment would pervade society and there would be no struggle for existence.

The *varna* system implies the obliteration of all distinctions of high and low. If the carpenter is held to be superior to the shoemaker and the pleader or doctor is superior to both of them, no one would willingly become a shoemaker or carpenter and all would try to become pleaders or doctors. They would be entitled to do so and to be praised for doing so. That is to say, the *varna* system would be looked upon as an evil and abolished as such.

But when it is suggested that everyone should practise his father's profession, the suggestion is coupled with the condition that the practitioner of every profession will earn only a living wage and no more. If the carpenter earns more than a shoemaker and the pleader or doctor more than both, everyone would become a lawyer or doctor. Such is the case at present, with the result that hatred has increased and there are more lawyers and doctors than are necessary. It may be that society needs the lawyer or doctor even as it needs the shoemaker and the carpenter. These four professions are here taken only as illustrations and for comparison. It would be irrelevant to stop to consider whether society has particular need or no need at all for this, that or the other profession.

This principle then is an integral part of the *varna* system, that learning is not a trade and may not be used in order to amass riches. Therefore in so far as his ministrations may be necessary, the lawyer or doctor ought by practising his profession to earn only a living wage. And such was actually the case formerly. The village vaidya (physician) did not earn more than the carpenter but only a living wage. In short the emoluments of all crafts and professions should be equal and amount to a living wage. The number of *varnas* has no sanctity about it; their value is due to the fact that they define the duties of man. *Varnas* may be supposed to be one or more just as we like. The scriptures enumerate four of them. But when once we have assigned equal status to all, it makes little difference whether we think that there are four of them or that there is only one.

Such is the *varna* system which the Ashram is trying to resuscitate. It is like Dame Partington with her mop, trying to push back the Atlantic Ocean. I have already mentioned its two fundamental principles, namely, that there are no high and low, and everyone is entitled to a living wage, the living wage being the same for all. In so far as these principles win acceptance, they will render a positive service to society.

It may be objected that if such a plan is accepted there will be no incentive for the acquisition of knowledge. But the object with which knowledge is acquired nowadays tends to corrupt it, and therefore the absence of an incentive will be entirely beneficial. Knowledge truly so called is intended for one's salvation, that is to say, service of mankind. Whoever has a desire to render service will certainly try to equip himself with the requisite knowledge, and his knowledge will be an ornament to himself as well as to society. Again when the temptation to amass riches is removed, there will be a change for the better in the curriculum of studies as well as in the methods of education. There is much misuse of knowledge at present. This misuse will be reduced to the minimum in the 'new order'.

Even then there will be scope for competition in trying to be good and helpful. And there will be no discontent or disorder as all will receive a living wage.

Varna is wrongly understood today. That wrong understanding must make way for the principles outlined above. Untouchability must go, and *varnas* should have nothing to do with intermarriage. A person will dine with and marry whom he likes. But as a rule he will marry someone who belongs to the same *varna* as himself. But if he marries a person belonging to another *varna*, his act will not count as a sin. A person will be boycotted not by the *varna* but by society at large when his conduct justifies such a measure. Society will be better constituted than it is at present, and the impurity and hypocrisy which infest it now will be dislodged.

Socialism And Trusteeship

My Path [11 December 1924]

[...] My path is clear. Any attempt to use me for violent purposes is bound to fail. I have no secret methods. I know no diplomacy save that of truth. I have no weapon but non-violence. I may be unconsciously led astray for a while but not for all time. I have therefore well-defined limitations, within which alone I may be used. Attempts have been made before now to use me unlawfully more than once. They have failed each time so far as I am aware.

I am yet ignorant of what exactly Bolshevism is. I have not been able to study it. I do not know whether it is for the good of Russia in the long run. But I do know that in so far as it is based on violence and denial of God, it repels me. I do not believe in short-violent-cuts to success. Those Bolshevik friends who are bestowing their attention on me should realize that however much I may sympathize with and admire worthy motives, I am an uncompromising opponent of violent methods even to serve the noblest of causes. There is, therefore, really no meeting ground between the school of violence and myself. But my creed of non-violence not only does not preclude me but compels me even to associate with anarchists and all those who believe in violence. But that association is always with the sole object of weaning them from what appears to me to be their error. For experience convinces me that permanent good can never be the outcome of untruth and violence. Even if my belief is a fond delusion, it will be admitted that it is a fascinating delusion.

Answers to Zamindars [25 July 1934]

Q. The Karachi Congress passed a resolution laying down the fundamental rights of the people and, since it recognized private property, nationalist zamindars have supported the Congress. But the new Socialist Party in the Congress threatens the extinction of private property. How would it affect the Congress policy? Do you not think that this will precipitate class war? Will you prevent it?

A. The Karachi resolution can be altered only by an open session of the next Congress, but let me assure you· that I shall be no party to dispossessing the propertied classes of their private property without just cause. My object is to reach your hearts and convert you so that you may hold all your private property in trust for your tenants and use it primarily for their welfare.

I am aware of the fact that within the ranks of the Congress a new party called the Socialist Party is coming into being and I cannot say what would happen if that party succeeds in carrying the Congress with it. But I am quite clear that if a strictly honest and unchallengeable referendum of our millions were to be taken, they would not vote for wholesale expropriation of the propertied classes. I am working for the co-operation and co-ordination of capital and labour and of landlords and tenants. It is open to you to join the Congress as much as it is open to the poorest by paying the fee of four annas and subscribing to the Congress creed.

But I must utter a note of warning. I have always told the mill-owners that they are not exclusive owners of the mills. Workmen are equal sharers in the ownership. In the same way, I would tell you that the ownership of your land belongs as much to the *ryots* as to you and you may not squander your gains in luxurious or extravagant living, but must use them for the well-being of the *ryots*. Once you make your *ryots* experience a sense of kinship with you and a sense of security that their interests as members of the family will never suffer at your hands, you may be sure that there cannot be a class war between you and them.

Class war is foreign to the essential genius of India which is capable of evolving a form of communism broad-based on the fundamental rights of all and equal justice to all. The Ramarajya of my dream ensures the rights alike of prince and pauper.

You may be sure that I shall throw the whole weight of my influence in preventing class war. I do not know what I am going to do after the termination of my self-imposed restriction on 3 August, but I shall try my best to avoid going back to prison. But it is difficult to predict anything with certainty in a situation of which I am unaware today. But supposing that there is an attempt unjustly to deprive you of your property, you will find me fighting on your side.

Q. We propose to support Congress candidates in the next Assembly elections. But we have our misgivings about the policy they will adopt in the Assembly. Could you persuade the Parliamentary Board to dispel our fears?

A. I invite you to discuss this thing with the members of the Parliamentary Board. I know, however, that no member will talk of expropriation or extinction of private property. They will certainly insist on a radical reform in your relations with the *ryots* but that should be no new thing to you. Even Sir Malcolm Hailey and Lord Irwin appealed to you to realize and live up to the spirit of the times. If you will only do this, you may be sure that we shall be able to evolve an indigenous socialism of the purest type.

Socialism and communism of the West are based on certain conceptions which are fundamentally different from ours. One such conception is their belief in the essential selfishness of human nature. I do not subscribe to it, for I know that the essential difference between man and brute is that the former can respond to the call of spirit in him and can rise superior to the passions that he owns in common with the brute and therefore superior to selfishness and violence which belong to brute nature and not to the immortal spirit of man.

That is the fundamental conception of Hinduism, which has years of penance and austerity at the back of the discovery of their truth. That is why whilst we had had saints who have burnt out their bodies and laid down their lives in order to explore the secrets of the soul, we have none as in the West who have laid down their lives in exploring the remotest or highest regions of earth. Our socialism or communism should therefore be based on non-violence and on the harmonious co-operation of labour and capital and the landlord and the tenant.

There is nothing in the Congress creed or policy that need frighten you. All your fears and misgivings, permit me to tell you, are those of a guilty conscience. Wipe out the injustice that you may have been consciously or unconsciously guilty of and shed all fear of the Congress and Congressmen.

Once you turn a new leaf in the relations between zamindars and *ryots*, you will find us on your side jealously guarding your private rights and property. When I say 'us', I have Pandit Jawaharlal also in mind, for I am sure that on this essential principle of non-violence there is no difference between us. He does indeed talk of nationalization of property, but it need not frighten you.

The nation cannot own property except by vesting it in individuals. It simply ensures its just and equitable use and prevents all possible misuses, and I do not think you can have any possible objection to holding your property for the benefit of the *ryots*. The *ryots* have themselves no greater ambition than to live in peace and freedom and they will never grudge you your possession of property provided you use it for them.

Extract from an Interview with Nirmal Kumar Bose [9/10 November 1934]

Q. Is love or non-violence compatible with possession or exploitation in any shape or form? If possession and non-violence cannot go together, then do you advocate the maintenance of private ownership of land or factories as an unavoidable evil which will continue so long as individuals are not ripe or educated enough to do without it? If it be such a step, would it not be better to own all the land through the State and place the State under the control of the masses?

A. Love and exclusive possession can never go together. Theoretically, when there is perfect love, there must be perfect non-possession. The body is our last possession. So a man can only exercise perfect love and be completely dispossessed if he is prepared to embrace death and renounce his body for the sake of human service.

But that is true in theory only. In actual life, we can hardly exercise perfect love, for the body as a possession will always remain with us. Man will ever remain imperfect, and it will always be his part to try to be perfect. So that perfection in love or non-possession will remain an unattainable ideal, as long as we are alive, but towards which we must ceaselessly strive.

Those who own money now are asked to behave like trustees holding their riches on behalf of the poor. You may say that trusteeship is a legal fiction. But if people meditate over it constantly and try to act up to it, then life on earth would be governed far more by love than it is at present. Absolute trusteeship is an abstraction like Euclid's definition of a point, and is equally unattainable. But if we strive for it, we shall be able to go further in realizing a state of equality on earth than by any other method.

Q. If you say that private possession is incompatible with non-violence, why do you put up with it?

A. That is a concession one has to make to those who earn money but who would not voluntarily use their earnings for the benefit of mankind.

Q. Why then not have State-ownership in place of private property and thus minimize violence?

A. It is better than private ownership. But that too is objectionable on the ground of violence. It is my firm conviction that if the State suppressed capitalism by violence, it will be caught in the coils of violence itself, and will fail to develop non-violence at any time. The State represents violence in a concentrated and organized form. The individual has a soul, but as the State is a soulless machine, it can never be weaned from violence to which it owes its very existence. Hence I prefer the doctrine of trusteeship.

Q. Let us come to a specific instance. Supposing an artist leaves certain pictures to a son who does not appreciate their value for the nation and sells them or wastes them, so that the nation stands to lose something precious through one person's folly. If you are assured that the son would never be a trustee in the sense in which you would like him to be, do you not think the State would be justified in taking away those things from him with the minimum use of violence?

A. Yes, the State will, as a matter of fact, take away those things, and I believe it will be justified if it uses the minimum of violence. But the fear is always there that the State may use too much violence against those who differ from it. I would be very happy indeed if the people concerned behaved as trustees; but if they fail, I believe we shall have to deprive them of their possessions through the State with the minimum exercise of violence. That is why I said at the Round Table Conference that every vested interest must be subjected to scrutiny, and confiscation ordered where necessary with or without compensation as the case demanded.

What I would personally prefer would be not a centralization of power in the hands of the State, but an extension of the sense of trusteeship; as in my opinion the violence of private ownership is less injurious than the violence of the State. However, if it is unavoidable, I would support a minimum of State-ownership.

Q. Then, sir, shall we take it that the fundamental difference between you and the Socialists is that you believe that men live more by self-direction or will than by habit, and they believe that men live more by habit than by will; that being the reason why do you strive for self-correction while they try to build up a system under which men will find it impossible to exercise their desire for exploiting others?

A. While admitting that man actually lives by habit, I hold that it is better for him to live by the exercise of will. I also believe that men are capable of developing their will to an extent that will reduce exploitation to a minimum. I look upon an increase of the power of the State with the greatest fear, because although while apparently doing good by minimizing exploitation, it does the greatest harm to mankind by destroying individuality, which lies at the root of all progress. We know of so many cases where men have adopted trusteeship, but none where the State has really lived for the poor.

Q. But have not those cases of trusteeship which you sometimes cite been due to your personal influence rather than to anything else? Teachers like you come infrequently. Would it not be better, therefore, to trust to some organization to effect the necessary changes in man, rather than depend upon the casual advent of men like yourself?

A. Leaving me aside, you must remember that the influence of all great teachers of mankind has outlived their lives. In the teachings of each prophet like Mohammed, the Buddha or Jesus, there was a permanent portion and there was another which was suited to the needs and requirements of the times. It is only because we try to keep up the permanent with the impermanent aspects of their teachings that there is so much distortion in religious practice today. But that apart, you can see that the influence of these men has sustained us after they have passed away. Moreover, what I disapprove of is an organization based on force which a State is. Voluntary organization there must be.

Q. What then, sir, is your social order?

A. I believe that every man is born in the world with certain natural tendencies. Every person is born with certain definite limitations which he cannot overcome. From a careful observation of those limitations the law of *varna* was deduced. It establishes certain spheres of action of certain people with certain tendencies. This avoided all unworthy competition. Whilst, recognizing limitations, the law of *varna* admitted of no distinctions of high and low, on the one hand it guaranteed to each the fruits of his labours and on the other it prevented him from pressing upon his neighbour.

This great law has been degraded and has fallen into disrepute. But my conviction is that an ideal social order will only be evolved when the implications of this law are fully understood and given effect to.

Q. Do you not think that in ancient India there was much difference in economic status and social privileges between the four *varnas*?

A. That may be historically true. But misapplication or an imperfect understanding of the law must not lead to the ignoring of the law itself. By constant striving we have to enrich the inheritance left to us. This law determines the duties of man. Rights follow from a due performance of duties. It is the fashion nowadays to ignore duties and assert or rather usurp rights.

Q. If you are so keen upon reviving *varnashrama*, why do you not favour violence as the quickest means?

A. Surely the question does not arise. Definition and performance of duties rule out violence altogether. Violence becomes imperative when an attempt is made to assert rights without reference to duties.

Extract from a Speech at a Meeting of Village Workers, Nagpur
[23 February 1935]

[...] There is a conflict of interest between capital and labour, but we have to resolve it by doing our own duty. Just as pure blood is proof against poisonous germs, so will labour, when it is pure, be proof against exploitation. The labourer has but to realize that labour is also capital. As soon as labourers are properly educated and organized and they realize their strength, no amount of capital can subdue them. Organized and enlightened labour can dictate its own terms. It is no use vowing vengeance against a party because we are weak. We have to get strong. Strong hearts, enlightened minds and willing hands can brave all odds and remove all obstacles. No, 'Love thy neighbour as thyself' is no counsel of perfection. The capitalist is as much a neighbour of the labourer as the latter is a neighbour of the former, and one has to seek and win the willing co-operation of the other. Nor does the principle mean that we should accept exploitation lying down. Our internal strength will render all exploitation impossible.

Excerpt from an Interview with an Egyptian
[22 January 1937]

Q. What do you think of communism? Do you think it would be good for India?

A. Communism of the Russian type, that is communism which is imposed on a people, would be repugnant to India. I believe in non-violent communism.

Q. But communism in Russia is against private property. Do you want private property?

A. If communism came without any violence, it would be welcome. For then no property would be held by anybody except on behalf of the people and for the people. The millionaire may have his millions, but he will hold them for the people. The State could take charge of them whenever they would need them for the common cause.

Q. Is there any difference of opinion between you and Jawaharlal in respect of socialism?

A. There is, but it is a difference in emphasis. He perhaps puts an emphasis on the result, whereas I put it on the means. Perhaps according to him I am putting over-emphasis on non-violence, whereas he, though he believes in non-violence, would want to have socialism by other means if it was impossible to have it by non-violence. Of course my emphasis on non-violence becomes one of principle. Even if I was assured that we could have independence by means of violence, I shall refuse to have it. It won't be real independence.

Answers to Questions at Gandhi Seva Sangh Meeting [6 May 1939]

Q. I am either unable to understand your theory of trusteeship or my reason cannot grasp it. Will you kindly explain it?

A. It is the same thing whether you are unable to understand it or your reason does not accept it. How can I explain such an important principle in a few minutes? Still I shall try to explain it in brief. Just imagine that I have a crore of rupees in my possession. I can either squander the amount in dissipation or take up the attitude that the money does not belong to me, that I do not own it, that it is a bequest, that it has been put in my possession by god and that only so much of it is mine as is enough for my requirements. My requirements also should be like those of the millions. My requirements cannot be greater because I happen to be the son of a rich man. I cannot spend the money on my pleasures. The man who takes for himself only enough to satisfy the needs customary in his society and spends the rest for social service becomes a trustee.

Ever since the idea of socialism became popular in India, we have been confronted with the question as to what our attitude should be towards the princes and millionaires. The socialists say that the princes and the millionaires should be done away with, that all must become workers. They advocate confiscation of the properties of all these people and say that they should be given the same wages as everyone else—from five rupees to eight annas a day or fifteen rupees a month. So much for what the socialists say. We too assert that the rich are not the owners of their wealth whereas the labourer is the owner of his labour. He is, therefore, from our point of view, richer than the rich. A zamindar can be recognized as the owner of one, two or ten *bighas* of land. That is to say, of as much as may be necessary for his livelihood. We also want that his wages should not be higher than those of the labourer, that he should maintain himself on eight annas a day and use the rest of his wealth for the welfare of society. But we would not take away his property by force. This is the most important point. We also wish that the princes and the millionaires too should do manual work and maintain themselves on eight annas a day, considering the rest of their property as national trust.

At this point it may be asked as to how many trustees of this type one can really find. As a matter of fact, such a question should not arise at all. It is not directly related to our theory. There may be just one such trustee or there may be none at all. Why should we worry about it? We should have the faith that we can, without violence or with so little violence that it can hardly be called violence, create such a feeling among the rich. We should act in that faith. That is sufficient for us. We should demonstrate through our endeavour that we can end economic disparity with the help of non-violence. Only those who have no faith in non-violence can ask how many trustees of this kind can be found.

You may say that such a thing can never happen. You may consider it as something not in keeping with human nature. But I cannot believe that you are not able to understand it or that your reason cannot grasp it.

Answers to Questions at Constructive Workers' Conference [24 January 1946]

Q. What exactly do you mean by economic equality? What is statutory trusteeship as conceived by you?

Gandhiji's reply was that economic equality of his conception did not mean that everyone would literally have the same amount. It simply meant that everybody should have enough for his or her needs. For instance, he required two shawls in winter whereas his grand-nephew Kanu Gandhi who stayed with him and was like his own son did not require any warm clothing whatsoever. Gandhiji required goat's milk, oranges and other fruit. Kanu could do with ordinary food. He envied Kanu but there was no point in it. Kanu was a young man whereas he was an old man of seventy-six. The monthly expense of his food was far more than that of Kanu but that did not mean that there was economic inequality between them. The elephant needs a thousand times more food than the ant, but that is not an indication of inequality. So the real meaning of economic equality was: 'To each according to his need.' That was the definition of Marx. If a single man demanded as much as a man with wife and four children, that would be a violation of economic equality. Gandhiji continued:

Let no one try to justify the glaring difference between the classes and the masses, the prince and the pauper, by saying that the former need more. That will be idle sophistry and a travesty of my argument. The contrast between the rich and the poor today is a painful sight. The poor villagers are exploited by the foreign Government and also by their own countrymen—the city-dwellers. They produce the food and go hungry. They produce milk and their children have to go without it. It is disgraceful. Everyone must have balanced diet, a decent house to live in, facilities for the education of one's children and adequate medical relief.

That constituted his picture of economic equality. He did not want to taboo everything above and beyond the bare necessaries but they must come after the essential needs of the poor are satisfied. First things must come first.

As for the present owners of wealth, they would have to make their choice between class war and voluntarily converting themselves into trustees of their wealth. They would be allowed to retain the stewardship of their possessions and to use their talent to increase the wealth, not for their own sakes, but for the sake of the nation and therefore without exploitation. The State would regulate the rate of commission which they would get commensurate with the service rendered and its value to society. Their children would inherit the stewardship only if they proved their fitness for it. He concluded:

Supposing India becomes a free country tomorrow, all the capitalists will have an opportunity of becoming statutory trustees. But such a statute will not be imposed from above. It will have to come from below. When the people understand the implications of trusteeship and the atmosphere is ripe for it, the people themselves, beginning with gram panchayats, will begin to introduce such statutes. Such a thing coming from below is easy to swallow. Coming from above, it is liable to prove a dead weight.

Q. What is the difference between your technique and that of the communists or socialists for realizing the goal of economic equality?

A. The socialists and communists say they can do nothing to bring about economic equality today. They will just carry on propaganda in its favour and to that end they believe in generating and accentuating hatred. They say, when they get control over the State, they will enforce equality. Under my plan, the State will be there to carry out the will of the people, not to dictate to them or force them to do its will. I shall bring about economic equality through non-violence, by converting the people to my point of view by harnessing the forces of love as against hatred. I will not wait till I have converted the whole society to my view but will straightaway make a beginning with myself. It goes without saying that I cannot hope to bring about economic equality of my conception if I am the owner of fifty motor-cars or even of ten *bighas* of land. For that I have to reduce myself to the level of the poorest of the poor. That is what I have been trying to do for the last fifty years or more, and so I claim to be a foremost communist although I make use of cars and other facilities offered to me by the rich. They have no hold no me and I can shed them at a moment's notice, if the interests of the masses demand it.

Q. What is the place of satyagraha in making the rich realize their duty towards the poor?

A. The same as against the foreign power. Satyagraha is a law of universal application. Beginning with the family, its use can be extended to every other circle. Supposing a land-owner exploits his tenants and mulcts them of the fruit of their toil by appropriating it to his own use. When they expostulate with him, he does not listen and raises objections that he requires so much for his wife, so much for his children and so on. The tenants, or those who have espoused their cause and have influence, will make an appeal to his wife to expostulate with her husband. She would probably say that for herself she does not need his exploited money. The children will say likewise that they would earn for themselves what they need.

Supposing further that he listens to nobody or that his wife and children combine against the tenants, they will not submit. They will quit, if asked to do so, but they will make it clear that the land belongs to him who tills it. The owner cannot till all the land himself, and he will have to give in to their just demands. It may, however, be that the tenants are replaced by others. Agitation short of violence will then continue till the replaced tenants see their error and make common cause with the evicted tenants. Thus satyagraha is a process of educating public opinion such that it covers all the elements of society and in the end makes itself irresistible. Violence interrupts the process and prolongs the real revolution of the whole social structure.

Talk with Zamindars [18 April 1947]

Zamindars or capitalists will not be able to survive if they continue to suppress peasants and labourers. Now you should behave towards them not as their masters but as partners and friends, and act as their trustees; then alone can you survive. For a long time during the British regime you have been exploiting the labourers and peasants. Therefore I advise you in your own interest that if you do not see the writing on the wall, it will be difficult for you to adjust.

Question Box [1 June 1947]

Q. You say that a raja, a zamindar or a capitalist should be a trustee for the poor. Do you think that any such exists today? Or do you expect them to be so transformed?

A. I think that some very few exist even today, though not in the full sense of the term. They are certainly moving in that direction. It can, however, be asked whether the present rajas and others can be expected to become trustees of the poor. I think it is worthwhile entertaining such a hope. If they do not become trustees of their own accord, force of circumstances will compel the reform unless they court utter destruction. When Pañchayat Raj is established, public opinion will do what violence can never do. The present power of the zamindars, the capitalists and the rajas can hold sway only so long as the common people do not realize their own strength. If the people non-co-operate, what can a raja, a zamindar or a capitalist do? In a Panchayat Raj only the panchayat will be obeyed and a panchayat can work only through the law of its making. If the panchayat follows non-violence in conducting its business, all the three would become trustees by law and if it resorts to violence it would mean the end of their power.

Who is a Socialist? [6 July 1947]

Socialism is a beautiful word and so far as I am aware in socialism all the members of society are equal—none low, none high. In the individual body the head is not high because it is the top of the body, nor are the soles of the feet low because they touch the earth. Even as members of the individual body are equal, so are the members of society. That is socialism.

In it the prince and the peasant, the wealthy and the poor, the employer and the employee are all on the same level. In terms of religion there is no duality in socialism. It is all unity.

Looking at society all the world over there is nothing but duality or plurality. Unity is conspicuous by its absence. This man is high, that one is low, that one is a Hindu, that one a Muslim, third a Christian, fourth a Parsi, fifth a Sikh, sixth a Jew. Even among these there are sub-divisions. In the unity of my conception there is perfect unity in the plurality of designs.

In order to reach this state we may not look on things philosophically and say that we need not make a move until all are converted to socialism. Without changing our life we may go on giving addresses, forming parties and hawk-like seize the game when it comes our way. This is no socialism. The more we treat it as a game to be seized, the further it must recede from us.

Socialism begins with the first convert. If there is one such, you can add zeros to the one and the first zero will account for ten and every addition will account for ten times the previous number. If, however, the beginner is a zero, in other words, no one makes the beginning, multiplicity of zeros will also produce zero value. Time and paper occupied in writing zeros will be so much waste.

This socialism is as pure as crystal. It, therefore, requires crystal-like means to achieve it. Impure means result in an impure end. Hence the prince and the peasant will not be equalized by cutting off the prince's head, nor can the process of cutting off equalize the employer and the employee. One cannot reach truth by untruthfulness. Truthful conduct alone can reach truth. Are not non-violence and truth twins? The answer is an emphatic 'no'. Non-violence is embedded in truth and vice versa. Hence has it been said that they are faces of the same coin. Either is inseparable from the other. Read the coin either way. The spelling of words will be different. The value is the same. This blessed state is unattainable without perfect purity. Harbour impurity of mind or body and you have untruth and violence in you.

Therefore, only truthful, non-violent and pure-hearted socialists will be able to establish a socialistic society in India and the world. To my knowledge there is no country in the world which is purely socialistic. Without the means described above the existence of such a society is impossible.

Hindu-Muslim Unity, Partition & Independence

Hindu-Muslim Unity [8 April 1919]

[...] If the Hindu and Muslim communities could be united in one bond of mutual friendship, and if each could act towards the other even as children of the same mother, it would be a consummation devoutly to be wished. But before this unity becomes a reality, both the communities will have to give up a good deal, and will have to make radical changes in ideas held heretofore. Members of one community when talking about those of the other at times indulge in terms so vulgar that they but acerbate the relations between the two.

In Hindu society we do not hesitate to indulge in unbecoming language when talking of the Mahomedans and vice versa. Many believe that an ingrained and ineradicable animosity exists between the Hindus and Mahomedans. In many places we see that each community harbours distrust against the other. Each fears the other. It is an undoubted fact that this anomalous and wretched state of things is improving day by day. The Time-Spirit is ceaselessly working on unchecked, and willy-nilly we have to live together. But the object of taking a vow is speedily to bring about, by the power of self-denial, a state of things which can only be expected to come in the fulness of time. How is this possible? Meetings should be called of Hindus—I mean the orthodox Hindus—where this question should be seriously considered. The standing complaint of the Hindus against the Mussalmans is that the latter are beef-eaters and that they purposely sacrifice cows on the Bakr-i-Id day. Now it is impossible to unite the Hindus and Mahomedans so long as the Hindus do not hesitate to kill their Mahomedan brethren in order to protect a cow. For I think it is futile to expect that our violence will ever compel that the Mahomedans to refrain from cow-slaughter. I do not believe that the efforts of our cow-protection societies have availed in the least to lessen the number of cows killed every day. I have had no reason to believe so. I believe myself to be an orthodox Hindu and it is my conviction that no one who scrupulously practises the Hindu religion may kill a cow-killer to protect a cow. There is one and only one means open to a Hindu to protect a cow and that is that he should offer himself as a sacrifice if he cannot stand its slaughter. Even if a very few enlightened

Hindus thus sacrificed themselves, I have no doubt that our Mussalman brethren would abandon cow-slaughter. But this is satyagraha, this is equity; even as, if I want my brother to redress a grievance, I must do so by taking upon my head a certain amount of sacrifice and not by inflicting injury on him. I may not demand it as of right. My only right against my brother is that I can offer myself as a sacrifice.

It is only when the Hindus are inspired with a feeling of pure love of this type that Hindu-Muslim unity can be expected. As with the Hindus, so with the Mussalmans. The leaders among the latter should meet together and consider their duty towards the Hindus. When both are inspired by a spirit of sacrifice, when both try to do their duty towards one another instead of pressing their rights, then and then only would the long-standing differences between the two communities cease. Each must respect the other's religion, must refrain from even secretly thinking ill of the other. We must politely dissuade members of both the communities from indulging in bad language against one another. Only a serious endeavour in this direction can remove the estrangement between us. Our vow would have value only when masses of Hindus and Mussalmans join in the endeavour. I think I have now made sufficiently clear the seriousness and magnitude of this vow. I hope that on this auspicious occasion and surely the occasion must be auspicious when a wave of satyagraha is sweeping over the whole country—we could all take this vow of unity. For this it is further necessary that leading Hindus and Mahomedans should meet together and seriously consider the question and then pass a unanimous resolution at a public meeting. This consummation will certainly be reached if our present efforts are vigorously continued. I think the vow may be taken individually even now and I expect that numerous people will do so every day. My warnings have reference to the taking of the vow publicly by masses of men. If it is taken by the masses, it should, in my humble opinion, be as follows:

> With God as witness we Hindus and Mahomedans declare that we shall behave towards one another as children of the same parents, that we shall have no differences, that the sorrows of each shall be the sorrows of the other and that each shall help the other in

removing them. We shall respect each other's religion and religious feelings and shall not stand in the way of our respective religious practices. We shall always refrain from violence to each other in the name of religion.

Hindu-Muslim Unity [15 May 1924]

Let me summarize the long statement issued last week on this the greatest of all questions for the Indian patriot. The posterity will judge both the faiths by the manner in which the followers of each acquit themselves in the matter. However good Hinduism or Islam may be in the abstract, the only way each can be judged is by the effect produced by each on its votaries considered as a whole.

The following then is the summary of the statement.

CAUSES

- The remote cause of the tension is the Moplah rebellion.
- The attempt of Mr Fazl Hussain to rearrange the distribution of posts in the education department consistently with the number of Mussalmans in the Punjab and consequent Hindu opposition.
- The *shudhi* movement.
- The most potent being tiredness of non-violence and the fear that the communities might, by a long course of training in non-violence, forget the law of retaliation and self-defence.
- Mussalman cow-slaughter and Hindu music.
- Hindu cowardice and consequent Hindu distrust of Mussalmans.
- Mussalman bullying.
- Mussalman distrust of Hindu fair play.

CURE

- The master-key to the solution is the replacement of the rule of the sword by that of arbitration. Honest public opinion should make it impossible for aggrieved parties to take the law into their own hands and every case must be referred to private arbitration or to law courts if the parties do not believe in non-co-operation.

- Ignorant fear of cowardly non-violence, falsely so called, taking the place of violence should be dispelled.
- Growing mutual distrust among the leaders must, if they believe in unity, give place to trust.
- Hindus must cease to fear the Mussalman bully and the Mussalmans should consider it beneath their dignity to bully their Hindu brothers.
- Hindus must not imagine they can force Mussalmans to give up cow-sacrifice. They must trust, by befriending Mussalmans, that the latter will, of their own accord, give up cow-sacrifice out of regard for their Hindu neighbours.
- Nor must Mussalmans imagine they can force Hindus to stop music or *aarti* before mosques. They must befriend the Hindus and trust them to pay heed to reasonable Mussalman sentiment.
- Hindus must leave to the Mussalmans and the other minorities the question of representation on elected bodies, and gracefully and whole-heartedly give effect to the findings of such referee. If I had my way I should appoint Hakim Saheb Ajmal Khan as the sole referee leaving him free to consult Mussalmans, Sikhs, Christians, Parsis, etc, as he considers best.
- Employment under national government must be according to merit to be decided by a board of examiners representing different communities.
- *Shuddhi* or *tabligh* as such cannot be disturbed, but either must be conducted honestly and by men of proved character. It should avoid all attack on other religions. There should be no secret propaganda and no offer of material rewards.
- Public opinion should be so cultivated as to put under the ban all the scurrilous writings, principally in a section of the Punjab Press.
- Nothing is possible without the Hindus shedding their timidity. Theirs is the largest stake and they must be prepared to sacrifice the most.

But how is the cure to be effected? Who will convince the Hindu maniac that the best way to save the cow is for him to do his duty by her and not goad his Mussalman brother? Who will convince the Mussalman fanatic that it is not religion but irreligion to break the head of his Hindu brother when he plays music in front of his mosque? Or, again, who will make the Hindu see that he will lose nothing by the minorities being even over-represented on the elective public secular bodies? These are fair questions and show the difficulty of working out the solution.

But if the solution is the only true solution, all difficulties must be overcome. In reality the difficulty is only apparent. If there are even a few Hindus and a few Mussalmans who have a living faith in the solution, the rest is easy. Indeed, even if there are a few Hindus only, or a few Mussalmans only with that faith, the solution would be still easy. They have but to work away single-heartedly and the others will follow them. And the conversion of only one party is enough because the solution requires no bargains. For instance, Hindus should cease to worry Mussalmans about the cow without expecting any consideration from the latter. They should yield to the Mussalman demand, whatever it may be, regarding representation, again without requiring any return. And if the Mussalmans insist on stopping Hindu music or *aarti* by force, the Hindus will continue playing it although every single Hindu should die at his post, but without retaliation. The Mussalmans will then be shamed into doing the right thing in an incredibly short space of time. Mussalmans can do likewise, if they choose, and shame the Hindus into doing the right thing. One has to dare to believe.

But in practice it will not be thus; on the contrary, both will act simultaneously as soon as the workers become true to themselves. Unfortunately they are not. They are mostly ruled by passion and prejudice. Each tries to hide the shortcomings of his co-religionists and so the circle of distrust and suspicion ever widens.

I hope that, at the forthcoming meeting of the All-India Congress Committee, it will be possible to find out a method of work which will bring a speedy end to the tension.

It has been suggested to me that the Government are fomenting these dissensions. I should hope not. But assuming that they are, surely it is up to us to neutralize such efforts by ourselves acting truly and faithfully.

Trust Begets Trust [29 May 1924]

For me the only question for immediate solution before the country is the Hindu-Mussalman question. I agree with Mr Jinnah that Hindu-Muslim unity means swaraj. I see no way of achieving anything in this afflicted country without a lasting heart unity between Hindus and Mussalmans of India. I believe in the immediate possibility of achieving it, because it is so natural, so necessary for both, and because I believe in human nature. Mussalmans may have much to answer for. I have come in closest touch with even what may be considered a "bad lot". I cannot recall a single occasion when I had to regret it. The Mussalmans are brave, they are generous and trusting the moment their suspicion is disarmed. Hindus, living as they do in glass houses, have no right to throw stones at their Mussalman neighbours. See what we have done, are still doing, to the suppressed classes! If *Kaffir* is a term of opprobrium, how much more so is *Chandal?* In the history of the world religions, there is perhaps nothing like our treatment of the suppressed classes. The pity of it is that the treatment still continues. What a fight in Vaikom for a most elementary human right!! God does not punish directly; His ways are inscrutable. Who knows that all our woes are not due to that one black sin? The history of Islam, if it betrays aberrations from the moral height, has many a brilliant page. In its glorious days it was not intolerant. It commanded the admiration of the world. When the West was sunk in darkness, a bright star rose in the Eastern firmament and gave light and comfort to a groaning world. Islam is not a false religion. Let Hindus study it reverently and they will love it even as I do. If it has become gross and fanatical here, let us admit that we have had no small share in making it so. If Hindus set their house in order, I have not a shadow of doubt that Islam will respond in a manner worthy of its liberal traditions. The key to the situation lies with the Hindus. We must shed timidity or cowardice. We must be brave enough to trust, all will be well.

Hindu-Muslim Unity
[26 December 1924]

Hindu-Muslim unity is not less important than the spinning-wheel. It is the breath of our life. I do not need to occupy much of your time on this question, because the necessity of it for swaraj is almost universally accepted. I say "almost" because I know some Hindus and some Mussalmans who prefer the present condition of dependence on Great Britain if they cannot have either wholly Hindu or wholly Mussalman India. Happily their number is small.

I share Maulana Shaukat's robust optimism that the present tension is a mere temporary distemper. The Khilafat agitation in which Hindus made common cause with their Mussalman brethren and the non-co-operation that followed it caused an awakening among the hitherto slumbering masses. It has given a new consciousness to the classes as well as the masses. Interested persons who were disappointed during the palmy days of non-co-operation, now that it has lost the charm of novelty, have found their opportunity and are trading upon the religious bigotry or the selfishness of both the communities. The result is written in the history of the feuds of the past two years. Religion has been travestied. Trifles have been dignified by the name of religious tenets which, the fanatics claim, must be observed at any cost. Economic and political causes have been brought into play for the sake of fomenting trouble. The culminating point was reached in Kohat. The tragedy was aggravated by the callous indifference of the local authority. I must not tarry to example the causes or to distribute the blame. I have not the material for the task even if I was minded for it. Suffice it to say that the Hindu refugees fled for fear of their lives. There is in Kohat an overwhelming Mussalman majority. They have in so far as is possible under a foreign domination effective political control. It is up to them, therefore, to show that the Hindus are as safe in the midst of their majority as they would be if the whole population of Kohat was Hindu. The Mussalmans of Kohat may not rest satisfied till they have brought back to Kohat every one of the refugees. I hope that the Hindus would not fall into the trap laid for them by the Government and would resolutely decline to go back till the Mussalmans of Kohat have given them full assurances as to their lives and property.

The Hindus can live in the midst of an overwhelming Mussalman majority only if the latter are willing to receive and treat them as friends and equals, just as Mussalmans, if in a minority, must depend for honourable existence in the midst of a Hindu majority on the latter's friendliness. A Government can give protection against thieves and robbers, but not even a swaraj government will be able to protect people against a wholesale boycott by one community of another. Governments can deal with abnormal situations. When quarrels become a normal thing of life, it is called civil war and parties must fight it out themselves. The present Government being foreign, in reality a veiled military rule, has resources at its command for its protection against any combination we can make and has, therefore, the power, if it has the will, to deal with our class feuds. But no swaraj government with any pretension to being a popular government can possibly be organized and maintained on a war footing. A swaraj government means a government established by the free joint will of Hindus, Mussalmans and others. Hindus and Mussalmans, if they desire swaraj, have perforce to settle their differences amicably.

The Unity Conference at Delhi has paved the way for a settlement of religious differences. The Committee of the All Parties Conference is among other things expected to find a workable and just solution of the political differences not only between Hindus and Mussalmans but between all classes and all castes, sects or denominations. Our goal must be removal, at the earliest possible moment, of communal or sectional representation. A common electorate must impartially elect its representatives on the sole ground of merit. Our services must be likewise impartially manned by the most qualified men and women. But till that time comes and communal jealousies or preferences become a thing of the past, minorities who suspect the motives of majorities must be allowed their way. The majority must set the example of self-sacrifice.

My Answer to Qaid-e-Azam
[26 March 1940]

Qaid-e-Azam Jinnah is reported to have said :

> Mr Gandhi has been saying for the last twenty years that
> there cannot be any swaraj without Hindu-Muslim unity.
> Mr Gandhi is fighting for a Constituent Assembly. May
> I point out to Mr Gandhi and the Congress that they are
> fighting for a Constituent Assembly which we cannot
> accept? Therefore, the idea of a Constituent Assembly is
> impracticable and unacceptable. Mr Gandhi wants a
> Constituent Assembly for purposes of ascertaining the
> views of Muslims, and if they do not agree, he would
> then give up all hope and then would agree with us. If
> there exists the will to come to a settlement with the
> Muslim League, then why does not Mr Gandhi, as I
> have said more than once, honestly agree that the
> Congress is a Hindu organization and that it does not
> represent anything but the solid body of Hindus? Why
> should Mr Gandhi not be proud to say: "I am a Hindu
> and the Congress is a Hindu body?" I am not ashamed
> of saying that I am a Muslim and that the Muslim
> League is the representative of Muslims. Why all this
> camouflage, why this threat of civil disobedience, and
> why this fight for a Constituent Assembly? Why should
> not Mr Gandhi come as a Hindu leader and let me meet
> him proudly representing the Mussalmans?

My position is and has been clear. I am proud of being a
Hindu, but I have never gone to anybody as a Hindu to secure
Hindu-Muslim unity. My Hinduism demands no pacts. My support
of the Khilafat was unconditional. I am no politician in the accepted
sense. But whatever talks I had with Qaid-e-Azam or any other have
been on behalf of the Congress which is not a Hindu organization.
Can a Hindu organization have a Muslim divine as President, and
can its Working Committee have four Muslim members out of
fifteen? I still maintain that there is no swaraj without Hindu-

Muslim unity. I can never be party to the coercion of Muslims or any other minority. The Constituent Assembly as conceived by me is not intended to coerce anybody. Its sole sanction will be an agreed solution of communal questions. If there is no agreement, the Constituent Assembly will be automatically dissolved. The Constituent Assembly or any body of elected representatives can alone have a fully representative status. The Congress representative capacity has been and can be questioned. But who can question the sole representative capacity of the elected delegates to the Constituent Assembly? I cannot understand the Muslim opposition to the proposed Constituent Assembly. Are the opponents afraid that the Muslim League will not be elected by Muslim voters? Do they not realize that any Muslim demand made by the Muslim delegates will be irresistible? If the vast majority of Indian Muslims feel that they are not one nation with their Hindu and other brethren, who will be able to resist them? But surely it is permissible to dispute the authority of the 50,000 Muslims who listened to Qaid-e-Azam to represent the feelings of eight crores of Indian Muslims.

A Baffling Situation [1 April 1940]

A question has been put to me :

> Do you intend to start general civil disobedience
> although Qaid-e-Azam Jinnah has declared war against
> Hindus and has got the Muslim League to pass a
> resolution favouring vivisection of India into two? If you
> do, what becomes of your formula that there is no
> swaraj without communal unity?

I admit that the step taken by the Muslim League at Lahore
creates a baffling situation. But I do not regard it so baffling as to
make civil disobedience an impossibility. Supposing that the
Congress is reduced to a hopeless minority, it will still be open to
it, indeed it may be its duty, to resort to civil disobedience. The
struggle will not be against the majority, it will be against the
foreign ruler. If the struggle succeeds, the fruits thereof will be
reaped as well by the Congress as by the opposing majority. Let
me, however, say in parenthesis that, until the conditions I have
mentioned for starting civil disobedience are fulfilled, civil
disobedience cannot be started in any case. In the present instance
there is nothing to prevent the imperial rulers from declaring their
will in unequivocal terms that henceforth India will govern herself
according to her own will, not that of the rulers as has happened
hitherto. Neither the Muslim League nor any other party can oppose
such a declaration. For the Muslims will be entitled to dictate their
own terms. Unless the rest of India wishes to engage in internal
fratricide, the others will have to submit to Muslim dictation if the
Muslims will resort to it. I know no non-violent method of
compelling the obedience of eight crores of Muslims to the will of
the rest of India, however powerful a majority the rest may
represent. The Muslims must have the same right of self-
determination that the rest of India has. We are at present a joint
family. Any member may claim a division.

Thus, so far as I am concerned, my proposition that there is no
swaraj without communal unity holds as good today as when I first
enunciated it in 1919.

But civil disobedience stands on a different footing. It is open even to one single person to offer it, if he feels the call. It will not be offered for the Congress alone or for any particular group. Whatever benefit accrues from it will belong to the whole of India. The injury, if there is any, will belong only to the civil disobedience party.

But I do not believe that Muslims, when it comes to a matter of actual decision, will ever want vivisection. Their good sense will prevent them. Their self-interest will deter them. Their religion will forbid the obvious suicide which the partition would mean. The "two nations" theory is an untruth. The vast majority of Muslims of India are converts to Islam or are descendants of converts. They did not become a separate nation as soon as they became converts. A Bengali Muslim speaks the same tongue that a Bengali Hindu does, eats the same food, has the same amusements as his Hindu neighbour. They dress alike. I have often found it difficult to distinguish by outward sign between a Bengali Hindu and a Bengali Muslim. The same phenomenon is observable more or less in the South among the poor who constitute the masses of India. When I first met the late Sir Ali Imam I did not know that he was not a Hindu. His speech, his dress, his manners, his food were the same as of the majority of the Hindus in whose midst I found him. His name alone betrayed him. Not even that with Qaid-e-Azam Jinnah. For his name could be that of any Hindu. When I first met him, I did not know that he was a Muslim. I came to know his religion when I had his full name given to me. His nationality was written in his face and manner. The reader will be surprised to know that for days, if not months, I used to think of the late Vithalbhai Patel as a Muslim as he used to sport a beard and a Turkish cap. The Hindu law of inheritance governs many Muslim groups. Sir Mahommed Iqbal used to speak with pride of his Brahmanical descent. Iqbal and Kitchlew are names common to Hindus and Muslims. Hindus and Muslims of India are not two nations. Those whom God has made one, man will never be able to divide.

And is Islam such an exclusive religion as Qaid-e-Azam would have it? Is there nothing in common between Islam and Hinduism or any other religion? Or is Islam merely an enemy of Hinduism?

Were the Ali Brothers and their associates wrong when they hugged Hindus as blood brothers and saw much in common between the two? I am not now thinking of individual Hindus who may have disillusioned the Muslim friends. Qaid-e-Azam has, however, raised a fundamental issue. This is his thesis:

> It is extremely difficult to appreciate why our Hindu friends fail to understand the real nature of Islam and Hinduism. They are not religions in the strict sense of the word, but are, in fact, different and distinct social orders, and it is a dream that the Hindus and Muslim can ever evolve a common nationality. This mis-conception of one Indian nation has gone far beyond the limits and is the cause of most of our troubles and will lead India to destruction if we fail to revise our notions in time.

> The Hindus and Muslims have two different religious philosophies, social customs, literatures. They neither intermarry, nor dine together, and indeed, they belong to two different civilizations which are based mainly on conflicting ideas and conceptions. Their aspects on life and of life are different. It is quite clear that Hindus and Mussalmans derive their inspiration from different sources of history. They have different epics, their heroes are different, and they have different episodes. Very often the hero of one is a foe of the other and, likewise, their victories and defeats overlap. To yoke together two such nations under a single State, one as a numerical minority and the other as majority, must lead to growing discontent and final destruction of any fabric that may be so built up for the government of such a State.

He does not say some Hindus are bad; he says Hindus as such have nothing in common with Muslims. I make bold to say that he and those who think like him are rendering no service to Islam; they are misinterpreting the message inherent in the very word Islam. I say this because I feel deeply hurt over what is now going on in the name of the Muslim League. I should be failing in my duty, if I did not warn the Muslims of India against the untruth that is being propagated amongst them. This warning is a duty because I have faithfully served them in their hour of need and because Hindu-Muslim unity has been and is my life's mission.

My Position [9 April 1940]

Nawabzada Liaquat Ali Khan has, in his criticism of my reply to Qaid-e-Azam, put some questions which I gladly answer. I must adhere to my statement that I have never spoken to anybody on the communal question as a Hindu. I have no authority. Whenever I have spoken to anybody I have spoken as a Congressman, but often only as an individual. No Congressman, not even the President, can always speak as a representative. Big things have always been transacted on this planet by persons belonging to different organizations coming together and talking informally in their non-representative capacity. I fear that even the answer I am about to give must be taken as representing nobody but myself. In the present instance I have reason to say that probably I do not represent any single member of the Working Committee. I am answering as a peacemaker, as a friend (and may I say brother) of the Mussalmans.

As a man of non-violence I cannot forcibly resist the proposed partition if the Muslims of India really insist upon it. But I can never be a willing party to the vivisection. I would employ every non-violent means to prevent it. For it means the undoing of centuries of work done by numberless Hindus and Muslims to live together as one nation. Partition means a patent untruth. My whole soul rebels against the idea that Hinduism and Islam represent two antagonistic cultures and doctrines. To assent to such a doctrine is for me denial of God. For I believe with my whole soul that the God of the Koran is also the God of the Gita, and that we are all, no matter by what name designated, children of the same God. I must rebel against the idea that millions of Indians who were Hindus the other day changed their nationality on adopting Islam as their religion.

But that is my belief. I cannot thrust it down the throats of the Muslims who think that they are a different nation. I refuse, however, to believe that the eight crores of Muslims will say that they have nothing in common with their Hindu and other brethren. Their mind can only be known by a referendum duly made to them on that clear issue. The contemplated Constituent Assembly can easily decide the question. Naturally on an issue such as this there

274

can be no arbitration. It is purely and simply a matter of self-determination. I know of no other conclusive method of ascertaining the mind of the eight crores of Muslims.

But the contemplated Constituent Assembly will have the framing of a constitution as its main function. It cannot do this until the communal question is settled.

I still believe that there can be no swaraj by non-violent means, without communal unity. And eight crores of Muslims can certainly bar the way to peaceful freedom.

If then I still talk of civil disobedience, it is because I believe that the Muslim masses want freedom as much as the rest of the population of this country. And assuming that they do not, civil disobedience will be a powerful means of educating public opinion whether Muslim, Hindu or any other. It will also be an education of world opinion. But I will not embark upon it unless I am, as far as is humanly possible, sure that non-violence will be observed both in spirit and in the letter. I hope the Nawabzada has no difficulty in believing that whatever is gained by civil disobedience will be gained for all. When India gets the power to frame her own constitution, the Muslims will surely have a decisive voice in shaping their own future. It will not be, cannot be, decided by the vote of the majority.

Lastly, I suggest to the Nawabzada that he wrote in haste the lines about the President of the Congress. For they are contrary to the history of our own times. And he was equally in haste in suggesting that "the sole objective of the Congress under Mr Gandhi's fostering care has been the revival of Hinduism and the imposition of Hindu culture on all and sundry." My own objective is not the issue in the terrible indictment. The objective of the Congress is wholly political. Nothing is to be gained by making statements that are incapable of proof. So far as my own objective is concerned my life is an open book. I claim to represent all the cultures, for my religion, whatever it may be called, demands the fulfilment of all cultures. I am at home wherever I go, for I regard all religions with the same respect as my own.

Interview to *The Hindu*
[Before 11 June 1942]

Q. Till the last day you said there can be no swaraj without Hindu-Muslim unity. Now why is it that you say that there will be no unity until India has achieved indepen-dence?

A. Time is a merciless enemy, if it is also a merciful friend and healer. I claim to be amongst the oldest lovers of Hindu-Muslim unity and I remain one even today. I have been asking myself why every wholehearted attempt made by all including myself to reach unity has failed, and failed so completely that I have entirely fallen from grace and am described by some Muslim papers as the greatest enemy of Islam in India. It is a phenomenon I can only account for by the fact that the third power, even without deliberately wishing it, will not allow real unity to take place. Therefore I have come to the reluctant conclusion that the two communities will come together almost immediately after the British power comes to a final end in India. If independence is the immediate goal of the Congress and the League then, without needing to come to any terms, all will fight together to be free from bondage. When the bondage is done with, not merely the two organizations but all parties will find it to their interest to come together and make the fullest use of the liberty in order to envolve a national government suited to the genius of India. I do not care what it is called. Whatever it is, in order to be stable, it has to represent the masses in the fullest sense of the term. And, if it is to be broad-based upon the will of the people, it must be predominantly non-violent. Anyway, up to my last breath, I hope I shall be found working to that end, for I see no hope for humanity without the acceptance of non-violence. We are witnessing the bankruptcy of violence from day to day. There is no hope for humanity if the senseless fierce mutual slaughter is to continue.

276

Speech at a Prayer Meeting
[7 September 1946]

The speeches being made by the Qaid-e-Azam and his followers cause me much pain. They say that they will take what they want by force. It is true that the reins of the Government are now in the hands of the Congress, but this only adds to their responsibilities and duties. During the struggle for freedom Congressmen were arrested, beaten and persecuted. They were even killed. These are now things of the past. Had the Congress taken to the path of violence it would have come to a bad end. In true suffering there is no room for revenge. Then alone can success be assured. The forty crores of Indian people, that is to say the teeming millions in the villages, do not think of violence. They are slaves. Violence is lodged only in the hearts of a handful of men in the cities.

I am a villager. I belong with the villagers. The Congress has accepted power for the sake of these downtrodden villagers. I had taken up the cause of Hindu-Muslim unity long before I joined the Congress. I had a number of Muslim friends when I was at school. I went to South Africa to plead the case of some Muslim friends of my brother. I had gone there to gain my livelihood, but soon after my arrival there I gave the first place to service. As a coolie-barrister I served my friends of the labouring class. I had gone as an employee of a Muslim firm and I served the Hindus through them. My memory of those days is a happy one. It is a matter of deep regret that even in South Africa communal differences have arisen. Nevertheless they are unitedly fighting for the rights of Indians. I still remember those hefty Muslims, and especially Seth Cachalia, who participated in the satyagraha and who said they would rather die than live as slaves. When the Qaid-e-Azam and his followers describe Hindus as their enemies I am surprised and pained. I am not a Muslim but I venture to say that Islam does not preach enmity towards anyone. I think I am as much a Christian, a Sikh and a Jain as I am a Hindu. Religion does not teach one to kill one's brother however different his belief. No one can treat another as his enemy until the latter has become his own enemy. Muslim League leaders were not right when they said that they would compel the Congress, the Hindus and the British to accede to their demand.

I am reminded of an incident during the Khilafat days. I was speaking at a meeting of Hindus. I said to them: 'If you want to protect the cow then protect Khilafat. If required even lay down your lives for it.' When I said this it brought tears of joy to the eyes of the Ali Brothers. But what a tragic change we see today. I wish the day may again come when Hindus and Muslims will do nothing without mutual consultation. I am day and night tormented by the question: what I can do to hasten the coming of that day. I appeal to the League not to regard any Indian as its enemy. I appeal to the English not to nurse the thought that they can divide Hindus and Muslims. If they do they will be betraying India and betraying themselves. Hindus and Muslims are both born of the same soil. They have the same blood, eat the same food, drink the same water and speak the same language. The Qaid-e-Azam says that all the Muslims will be safe in Pakistan. In Punjab, Sind and Bengal we have Muslim League Governments. Can one say that what is happening in those provinces augurs well for the peace of the country? Does the Muslim League believe that it can sustain Islam by the sword? If it does it is committing a great error. The very meaning of the word 'Islam' is peace and I am certain that no religion worth the name can be kept alive except through peace.

Excerpts from Gandhi's Prayer Speeches
[12 September 1947]

Anger breeds revenge and the spirit of revenge is today responsible for all the horrible happenings here and elsewhere. What good will it do the Muslims to avenge the happenings in Delhi or for the Sikhs and the Hindus to avenge cruelties on our co-religionists in the Frontier and West Punjab? If a man or a group of men go mad, should everyone follow suit? I warn the Hindus and Sikhs that by killing and loot and arson they are destroying their own religions. I claim to be a student of religion and I know that no religion teaches madness. Islam is no exception. I implore you all to stop your insane actions at once. Let not future generations say that we lost the sweet bread of freedom because we could not digest it. Remember that unless we stop this madness the name of India will be mud in the eyes of the world.

[26 September 1947]

There was a time when India listened to me. Today I am a back number. I have been told I have no place in the new order, where we want machines, navy, air force and what not. I can never be a party to that. If you can have the courage to say that you will retain freedom with the help of the same force with which you have won it, I am your man. My physical incapacity and my depression will vanish in a moment. The Muslims are reported to have said, '*Hanske liya Pakistan, ladke lenge Hindustan*' (Laughing we took Pakistan, fighting we will take Hindustan.) If I had my way, I would never let them have it by force of arms. Some dream of converting the whole of India to Islam. That will never happen through war. Pakistan can never destroy Hinduism. The Hindus alone can destroy themselves and their faith. Similarly, if Islam is destroyed, it will be destroyed by the Muslims in Pakistan, not by the Hindus in Hindustan.

[13 November 1947]

Freedom without equality for all, irrespective of race or religion, is not worth having for the Congress. In other words, the Congress and any government representative of the Congress must remain a purely democratic, popular body, leaving every individual to follow that form of religion which best appeals to him without any interference from the State. There is so much in common between people living in the same State under the same flag owing undivided allegiance to it. There is so much in common between man and man that it is a marvel that there can be any quarrel on the ground of religion. Any creed or dogma which coerces others into following one uniform practice is a religion only in name, for a religion worth the name does not admit of any coercion. Anything that is done under coercion has only a short lease of life. It is bound to die. It must be a matter of pride to you, whether you are four-anna Congress members or not, that you have in your midst an institution without a rival which disdains to become a theocratic state, and which always believes and lives up the belief that the state of your conception must be a secular, democratic state having perfect harmony between the different units composing the state. When I think of the plight of the Muslims in the Union, how in many places life has become difficult for them and how there is a continuing exodus of the Muslims from the Union, I wonder whether the people who are responsible for creating such a state of things could ever become a credit to the Congress. I therefore hope that during the year which has just commenced, the Hindus and Sikhs will so behave as to enable every Muslim, whether a boy or a girl, to feel that he or she is as safe and free as the tallest Hindu or Sikh.

[14 January 1948]

I have come to the prayer meeting in spite of the doctor's objections. But from tomorrow I shall probably not be able to walk to the prayer ground. I have the strength today and I use it though the doctors have advised me to conserve it. I am in God's hands. If

He wants me to live I shall not die. I do not want my faith in God to weaken.

Before I ever knew anything of politics in my early youth, I dreamt the dream of communal unity of the heart. I shall jump in the evening of my life, like a child, to feel that the dream has been realized in this life. This wish for living the full span of life, portrayed by the seers of old and which they permit us to set down at 125 years, will then revive. Who would not risk sacrificing his life for the realization of such a dream? Then we shall have real swaraj. Then, though legally and geographically we may still be two states, in daily life no one will think that we were separate states. The vista before me seems to me to be, as it must be to you, too glorious to be true. Yet like a child in a famous picture, drawn by a famous painter, I shall not be happy till I have got it. I live and want to live for no lesser goal. Let the seekers from Pakistan help me to come as near the goal as it is humanly possible. A goal ceases to be one, when it is reached. The nearest approach is always possible. What I have said holds good irrespective of whether others do it or not. It is open to every individual to purify himself or herself so as to render him fit for that land of promise. I remember to have read, I forget whether in the Delhi Fort or the Agra Fort, when I visited them in 1896, a verse on one of the gates, which when translated reads: 'If there is paradise on earth, it is here, it is here, it is here.' That fort with all its magnificence at its best, was no paradise in my estimation. But I should love to see that verse with justice inscribed on the gates of Pakistan at all the entrances. In such a paradise, whether it is in the Union or in Pakistan, there will be neither paupers nor beggars, nor high nor low, neither millionaire employers nor half-starved employees, nor intoxicating drinks or drugs. There will be the same respect for women as vouchsafed to men, and the chastity and purity of men and women will be jealously guarded. Where every woman except one's wife will be treated by men of all religions as mother, sister or daughter according to her age. Where there will be no untouchability and where there will be equal respect for all faiths. They will be all proudly, joyously and voluntarily bread labourers. I hope everyone who listens to me or reads these lines will forgive me if stretched on my bed and basking in the sun, inhaling life-giving sunshine, I allow myself to indulge in this ecstasy. Let this assure the doubters and sceptics that I have not the slightest desire that the fast should be ended as quickly as possible. It matters little if the ecstatic wishes of a fool like me are never realized and the fast is never broken. I am content to wait as long as it may be necessary, but it will hurt me to think that people have acted merely in order to save me. I claim that God has inspired this fast and it will be broken only when and if He wishes it. No human agency has ever been known to thwart, nor will it ever thwart the Divine Will.

[26 January 1948]

This day, 26th January, is Independence Day. This observance was quite appropriate when we were fighting for independence we had not seen nor handled. Now! We have handled it and we seem to be disillusioned. At least I am, even if you are not.

What are we celebrating today? Surely not our disillusionment. We are entitled to celebrate the hope that the worst is over and that we are on the road to showing the lowliest villager that it means his freedom from serfdom and that he is no longer a serf born to serve the cities and towns of India, but that he is destined to exploit the city-dwellers for the advertisement of the finished fruits of well-thought-out labours, that he is the salt of the Indian earth, that it means also equality of all classes and creeds, never the domination and superiority of the major community over a minor, however insignificant it may be in number or influence. Let us not defer the hope and make the heart sick. Yet what are the strikes and a variety of lawlessness but a deferring of the hope? These are symptoms of our sickness and weakness. Let labour realize its dignity and strength. Capital has neither dignity nor strength compared to labour. These the man in the street also has. In a well-ordered democratic society there is no room, no occasion for lawlessness or strikes. In such a society there are ample lawful means for vindicating justice. Violence, veiled or unveiled must be taboo. Strikes in Cawnpore, coal-mines or elsewhere mean material loss to the whole society not excluding the strikers themselves. I need not be reminded that this declamation does not lie well in the mouth of one like me who has been responsible for so many successful strikes. If there be such critics they ought not to forget that then there was neither independence nor the kind of legislation we have now. I wonder if we can remain free from the fever of power politics or the bid for power which afflicts the political world, the East and the West. Before leaving this topic of the day, let us permit ourselves to hope that though geographically and politically India is divided into two, at heart we shall ever be friends and brothers helping and respecting one another and be one for the outside world.

Appendices

Appendix A

EXTRACT FROM A LETTER TO W.J. WYBERGH
[10 MAY 1910]

[...] I have ventured utterly to condemn modern civilization because I hold that the spirit of it is evil. It is possible to show that some of its incidents are good, but I have examined its tendency in the scale of ethics. I distinguish between the ideals of individuals who have risen superior to their environment, as also between Christianity and modern civilization. Its activity is by no means confined to Europe. Its blasting influence is now being exhibited in full force in Japan. And it now threatens to overwhelm India. History teaches us that men who are in the whirlpool, except in the cases of individuals, will have to work out their destiny in it; but I do submit that those who are still outside its influence, and those who have a well-tried civilization to guide them, should be helped to remain where they are, if only as a measure of prudence. I claim to have tested the life which modern civilization has to give, as also that of the ancient civilization, and I cannot help most strongly contesting the idea that the Indian population requires to be roused by "the lash of competition and the other material and sensuous, as well as intellectual, stimuli"; I cannot admit that these will add a single inch to its moral stature. Liberation in the sense in which I have used the term is undoubtedly the immediate aim of all humanity. It does not, therefore, follow that the whole of it can reach it in the same time. But if that liberation is the best thing attainable by mankind, then, I submit, it is wrong to lower the ideal for anyone[...]

Appendix B

The Indian States are even now changing their character, be it ever so imperceptibly. They cannot be autocratic when the bulk of India becomes democratic. What, however, Indian democracy will be no one can tell. It is easy enough to forsee the future, if English were our common language. For it would be then the democracy of a mere handful. But if we desire to realize, as we must, the political unity of the vast mass of Indian humanity, he must be a prophet who would foretell the future. And the common language of the vast mass can never be English. It is as a matter of course a resultant of Hindi and Urdu or Hindustani as I would call it. Our English speech has isolated us from the millions of our countrymen. We have become foreigners in our own land. The manner in which English speech has permeated the political-minded men of India constitutes in my humble opinion a crime against the country, indeed humanity; because we are a stumbling-block in the progress of our own country, and the progress of what is after all a continent must mean the progress of humanity and vice versa. Every English-educated Indian who has penetrated the villages has realized this burning truth, even as I have. I have profound admiration for the English language and many noble qualities of the English people, but I have no manner of doubt in my mind that the English language and the English people occupy a place in our life which retards our progress and theirs as well.

285

Appendix C

THE IMMORAL FOUNDATION

This Indian Empire was conceived in immorality for it was to perpetuate the exploitation of India's resources that it was founded. The pages of history written by Englishmen amply prove the assertion that no fraud was considered too much, no force too frightful by Englishmen, to gain the end. There is perhaps not an inch of ground lawfully acquired by or for the British crown in India.

The rule is nurtured by immoral means. English statesmen assure us that it is the British bayonet that keeps the Empire free from attack both from without and within.

It is supported by revenues derived from immoral sources. I have sufficiently demonstrated the hideous immorality, because inhumanity, of the salt-tax. The immorality of the drink and drug revenue is self-demonstrated.

The immorality of the land revenue is not self-demonstrated. But those who have followed the Bardoli agitation, who have studied the so-called revenue laws and their administration, cannot fail to perceive the immorality of the system. I call the revenue laws so-called because they give arbitrary powers to revenue officers whose decisions are not subject to judicial control. This land revenue, like the salt-tax, presses most heavily upon the poor *ryot* whether under the *ryotwari* system or the permanent system. How it oppresses the peasant under the *ryotwari* system we saw in Bardoli and recently in Matar and Mehemedabad. The permanent settlement crushes the *ryot* more than those affected by the *ryotwari* system. That the *ryot* himself is partly to blame for his woes I have no hesitation in admitting. But that fact is irrelevant to the present consideration. There is no inherent or independent right belonging to the State to tax the land, whether it be considered to be the State property or the individual's. The State has no more right to exact its toll from land under any circumstance than the owner of an ox has a right to exact work from it irrespective of its capacity. That there is a kind of classification of land and some regulations about remissions, etc., is no answer to the charge here made. The claim here made is that in the vast majority of cases the *ryot* is wholly unable to pay any tax. In shaping its taxation policy a wise State will always take note of the citizen's habits, customs and even his weaknesses. This Government had no time for such consideration. It had its fixed minimum to exact anyhow; and so in the words of the late Lord Salisbury the lancet had to be applied where there was yet any blood to be drawn.

So much about some of the visible sources of revenue. The invisible sources are equally tainted if not much more so. The unconscionable forced inflation of the rupee has by a stroke of the pen drained India of millions. The favoured treatment of British cloth in a variety of unseen ways drains India of sixty crores of rupees annually, leaving behind partial unemployment of the starving millions.

Thus the Government trades upon our vices and exacts payment by questionable methods principally from those who are least able to make it.

There is therefore no way open to the people save to end a system whose very foundations are immoral. Let us therefore pray and work for the destruction of this demonstrably immoral system and for ending it take the boldest risks consistently with the national creed or policy (as the case may be) of non-violence.

Appendix D

Extract From A Letter To Jawaharlal Nehru
[5 October 1945]

CHI. JAWAHARLAL,

I have long been intending to write to you but can do so only today. I have also been wondering whether I should write in English or Hindustani. In the end I have decided to write in Hindustani.

I take first the sharp difference of opinion that has arisen between us. If such a difference really exists people should also know about it , for the work of swaraj will suffer if they are kept in the dark. I have said that I fully stand by the kind of governance which I have described in *Hind Swaraj*. It is not just a way of speaking. My experience has confirmed the truth of what I wrote in 1909. If I were the only one left who believed in it, I would not be sorry. For I can only testify to the truth as I see it. I have not *Hind Swaraj* in front of me. It is better that I redraw the picture today in my own language. Then it would not matter to me whether or not the picture tallies with that of 1909 nor should it to you. I do not have to establish what I had said before. What is worth knowing is only what I have to say today. I believe that if India, and through India the world, is to achieve real freedom, then sooner or later we shall have to go and live in the villages—in huts, not in palaces. Millions of people can never live in cities and palaces in comfort and peace. Nor can they do so by killing one another, that is, by resorting to violence and untruth. I have not the slightest doubt that, but for the pair, truth and non-violence, mankind will be doomed. We can have the vision of that truth and non-violence only in the simplicity of the villages. That simplicity resides in the spinning-wheel and what is implied by the spinning-wheel. It does not frighten me at all that the world seems to be going in the opposite direction. For the matter of that, when the moth approaches its doom it whirls round faster and faster till it is burnt up. It is possible that India will not be able to escape this moth-like circling. It is my duty to try, till my last breath, to save India and through it the world from such a fate. The sum and substance of what I want to say is that the individual person should have control over the things that are necessary for the sustenance of life. If he cannot have such control the individual cannot survive. Ultimately, the world is made up only of individuals. If there were no drops there would be no ocean. This is only a rough and ready statement. There is nothing new in this.

But even in *Hind Swaraj* I have not said all this. While I appreciate modern thought, I find that an ancient thing, considered in the light of this thought looks so sweet. You will not be able to understand me if you think that I am talking about the villages of today. My ideal village still exists only in my imagination. After all every human being lives in the world of his own imagination. In this village of my dreams the villager will not be dull—he will be all awareness. He will not live like an animal in filth and darkness. Men and women will live in freedom, prepared to face the whole world. There will be no plague, no cholera and no smallpox. Nobody will be allowed to be idle or to wallow in luxury. Every-one will have to do body labour. Granting all this, I can still envisage a number of things that will have to be organized on a large scale. Perhaps there will even be railways and also post and telegraph offices. I do not know what things there will be or will not be. Nor am I bothered about it. If I can make sure of the essential thing, other things will follow in due course. But if I give up the essential thing, I give up everything.

The other day, at the final day's meeting of the Working Committee, we had taken a decision to the effect that the Working Committee would meet for two or three days to work out this very thing. I shall be happy if it meets. But even if it does not meet, I want that we two should understand each other fully. And this for two reasons. Our bond is not merely political. It is much deeper. I have no measure to fathom that depth. This bond can never be broken. I therefore want that we should understand each other thoroughly in politics as well. The second reason is that neither of us considers himself as worthless. We both live only for India's freedom and will be happy to die too for that freedom. We do not care for praise from any quarter. Praise or abuse are the same to us. They have no place in the mission of service. Though I aspire to live up to 125 years rendering service, I am nevertheless an old man, while you are comparatively young. That is why I have said that you are my heir. It is only proper that I should at least understand my heir and my heir in turn should understand me. I shall then be at peace[...]

Notes

Introduction

1. See Romain Rolland, *Mahatma Gandhi: A Study in Indian Nationalism*, Madras: S. Ganesan, 1923; Raghavan N. Iyer, *The Moral and Political Thought of Mahatma Gandhi*, OUP, 1973; Partha Chatterjee, *Nationalist Thought and the Colonial World: A Derivative Discourse?*, London: Zed Press, 1986.
2. See *Collected Works of Mahatma Gandhi*, New Delhi: Publications Divisions, 1958, Vol. 10, p.7.
3. *ibid.*, Vol. 57, p.498.
4. See Edward Carpenter, *Civilization: Its Cause and Cure*, London: George Allen & Unwin, 1921, pp.46-49.
5. See John Ruskin, *Unto This Last*, London: W.B. Clive, 1931, p.83.
6. See R.G. Collingwood, *Ruskin's Philosophy*, Chinchester: Quentin Nelson, 1971, p.20.
7. *ibid.*, p.28.
8. See *Collected Works*, Vol. 66, p.245.
9. *ibid.*, Vol. 10, p.478.
10. *ibid.*, p.37.
11. See Partha Chatterjee, op, cit., pp.98-100.
12. See *Collected Works*, Vol. 10, p.51.
13. *ibid.*
14. *ibid.*, p.39.
15. *ibid.*, p.52.
16. *ibid.*, Vol. 68, p.265.
17. *ibid.*, Vol. 35, pp.489-90.
18. *ibid.*, Vol. 59, pp.65-66.
19. *ibid.*, Vol. 10, p.62.
20. See Jawaharlal Nehru, *An Autobiography*, London: Bodley Head, 1936, p.52.
21. *ibid.*, p.510.
22. See Shahid Amin, "Gandhi as Mahatma: Gorakhpur District, Eastern U.P., 1921-1922", in R. Guha, ed., *Subaltern Studies*, Vol. 3, Delhi: OUP, 1985, p.61.
23. *ibid.*, p.55.

24. See Sumit Sarkar, *Modern India*, Delhi: Macmillan, 1983, pp.310-11.
25. Chatterjee., *op.cit.*, p.
26. See Sumit Sarkar, *op.cit.*, chapter 8.

Critique of Modern Civilization

1. *Hind Swaraj* was originally written during M.K. Gandhi's return journey from England and was published in *Indian Opinion* in December 1909. In January 1910, it was proscribed in India by the government of Bombay on 24 March 1910. This made Gandhi decide on an English translation.

The Creed of Non-violence

1. The relevant part of the Working Committee resolution read: 'While the Working Committee hold [sic] that the Congress must continue to adhere strictly to the principle of non-violence in their struggle for independence, the Committee cannot ignore the present imperfections and failings in this respect of the human elements they have to deal with . . . The Committee have [sic] deliberated over the problem that has thus arisen and have come to the conclusion that they are unable to go the full length with Gandhiji. But they recognize that he should be free to pursue his great ideal in his own way, and therefore absolve him from responsibility for the programme and activity which the Congress has to pursue under the conditions at present prevailing in India and the world in regard to external agression and internal disorder.'

Women and Sex

1. This section is taken from a larger essay entitled, "History of the Satyagraha Ashrama."

Caste and Untouchability

1. This section is taken from a larger essay entitled, "History of the Satyagraha Ashrama."

Index

READ MORE IN PENGUIN

In every corner of the world, on every subject under the sun, Penguin represents quality and variety—the very best in publishing today.

For complete information about books available from Penguin—including Puffins, Penguin Classics and Arkana—and how to order them, write to us at the appropriate address below. Please note that for copyright reasons the selection of books varies from country to country.

In India: Please write to *Penguin Books India Pvt. Ltd. 210 Chiranjiv Tower, Nehru Place, New Delhi, 110019*

In the United Kingdom: Please write to *Dept JC, Penguin Books Ltd. Bath Road, Harmondsworth, West Drayton, Middlesex, UB7 ODA. UK*

In the United States: Please write to *Penguin USA Inc., 375 Hudson Street, New York, NY 10014*

In Canada: Please write to *Penguin Books Canada Ltd. 10 Alcorn Avenue, Suite 300, Toronto, Ontario M4V 3B2*

In Australia: Please write to *Penguin Books Australia Ltd. 487, Maroondah Highway, Ring Wood, Victoria 3134*

In New Zealand: Please write to *Penguin Books (NZ) Ltd. Private Bag, Takapuna, Auckland 9*

In the Netherlands: Please write to *Penguin Books Netherlands B.V., Keizersgracht 231 NL-1016 DV Amsterdom*

In Germany : Please write to *Penguin Books Deutschland GmbH, Metzlerstrasse 26, 60595 Frankfurt am Main, Germany*

In Spain: Please write to *Penguin Books S.A., Bravo Murillo, 19-1'B, E-28015 Madrid, Spain*

In Italy: Please write to *Penguin Italia s.r.l., Via Felice Casati 20, I-20104 Milano*

In France: Please write to *Penguin France S.A., 17 rue Lejeune, F-31000 Toulouse*

In Japan: Please write to *Penguin Books Japan. Ishikiribashi Building, 2-5-4, Suido, Tokyo 112*

In Greece: Please write to *Penguin Hellas Ltd, dimocritou 3, GR-106 71 Athens*

In South Africa: Please write to *Longman Penguin Books Southern Africa (Pty) Ltd, Private Bag X08, Bertsham 2013*

UNDERSTANDING THE
MUSLIM MIND
Rajmohan Gandhi

Through the lives and philosophies of eight prominent Muslim personalities—Sayyid Ahmed Khan, Fazlul Haq, Muhammad Ali Jinnah, Muhammad Iqbal, Muhammad Ali, Abul Kalam Azad, Liaqat Ali Khan and Zakir Hussain—the author sketches a fascinating and insightful picture of the Islamic community in the subcontinent today.

'Rajmohan Gandhi's excellent book should waken us to the many why's of Hindu-Muslim relationships that remain unanswered to this day'. —M.V. Kamath in the *Telegraph*

'At long last we have a dispassionate analysis of the making of Indian Muslims psyche' —*The Hindustan Times*